A NOTE ON THE AUTHOR

PAUL ROBERTS is the author of *The End of Oil* and *The End of Food*. As a journalist, he has written for the *Los Angeles Times*, the *Washington Post*, and the *Guardian*, and his work has appeared in *Slate*, *The New Republic*, *Newsweek*, *Rolling Stone*, and elsewhere. Roberts also appears regularly on TV and radio. He lives in Washington State, USA.

D1322648

BY THE SAME AUTHOR

The End of Oil

The End of Food

THE
IMPULSE
SOCIETY

What's Wrong With Getting What We Want?

Paul Roberts

BLOOMSBURY

LONDON · OXFORD · NEW YORK · NEW DELHI · SYDNEY

Bloomsbury Paperbacks
An imprint of Bloomsbury Publishing Plc

50 Bedford Square
London
WC1B 3DP
UK

1385 Broadway
New York
NY 10018
USA

www.bloomsbury.com

BLOOMSBURY and the Diana logo are trademarks of Bloomsbury Publishing Plc

First published in Great Britain 2014
This paperback edition first published in 2015

Copyright © Paul Roberts 2014

Paul Roberts has asserted his right under the Copyright, Designs and Patents Act, 1988,
to be identified as Author of this work.

No part of this book may be used or reproduced in any manner whatsoever
without written permission from the publisher except in the case of brief quotations
embedded in critical articles or reviews. Every reasonable effort has been made
to trace copyright holders of material reproduced in this book, but if any have
been inadvertently overlooked the publisher would be glad to hear from them.

No responsibility for loss caused to any individual or organization acting on or refraining from
action as a result of the material in this publication can be accepted by Bloomsbury or the author.

British Library Cataloguing-in-Publication Data
A catalogue record for this book is available from the British Library.

ISBN: HB: 978-1-4088-3046-8
TPB: 978-1-4088-5160-9
PB: 978-1-4088-6427-2
ePub: 978-1-4088-3994-2

2 4 6 8 10 9 7 5 3 1

Typeset by Hewer Text UK Ltd, Edinburgh
Printed and bound in Great Britain by CPI Group (UK) Ltd, Croydon CR0 4YY

MIX
Paper from
responsible sources
FSC® C020471

To find out more about our authors and books visit www.bloomsbury.com.
Here you will find extracts, author interviews, details of forthcoming events
and the option to sign up for our newsletters..

To Lynn, Molly, Mathew, and Annie—my old neighborhood.

Haringey Libraries	
YY	
Askews & Holts	30-Nov-2015
306.3097	
	HAOL11/11/15

Contents

Introduction

A half hour east of Seattle, not far from the headquarters of Microsoft, Amazon, and other pillars of the digital age, a winding country road brings a visitor to reSTART, the nation's first rehab for technology addicts and a window onto the wider world to come. Most of the patients here are trying to quit Internet gaming, which they once played so obsessively that careers, relationships, and prospects for happiness were in shambles. For the outsider, the addiction can be incomprehensible. But as you hear the patients' stories, the appeal comes into focus. In a living room overlooking a sward of lawn, twenty-nine-year-old Brett Walker talks about his time in *World of Warcraft*, a popular online role-playing game where participants become warriors in a steampunk medieval world. For four years, even as his real life collapsed, Walker enjoyed a near-perfect online existence, with virtually unlimited power and status akin to that of a Mafia boss crossed with a rock star. "I could do whatever I wanted, go where I wanted," Walker tells me with a mixture of pride and self-mockery. "The world was my oyster."

Walker appreciates the irony here. His endless hours as an online superhero left him physically weak, financially destitute, and so socially isolated he could barely hold a face-to-face conversation.

There may also have been deeper effects. Studies suggest that heavy online gaming actually alters brain structures involved in decision making and self-control, much as drug and alcohol use does. Emotional development can be delayed or derailed, leaving the player with a sense of self that is incomplete, fragile, and socially disengaged—more id than superego. Or as Hilarie Cash, reSTART cofounder and an expert in online addiction, told me, "We end up being controlled by our impulses."

Which, for gaming addicts, means being even more susceptible to the complex charms of the online world. Gaming companies want to keep players playing as long as possible—the more you play, the more likely you'll upgrade to the next version. To this end, game designers have created sophisticated data feedback systems that tie players to an upgrade treadmill. As players move through these virtual worlds, the data they generate is captured and used to make subsequent game iterations even more "immersive." (*World of Warcraft*, for instance, releases periodic upgrades, or "patches," with new weapons and skills that players must have to retain their godlike status.) As a result, players play more, and generate still more data, which leads to even more immersive iterations, and so on. The result is a perpetual-motion machine, driven by companies' hunger for revenues, but also by players' insatiable appetite for self-expression. Until the day he quit, Walker never once declined the chance to "level up," but instead consumed each new increment of power as soon as it was offered—even as it sapped his power in real life.

On the surface, the tale of someone like Brett Walker may not seem relevant to those of us who *don't* spend our days waging virtual war. But the truth is that these digital narratives center on a dilemma that every citizen in postindustrial society will eventually confront: namely, how to cope with a socioeconomic system that is almost too good at giving us what we want. I don't just mean the way smartphones and search engines and Netflix and Amazon now anticipate our preferences. I mean how the entire edifice of the consumer economy has reoriented itself around our personal agendas, self-images, and inner fantasies. In North America and the United Kingdom, and to lesser degrees in Europe and Japan, it is now completely normal to demand a personally customized life. We fine-tune our moods with pharmaceuticals and classic rock. Craft our meals around our allergies and ideologies. Customize our bodies with cross training, with ink and metal, with surgery and wearable technologies. We can choose a vehicle to express our hipness or hostility. We can move to a neighborhood that matches our social values, find a news outlet that mirrors our politics, create a social network that "likes" everything we say or post. With each transaction and upgrade, each choice and click, life moves closer to us, and the world becomes *our* world.

And yet . . . one needn't be a gaming addict to recognize that the world we're so busily refashioning in our own image has some serious problems. Certainly, our march from one level of gratification to the next has cost us—most recently in a real estate-and-credit binge that nearly sunk the global economy. But the problem here isn't simply one of overindulgence. Even as the economy slowly recovers, many of us still feel out of balance and unsteady—as if our quest for constant, seamless self-expression has become so advanced and pervasive that it is undermining the essential structures of everyday life. In everything from eating and socializing to marriage and parenting to politics, the norms and expectations of our self-centered culture are making it steadily harder to behave in civic, *social* ways. We struggle to make, or keep, long-term commitments. We find it harder to engage with, or even tolerate, people or ideas that don't relate directly and immediately to us. Empathy weakens, and with it, our faith in the idea, essential to a working democracy, that we have anything in common.

Our unease isn't new, exactly. Some forty years ago, social critics such as Daniel Bell, Christopher Lasch, and Tom Wolfe warned that our growing self-absorption was steamrollering the idealism and aspirations of the postwar era. The "logic of individualism," argued Lasch in his 1978 polemic, *The Culture of Narcissism*, had transformed daily life into a brutal social competition, a Hobbesian "war of all against all," that was sapping our days of meaning or joy. Today, one could argue that the pessimists weren't pessimistic enough. They couldn't have imagined how self-absorption and full-blown narcissism would become so inseparable from mainstream culture. Nor would they have guessed the degree to which the selfish reflexes of the individual would become the reflexes of an entire society. Government, the media, academia, and especially business—the very institutions that once helped to temper the individual pursuit of quick, self-serving rewards are themselves increasingly engaged in the same pursuit. In sector after sector, at scales small and large, we are becoming a society that wants it *now*, regardless of the consequences. We are becoming an Impulse Society.

What we're describing here goes beyond a wayward consumer culture. Under our escalating drive for quick "returns," our whole socioeconomic system is turning on itself. Our traditions of collective action and personal commitment are fraying. Our economy struggles to generate the kind of long-term, broadly based prosperity it once provided—and worse, now seems locked in an intensifying cycle of overshoot and collapse. Most alarmingly, our political institutions, which not so long ago could mobilize resources and people to make real progress, now shy away from complex, long-term challenges such as education reform or resource depletion—or the financial reforms needed to prevent the next meltdown. Consider this one fact: the worst recession in three-quarters of a century should have served as a society-wide reset, a chance to rethink a socioeconomic model based on automatic upgrades and short-term gains. Instead, we've continued to focus our economic energies, entrepreneurial talents, and innovation on getting the biggest returns in the shortest time possible. Worse, we've done so despite the fact that, thanks to our failing economic model, more and more of us can no longer afford to keep up with the treadmill of ever-faster gratification—a frustration not unconnected to the strains of angry populism now paralyzing our politics.

How did we get to this point? How did entire societies that once celebrated their prudence, unity, and concern for the future become so impulsive, self-centered, and shortsighted? And how will these changes play out for us, as people and as a people, in the years and decades ahead? These questions are at the heart of *The Impulse Society*.

On one level, this is a deeply personal story. Like many first-worlders, I've spent much of my life in a not-always-successful effort to cope with an economic system that routinely mistakes want for need. For that reason, a lot of my initial research focused on the almost comic mismatch between an individual adapted for scarcity and an economic system wired for abundance. But the real story here wasn't merely about mischievous marketers or gullible consumers; it was about a much larger historic shift in the essential and complicated relationship between the individual and our entire socioeconomic system. It's clear, for example, that the selfishness of today's culture wasn't nearly so apparent in the postwar period—and it's fair to argue that our rising self-centeredness stems, at least in part, from the weakening of institutions, such as religion and family, that once tempered self-absorption. But there is a more strictly economic narrative here as well. It's hardly coincidental that the famous selflessness of the postwar era began to crumble with the economic upheavals of the 1970s. I mean the recessions, which made us more self-preserving and insecure—but also the successes: the explosion of new economic ideas and technologies that enabled the economy to, in effect, satisfy our desires more rapidly and efficiently and personally—so much so that we often have difficulty knowing where we stop and the market begins. In other words, what we're experiencing now isn't simply the normal retrenchment that follows an economic downturn; rather, we are in the midst of an invasion—the end stages in an accelerating drive by the marketplace to break down all barriers between itself and us. Simply put, the marketplace and the self, our economy and our psychology, are merging in ways we've never before experienced.

If we could step back a century, before the rise of the consumer economy, we would be struck not only by the lack of affluence and technology, but also by the *distance* between ourselves and our economy, the separation of our economic and emotional lives. It isn't that people were any less wrapped up in economic activities. The difference, rather, lay in where, psychically speaking, the majority of that activity took place. A century ago, most economic activity occurred in our *outer* lives—that is, in the physical world of *production*. We made things: we farmed, crafted, cobbled, nailed, baked, brined, brewed. We created tangible goods and services whose value was reasonably objective and quantifiable, determined not only by the marketplace but by the measurable needs and requirements of our physical, outer lives. Today the situation is almost reversed. Although our economy is vastly larger, most economic activity (70 percent in the United States) centers on *consumption*. Much of that consumption is discretionary and is thus driven not by need, but by the intangible criteria of our inner worlds: our aspirations and hopes, our identities and secret cravings, our anxieties and our boredom. And as these inner worlds have come to play a larger role in the economy—and more particularly, as company profits have come to depend on our ephemeral (but conveniently endless) appetites—the entire marketplace has become more attuned to the mechanics of the self. Bit by bit, product by product, the marketplace has drawn closer to the self. Some would even argue that, since the computer revolution of the 1970s, the consumer marketplace has effectively moved *inside* the self, and is now inseparable from not only our desires and decisions, but also our very identities.

In the usual telling, this merger of market and self was a hostile takeover—as if we'd all still be in the idyll of a producer economy were it not for decades of marketing and *Mad Men* manipulation. But the merger of market and self was always on the horizon. Once the consumer became the center of economic activity and corporate profitability, the die was cast. The market would, inexorably and naturally, reorient its vast structures and processes around the self, because only the bottomless appetites of the self could contain all the output of a maturing industrial capitalist economy, which can never stop growing. And just as inevitably, the self would welcome the market's advances, because without that relentless output, our inner lives wouldn't have access to all these fantastic, endlessly shifting and diverting powers of self-expression. It was the original win-win.

We can argue about the ultimate desirability of this merger—about the morality and sustainability of it, and whether another sort of relationship between the market and the self might be preferable or even possible. But the merger itself was destiny. Today the self-centeredness of our socioeconomic system is so complete and normalized that it has redefined the meaning of progress. It shapes our expectations, controls how we measure success and failure. It guides the allocation of resources and talent and, especially, determines how we exploit our massive capacity for innovation: it is surely telling that the company with the most market value and brand recognition, Apple, has achieved that success by positioning itself at the very center of the me-centered economy. And none of these trends shows any signs of slowing. To the contrary, without a serious course correction, the entire merger will only accelerate as new technologies let the market gratify ever-more esoteric appetites on a nearly continuous basis. Market and self are becoming one.

But is this such a bad thing? Surely, if we were to bring someone from the 1890s, or even the 1970s, to the present moment, he would struggle to see the crisis in a socioeconomic system that wants nothing more than to please. In fact, there is no shortage of experts today who suggest that the proper response to all this efficient gratification is to relax and enjoy it. Not only is a society shaped by our impulses the very manifestation of freedom; but an economy shaped by our desires is the best possible economy precisely because it is desire-shaped. As Adam Smith argued more than two centuries ago, when individuals freely pursue their own self-interests—presumably, even their most trivial desires—the aggregate effect is an economy that most efficiently and naturally delivers the most benefits to the greatest majority. (In Smith's famous phrasing, by pursuing our own self-interests, it's as if we "are led by an invisible hand to promote an end that was no part of [our] intention.") And the truth is our self-centered economy delivers a lot of benefits. It generates a lot of wealth, a lot of innovation, and, perhaps most important, a lot of individual adaptability, which you and I can use to shape our lives, our feelings, and our very identities. For these unprecedented powers of self-creation, shouldn't we be willing to tolerate periodic meltdowns, partisan politics, and a selfish, narcissistic culture?

Perhaps not. An economy reoriented to give us what we want, it turns out, isn't the best for delivering what we *need*. The more efficient we have gotten at gratifying immediate individual desire, the worse we have become at meeting other, longer-term *social* necessities. Yes, our economy generates scads of wealth, but it is no longer the steady, broadly distributed wealth that once lifted all social classes. Yes, our economy cranks out a parade of astonishing personal goods (from smartphones to financial "instruments" to miraculous medical treatments), but it no longer produces enough of the *public* goods (roads and bridges, for example, or education or science, or preventative medicine or alternative energy) that are essential for long-term economic stability, and whose absence is already feeding back, negatively, into our economy and society. We can make great plasma screens and seat warmers and teeth whiteners and apps that will guide you, turn by turn, to the nearest edgy martini bar. But when it comes to, say, reforming the financial system, dealing with climate change, or fixing health care or some other large-scale problem out in the real world, we have little idea where to start.

We often explain this dilemma in terms of policy failures, and it is a failure. But it is a failure rooted in a marketplace that is now so married to the psychology of the consumer that it mirrors that psychology's least attractive attributes—not least the tendency, wired in by evolution, to prize immediate rewards and ignore future costs. You can see this have-it-now reflex in the way our entire consumer culture treats immediate gratification as if it were life's primary goal, to be pursued as efficiently and unapologetically as possible. But you can also see it among the institutions in charge of the consumer economy, not least the institutions of business. We may always have been a profit-maximizing species, but there was a time when profit was regarded as inseparable from broader social goals and obligations. Today, those obligations are treated increasingly as "inefficiencies" to be minimized or eliminated entirely with cost-cutting technologies and lean strategies. This intensifying emphasis on the bottom line helps explain the unprecedented level of corporate earnings, which have more than recovered from the Great Recession. But it also helps us understand the unprecedented insecurity of workers, communities, and other "constituencies" that once regarded the corporate world as a stabilizing anchor.

And it was an anchor—the source of much of our material progress. So we aren't necessarily being antibusiness or antitechnology to be worried by the way business now reflexively applies technology to raise profits with almost no consideration for the broader consequences. Or to feel uneasy at the fact that more and more of our technological skills and resources—which once lifted all society and advanced very broad social goals (and which remain crucial to solving our looming challenges)—are now devoted to fields such as financial "engineering," whose social costs are now painfully well known. It is instructive that both the United States and the United Kingdom, which once generated most of their profits in their manufacturing sectors, now get their biggest profits from the financial industry. Telling, too, that most of the excitement around Big Data comes, not from its potential to solve the very complex problems of our times (nor even its potential to be abused), but for the way it is already letting the marketplace move closer to the self, with more immersive games, more adaptive personal technologies—even, fittingly, eyeglasses that place the entire digital economy just centimeters from your brain.

This isn't how an advanced society is supposed to work. Yet what else should we expect from a socioeconomic system that has come to take its marching orders from our fantasies and fears? More funda- mentally, what else should we expect from a culture that now all but mocks the values of cooperation, patience, and self-sacrifice? A culture in which self-indulgence and self-absorption, far from being treated as character flaws to be remedied, are celebrated and legiti- mized as lifestyle choices and "product categories." This is what a society based on the self actually looks like—and not the strong, assured, confident self that Americans once proudly extolled or of which Walt Whitman sang, but rather a self that has become corrupted, insecure, and deeply compromised.

The irony of the Impulse Society is that, for all the emphasis on pleas- ure and gratification, the main output seems to be anxiety. Most of us understand, if only at a gut level, that a culture geared for short-term self-interest is a disaster waiting to happen. We see the growing social risks of an economic system that generates more inequality each year—and of a political system too shortsighted and "bought" to do anything about it. And on a personal, emotional level, we are increas- ingly aware that the Impulse Society, despite its relentless prioritizing of self-interest, of "I" over "we," is actually making it harder for each of us to be truly satisfied. The freedom to live as we wish is a marvelous privilege, but the harder we strive for self-gratification, the more we are reminded of the old truth—that to live only for the moment and the self is to fall far short of one's potential.

Yet we're hardly paralyzed. Brett Walker, the former digital junkie, saved himself by going clean—by breaking away from continuous gratifications of gaming "economy" long enough to discover that he was happier without that degree of self-indulgence. Perhaps we should take note. Like Walker, this society has let the expectation of narrowly self-serving gratification drive us into a social and economic crisis so deep we still haven't recovered. But unlike Walker, we still haven't broken free. To the contrary, our "solution" has been to resurrect the status quo and revive the same self-centered economy that caused us such grief in the first place—and will only do so again.

But we needn't stick to that plan. Were we serious about interrupting our downward spiral, we would start by recognizing the social limits of immediate gratification and of an economic strategy that always prioritizes the largest, quickest, cheapest payoff. This isn't to question the idea of *efficiency*—of exploiting technology and technique to get the biggest bang for our buck. Efficiency is what made our civilization possible, and we'll need more and more of it as we navigate the crises of income inequality, ecological degradation, and resource scarcity that the Impulse Society has been unable to address effectively—or has simply made worse.But it is to criticize the *ideology* of efficiency—or the belief, sacred in contemporary politics and especially business, that the greatest output at the lowest cost should *always* be society's aim. That dogma, though we credit it for our prosperity, is now destroying that prosperity. How can we mend the job market if we're doing everything possible to eliminate labor? How can we build anything of real value when everything we make—every product and service, every achievement, experience, and emotional state—is by definition obsolete the moment we create it? Where under such a model of endless upgrades is there a place for tradition, or a sense of permanence, or a conception of individual commitment to the long term?

Here, I think, we find the story behind the increasing fragility of the self. Here, too, is the real reason our economic recovery has dragged on for the better part of a decade. What we're trying to recover from isn't just the collapse of an asset bubble or an episode of irrational exuberance. It's the exhaustion of a socioeconomic program so focused on short-term goals, and so hostile to the notion of long-term investment, or commitment, or permanence, that it is becoming incapable of producing anything of durable social or economic value. In an era of ambitious "emerging" societies—such as China, Brazil, India, or Indonesia, which still value the making of things very much as we used to—this impulse toward the short term and the provisional may be a fatal flaw.

In the post–Cold War world, it is unfashionable to call for any alternative to capitalism, or even to imagine that such an alternative might exist. But shouldn't we at least retain the prerogative to choose the sort of capitalism we want? Shouldn't we be able to demand that our capitalism produce things of real value and be capable of sustaining a society that is equitable and *deliberate*? We are rightly skeptical of the heavy-handed top-down government style in places such as China, Brazil, India, and Indonesia. But these societies, at the very least, have tried to make their economies take them in specific directions, as opposed to simply following where the ideology of efficiency leads. More fundamentally, they have consciously defined economic success and wealth in explicitly social terms. One needn't agree with those terms to recognize that *our* terms—the way we measure progress in much of the "first world"—is no longer sustainable. We badly need a new metric for economic success and wealth that goes beyond earnings per share.

So our solution to the Impulse Society begins with questions: Where do we want our economy to take us? What kind of wealth are we hoping to produce? How should we redefine wealth to include the values that sustain a society and can balance short- and long-term goals, such as education and energy and scientific research? Can we find a program that renders the economy more "conscious" of its social impacts? A program that inspires citizens to leave the mind-set of immediate gratification and narrow self-interest and recover a sense of long-term responsibility and permanent, stable selfhood?

Admittedly, in the current political culture, developing a program to balance these objectives seems flatly impossible. Witness our tortured efforts to reform health care, or to enact strategies that meaningfully address climate change. These failures, we're told, reflect not just the complexity of the task, but also fundamentally irreconcilable differences in the way "the right" and "the left" understand the purpose of the market, the role of government, and the rights and responsibilities of the individual. In the politics of the Impulse Society, there is no middle ground.

But this idea of an insurmountable divide is itself a political contrivance. When I set out to understand the Impulse Society, I did so as an unapologetic liberal, deeply distrustful of laissez-faire economics and the reflexive leap for quick, efficient returns that is grinding entire economies and cultures into the dust. And yet, while my economic stance remains largely unchanged, the more closely I've looked at the social and cultural drivers behind the Impulse Society, the more I've found myself reaching conclusions that are distinctly conservative. The social elements that are most essential to maintaining a stable, sustainable society—among them, the emphasis on strong families and intact communities and an appreciation for personal virtues such as self-discipline—these are traditionally conservative objectives. What I ended up with is a political amalgam: an economy that has been rendered, through regulation and incentive, more sensitive to its social impacts, combined with a public that has been persuaded, even inspired, to look beyond narrow self-interest.

My own evolution toward a politically amalgamated approach is hardly unique—many of the social critiques of the past four decades have reached similarly hybridized conclusions. But it leads me to believe that the current divides—right versus left, free markets versus socialism, the all-powerful state versus the unfettered individual—represent not fundamental differences but false choices. These hardened positions are themselves impulsive: they are the result of political parties choosing the quick payoff of partisanship instead of committing to the longer-term political processes that once characterized industrial society—before our economic models and technological successes persuaded us that such behavior was inefficient. Yet that older, more farsighted political process isn't extinct: despite the partisan extremism that has flourished under the Impulse Society, most of us remain somewhere in the middle—and more than ready for change.

And here, in the historical comparison, is my real source of optimism. As a society, we used to tackle large, complicated problems (world wars, economic depression, racial injustice), and we can do so again. In some respects, the challenge we face today is more difficult. But the alternative, the status quo, is no longer an option.

Part One

I Society

CHAPTER 1

More Better

It's late on a Friday afternoon in the Apple Store in North Seattle and I'm sitting with a half dozen other middle-aged customers in a "workshop" for new iPhone owners. Late Friday afternoons were once a time for half-priced drinks and flirting, but buying personal technology now counts as leisure, and the store is so jammed that our instructor, Chip, a wispy twentysomething with hipster glasses and the quiet despair of a tour guide on an old folks' bus trip, is using a PA to be heard. Just now Chip is tutoring us on Siri, the iPhone digital assistant that can, according to Apple, help us with everything from writing texts to finding hotels to locating the best Kansas City–style barbecue. Siri delivers this cutting-edge functionality by means of "adaptive intelligence,"[1] which, Chip explains, means that the more we talk to Siri, the more responsive and understanding she becomes, and the more she can do for us. Siri has been billed as a "human-centered productivity app"—that is, software that makes us more efficient by letting us get more done in less time—and thus a critical step in the evolution of the machine-human relationship. But such power, Chip warns, can be disconcerting. "It's a little weird to be talking to our device, frankly, and have it talk back to you and do what you want," he says in tones of rehearsed empathy, as if he, too, once felt awkward and shy around Siri. Chip suggests that we avoid using Siri in public until we've practiced at home. "But you'll find after a couple of days, you'll be comfortable using it."

The solemnity of Chip's spiel contrasts sharply with some of the ribald commentary that accompanied Siri's release in 2011. Beyond the specific complaints—that Siri cannot understand Bronx, for example—were broader, often mocking critiques of the notion of Siri as a productivity booster. Many of Siri's advertised uses[2] ("Siri, find me a latte" or "Siri, play my running mix") seem less about raising output than providing digital parlor tricks for bored yuppies. Given the way Apple uses cloying techno-utopian hype (the iPad is "a magical window where nothing comes between you and what you love") to grease its famously aggressive release schedule (new versions rolled out precisely as profit margins on existing ones are fading), it doesn't take a cynic to see Siri as an unusually elaborate carrot.

And yet . . . it's hard to ignore the *thrill* I get when, a few days later, I tell Siri to set a timer for five minutes, and she does it. Or when I ask her to tell my son I'll be late picking him up from cross-country practice, and she sends him a text with *those exact words*. Or ask her to find the score for last night's Mariners game, or to check tomorrow's weather, or to read my text messages aloud, and she does all these things—a bit awkwardly at first, but more smoothly as she learns my patterns of speech. Nor can I deny the weirdly visceral pleasure I get once I start downloading those other productivity apps—apps that, for example, aggregate all my banking; or track my caloric output when I jog; or let me hover, virtually, over my hometown and peek into my neighbors' backyards. I still can't quite see how these "tools" boost productivity—in fact, I'm pretty sure I'm actually getting *less* work done—but they make me *feel* great, and the sensation is deep and visceral and no doubt involves the same neural chemistry that once helped my ancestors locate food, shelter, and sex as fast and with as little effort as possible. And it occurs to me that this biochemical rush is Apple's *real* product. The company gets criticized for pitching style over substance. But much of what Apple and most other purveyors of personal technology, from Google to Microsoft to Facebook, are selling really *is* a kind of productivity: the ability to generate the highest level of momentary pleasure for the least effort.

Granted, this isn't Adam Smith's sort of productivity. For economists, productivity means the sort of utility-maximizing, cost-reducing, survival-enhancing stuff (such as a more efficient way of growing more calories with fewer hours of labor) that helped our predecessors escape starvation, poverty, and scarcity generally. But to judge by Apple's massive success (its market value is larger than that of ExxonMobil, whose products are arguably far more essential to humanity) or the viral growth in personal technology (a quarter of a *trillion* dollars spent annually on smartphones and tablets), this new, more personal productivity is, at some deep level, as vital as any other sort. Not only are we willing to pay large amounts for it, but we also anticipate, with the hyper-alert focus of a hunter-gatherer, each new increment of productivity, and we snap it up, as soon as it goes on sale, as quickly and automatically as our forebears might have embraced a new weapon or tool. It is this reflexive move toward more efficiency and greater productivity, whenever and wherever we find it, that lies at the heart of the Impulse Society—and it's here that our story begins.

Today's big technology companies are hardly the first to cash in on our appetite for productivity. More than a century ago, as the chaotically industrializing economies of the United States and Europe were still dragging us through routine crashes and shortages, an entire industry arose to help us get the most from the least. There were self-styled productivity gurus—Frederick Taylor, who showed managers how to coax more output from workers. There was Edward Purinton, author of "The Efficient Optimist,"[3] who advised his millions of readers to purge their lives of all inefficient activities, including pink teas, polite conversation, and four-fork etiquette. But there were also the big-time players, the industrialists, whose vast, ultraefficient factories let them mass-produce the world's first productivity apps: lamp oil and canned soup and repeating rifles and typewriters and washing machines and other instruments that let us get more done in less time. Of these players, the most significant was Henry Ford, whose creation, the mass-produced car, offered such an unprecedented boost in personal output that it transformed what it meant to be an individual.

Henry Ford was born to the mission of personal productivity. Raised on a farm outside Detroit, he had absorbed the farmer's obsession for any tool or technique that let you get more bushels or other outputs from the same hour of labor, and he made that principle the centerpiece of his new company. Where rival carmakers were hand-crafting luxury sedans for the scions of the Gilded Age, Ford created his Model T to be cheap enough "for the multitudes." To do this, he not only designed a simple, durable vehicle, but he also created a new system, centered on the world's first moving assembly line, that let him produce that car in enormous volumes and thus exploit the very powerful efficiencies of scale. As Ford churned out more cars every month, each car's share of the "fixed" cost of Ford's factories became proportionately smaller. As Ford's costs fell, he was able to cut his selling price, thereby attracting more buyers and generating even more volume, leading to even lower prices, and so on. By 1923, Ford had lowered the price of a Model T from $850 (around $21,000 today) to just $290 ($4,000), or around a third of the average workingman's annual salary and, as crucially, around half the price of a horse and buggy, then the standard in personal mobility.

Put another way, a citizen of even modest means could now afford an unprecedented upgrade in personal power. Where a horse and buggy were lucky to do a glacial eight miles an hour (with pauses for rest, feed, and water), the Model T could maintain a pace of forty miles per hour and cover perhaps two hundred miles between fill-ups—a fivefold increase in personal mobility. Granted, the full effects of this upgrade were muted in the congested cities. But in rural America, where most people still lived, and where vast distances imposed deep economic and social isolation, this surge in personal power was life-changing. A farm family could make a trip into town and back in an hour, instead of needing all day. A doctor could reach a rural homestead in time actually to save a patient. A salesman could cover five times the territory. A young couple (your great-grandparents, perhaps) could escape the oppressive, puritanical watchfulness that dictated rural life. As sociologist Daniel Bell put it, within a few years of Ford's breakthrough, mechanized mobility was so cheap and ubiquitous and normal that small-town "boys and girls thought nothing of driving 20 miles to dance at a roadhouse, safe from the prying eyes of neighbors."[4] Freedom of a kind previously reserved for the upper classes was now accessible to virtually anyone—and with it, came an entirely new conception of what was possible for the individual.

The empowering effects of Ford's system went beyond personal mobility. By the 1920s this new business model had given rise to an entirely new economy. As other manufacturers copied Ford's methods, the marketplace positively swelled with affordable new "tools," from household appliances and prepared foods to telephones and radios, each providing another increment of individual power. Not all delivered as much sovereignty as the car. But in an era when the average person was still at the mercy of large, impersonal forces (not least a corrupt business elite that blithely steamrollered the little people in the pursuit of personal profits), even small increases in personal power were life-changing. We clamored for them, and to satisfy this surging demand, new entrepreneurs came out with new products. More factories were built, with even more efficient assembly lines and processes, and the wages paid to the workers in those new factories fueled even more demand, which led to more factories, more wages, and more personally empowering products.

The entire economy was changing, and with it, our conception of ourselves as economic actors. Where once we had been a nation of producers, operating on the slow schedule of the farmer or the craftsman, and living within the limits of our own output, we were becoming a nation of consumers. More and more of us now used our time to earn wages, and used those wages to buy our necessities premade—products that were often cheaper and of better quality than homemade. A century later, it's fashionable to pine for that producer economy, with its imagined authenticity and simplicity and innocence. At the time of its demise, however, there was little sorrow. Most of the new consumers had grown up, like Henry Ford, in the nineteenth century and had known mainly hard labor, chronic shortages, and the colossal inequality of the Gilded Age. For them, the new consumer economy represented not just a massive improvement in living standards, but also the means to ensure that such improvement continued. The consumer economy was a veritable perpetual-motion machine capable, it seemed, of churning out more power for ordinary individuals with every passing year.

But the revolution in personal power was only half complete. As it turned out, the circular strategy that Ford had perfected—using low prices to generate volume and using volume to maintain low prices—was a bit like being on a treadmill. It was profitable only as long as he could keep selling more and more increments of personal power every year. And this was a problem because, past a certain point, consumers couldn't use any more. Wages might be getting higher, but most wage earners maintained a frugal, nineteenth-century attitude, under which a tool was used until it broke (at which point it was fixed and used until it broke again). By the mid-1920s, most American families not only owned a car,[5] but, because Ford had built his so sturdily, were rarely in the market for another. Sales growth slowed, and Ford's profits plunged, and he was forced to reduce his output, which cost him some of his precious scale efficiencies and threatened to unravel his entire model. Ford wasn't alone. Most manufacturers were confronting the same potentially ruinous paradox. In the scramble to achieve Ford-like scale and market share, they had spent billions of dollars on factories and assembly lines and distribution networks and showrooms. But the volumes needed to repay those investments markedly exceeded consumers' appetites. Ford and his fellow industrialists faced a stark choice: either dramatically reduce output, and write off billions of dollars in investments, or somehow persuade people to use more personal power.

The persuader would turn out to be another carmaker, Alfred Sloan, president of General Motors and Ford's biggest rival both commercially and philosophically. Where Ford was an austere farmer's son who shunned ostentatious display, Sloan had been raised in wealth and educated at the best schools, and was accustomed to living in high style. More to our point, where Ford fixated on the practical, nuts-and-bolts aspects of individual mobility, Sloan realized that the key to mass-producing consumer goods was no longer just technology but *psychology*: making consumers feel comfortable spending their new wages.

Sloan's psychological strategy came in two stages. First, General Motors offered a radical new service: cheap consumer financing through an in-house bank. At a time when consumer credit was still widely seen as the financial equivalent to opium—Ford considered credit to be immoral, and accepted only cash—Sloan's move was brash but brilliant. At a stroke, he provided his customers the capacity not only to buy a car sooner (without having to save for it), but also to buy considerably *more* car. And more car is what Sloan proceeded to sell them. Where traditional manufacturers offered customers few

choices—Ford made one basic model in one color, blackish green—
General Motors brought out a range of options, from the budget
Chevrolet to the top-of-the-line Cadillac. GM's product mix was
carefully designed to let motorists choose a car to match their socioeconomic status and then *elevate* that status by upgrading to the
fancier model. Sloan was, in effect, offering his customers the power
to move themselves not just physically but *socially*—a shrewd proposition at a time when Americans were becoming increasingly status
conscious.

Further, Sloan gave consumers the means to go on elevating
their status forever. In 1926, General Motors introduced what came
to be known as the "annual model change," or yearly modifications to
each model. Some of these changes represented measurable, *material*
improvements, such as better brakes and more reliable transmissions.
But most were cosmetic or stylistic and intended to provide an
emotional reward—the pleasure of owning the newest car on the
block, say, or the thrill of a more powerful engine or some clever new
gadget or convenience. (As Harley Earl, Sloan's chief car "stylist," told
an interviewer, "I try to design a car so that every time you get in it, it's
a relief—you have a little vacation for a while."[6]) Sloan was hardly the
first to target these softer appetites. For centuries, the wealthy had
been purchasing status and other preferred emotional states via
"conspicuous consumption," in Thorstein Veblen's famous term. But
with mass production, annual design changes, and easy financing,
Sloan gave the average consumer the same capacity for self-
gratification. Now nearly anyone could upgrade to a higher level of
emotional fulfillment—and do so more quickly and efficiently than
had been possible under the old producer economy, when moments
of intense satisfaction were less frequent and more likely to require
some serious effort or discipline. In a way, Sloan was offering
a new kind of personal productivity, an emotional or *aspirational*
productivity, where individuals could create a desired emotional state

with far less exertion—and we embraced it as eagerly and reflexively as farmers might have embraced a more efficient tractor.

It's worth noting that the urges Sloan was exploiting were not entirely manufactured. We like novelty for the same reasons our ancestors did: it represents a change in the environment that might prove to be advantageous. Likewise, we have an inborn desire to improve our social status because status would have been crucial in a world where individuals depended utterly on power relations within our group. Sloan, it's safe to assume, knew little about prehistoric neurochemistry or tribal dynamics, but he clearly understood that people gravitate naturally to novelty and status. More to the point, he recognized that these desires can be satisfied only fleetingly. The pleasures of novelty begin to fade as soon as you leave the showroom. The thrill of a high-status product vanishes with next year's model. The only way to maintain those joys was to keep upgrading—a convenient requirement indeed for any large-scale manufacturer desperate for ever-larger sales volumes. The consumer, too, would now be on a treadmill—one that, with the right product design and advertising and incentives, could be perfectly matched to the treadmill of the manufacturer. Sloan dubbed his strategy "dynamic obsolescence," and he was quite candid about its purpose. "Each year we build the best car we possibly can to satisfy the customer," he later explained. "And then the next year we build another to make him dissatisfied."[7] Sloan had found the perfect repository for the inherent surpluses of the modern industrial machine: from here on out, those surpluses would go into the bottomless psyche of the consumer.

The genius of Sloan's strategy was soon visible to all. General Motors grew into the largest company of any kind, and dynamic obsolescence—the linking of psychological and industrial appetites, the self and the marketplace—became the new economic paradigm. Manufacturing companies long dominated by engineers and accountants now hired armies of sociologists, psychologists, and even Freudian analysts to catalogue, as one practitioner put it, "the whole battery of inner conditions that play a dynamic part in a person's buying or not buying."[8] And what a battery it was. We bought, it was discovered, not simply for novelty or status, but to salve our battered self-esteem; to assuage the disappointment of our mediocre marriages; to escape the frustrations of our office jobs, the cloying, suffocating conformity of our suburban lives, and the humiliations of age and infirmity. As Robert Lynd, the Columbia University sociologist and early critic of consumer culture, observed, consumer products were now marketed, and consumed, almost like pharmaceutical treatments: to assist our "adjustment" to every sort of emotional or social problem.[9] Lynd and other academics were scornful of the new therapeutic consumerism. Yet it was hard to argue with success. With every product cycle and model change, consumer products were giving us the power to rule not only our external worlds, but our internal worlds as well.

There was one detail missing before the era of the empowered individual could fully be under way. Having made the leap from producers to consumers, we were now entirely at the mercy of the marketplace for not only the things we consumed but also the wages to buy those things, and this was a precarious position indeed. As wage earners, we were even more beholden to a corporate world that still treated labor solely as a means to an end. Manufacturers routinely cut wages and used violence (and bribes to politicians) to crush any attempts by workers to unionize. Not surprisingly, the gap between the richest Americans and the rest was large and growing larger. As consumers, on the other hand, we confronted a marketplace that, to put it politely, did not always share our interests. Many new products and services were defective, dangerous, or fraudulent. The larger problem, however, was that many of the new products worked *too* ll, and provided us with more individual power than could often be ly or sustainably used. Our cars, for example, now went faster than our primitive road systems could safely support.* The newly accessible consumer credit, meanwhile, encouraged massive growth in household debt and helped set the stage for the 1929 crash and subsequent Depression. More and more, individuals had the capacity to gratify their desires at society's expense—a situation that is entirely familiar today, but which in those days was a "privilege" that had heretofore been limited to the very wealthy.

Our economy was moving dangerously out of balance. The further we shifted from a nation of producers to one of consumers, the more the output of private goods, such as powerful cars or consumer credit, was outpacing the output of "public goods," such as highway safety or stable credit markets. The market was tilting, gradually but relentlessly, toward the interests of the individual and away from the interests of society. Granted, this shift was entirely logical. From a purely economic standpoint, producing private goods, and especially those that delivered more personal power, was far more profitable than producing public goods. Yet, logical or not, this shift from public to private goods forced society to confront what would become the central modern dilemma: without some sort of recalibration, the economic interests of society would be obliterated, slowly but inexorably, by those of the self.

Yet this imbalance between public and private wasn't locked in place. Even before the crash of 1929, reformers such as Theodore Roosevelt and Woodrow Wilson had sought to use government's vast scale and power to reorder a marketplace too focused on short-term gratification, both corporate and individual. Monopolies such as Standard Oil and the railroad trusts were broken up and regulated. Workers were slowly empowered by a minimum wage and laws protecting collective bargaining (which gradually forced corporations to make peace with

---

* Traffic fatalities in the 1920s were about seventeen times higher, per mile traveled, than today.

their unions). Consumers were shielded with regulations from unsafe products, tainted food, and predatory lenders, and from the volatility of shortsighted speculators. Government also countered the underinvestment in public goods by spending heavily on education, research, and especially infrastructure (everything from roads and bridges to irrigation and reclamation projects), which then encouraged private industry to step up its own investments. Even the nascent culture of instant gratification and narrow self-interest could be attacked, if only rhetorically, through relentless political appeals—as when Franklin Roosevelt declared, in his 1933 inaugural address, that Americans "must move as a trained and loyal army willing to sacrifice for the good of a common discipline" and be "ready and willing to submit our lives and property to such discipline."[10] In other words, what the increasingly self-centered economy could not, or would not, produce on its own, government would now seek to *make* it produce.

The results of this ambitious rebalancing of social and private needs—a "New Deal," as Roosevelt called it—were striking. By the time the United States entered the Second World War in 1941, U.S. economic output had not only recovered from the crash, but was poised, thanks to both government and corporate investments, to launch a new generation of high-tech consumer goods and a new level of prosperity.[11] That launch was postponed by the war, but the delay merely allowed the consumer economy to reload and enlarge. Over the next four years, the government spent the modern equivalent of $4.3 trillion to ramp up industrial output,[12] with new factories, new manufacturing processes, and new technologies—while curbing consumption with rationing and other wartime restrictions. By the war's end, in 1945, Americans had put away the equivalent of $1.5 trillion in savings, waiting to be spent.[13] As the postwar era dawned, all that money, and all the pent-up desire it represented, poured through an industrial apparatus that was now much larger, more sophisticated, and far more responsive to consumer desire.

Conditions in the postwar period could not have been more ideal for a massive economic boom. Consumer demand was high. American companies such as General Motors, Ford, Esso, General Electric, AT&T, IBM, and DuPont not only were much bigger and more efficient, but had largely free rein in a global economy swept clean of foreign competition by the war. Natural resources were cheap—oil prices were just a quarter of today's level—and the technologies to use those resources were advancing so rapidly that industrial productivity (the amount of output per labor hour) was increasing by 3 to 4 percent a year. Over the next quarter century, the U.S. economy nearly tripled in size,[14] while GDP per capita more than doubled.[15] (The story would be similar in Japan and Western Europe, where postwar rebuilding programs, funded largely by U.S. taxpayers, would eventually triple per capita incomes.[16]) And critically, this new prosperity was much more broadly based than anything that had come before. Incomes at the bottom of the economic ladder actually grew faster than those at the top: "moving up" was now a central theme in American society. By the 1960s, median family incomes had increased by more than half,[17] meaning that two of every three American families were now in the middle class.[18]

Significantly, much of this increased economic equality reflected a continued willingness by government to intervene in the market. Washington was eager to avoid the often-violent labor strife that marked the prewar era.[*] As important, Washington was anxious to advance a "pro-worker" American labor policy that could, in effect, outshine the "workers' paradise" ostensibly proffered by America's new geopolitical rival, the Soviet Union. As a result, when unions and companies negotiated, the White House now openly supported generous contracts entitling workers to pensions, medical benefits, and, most important, a share in companies' productivity gains: for much of

[*] Violence that, shamefully, federal and state authorities often contributed to.

the postwar period, union contracts linked wage increases to the yearly growth in industrial productivity.[19] Likewise, government maintained a top marginal tax rate of 70 to 80 percent, which discouraged companies from returning to the high executive salaries of the Gilded Age. (Through the 1970s, the average CEO earned roughly twenty times the salary of the median employee—a small fraction of the gap today.)

But there was more at work than government meddling. By the 1950s and early 1960s, many corporations had, even if only grudgingly, accepted the reality of a more socially oriented economy. Many firms made peace with labor unions. They began making long-term investments in their workforces (for example, offering extensive employee training so workers could keep pace with rapidly changing technology). Health care and benefits became increasingly common. More and more, large firms were coming to resemble private welfare states. Their executives and boards may not have bought into the rhetoric of corporate social responsibility from management gurus such as Peter Drucker, but as makers of products for consumers, companies seemed to have grasped that their own prosperity was inseparable from the prosperity of those consumers. When General Motors CEO Charles Wilson, nominated by President Eisenhower to be defense secretary, was asked during his Senate confirmation hearing whether he would be able to make policy decisions that might harm his former employer, Wilson said yes, but insisted that such a decision was unlikely to come up, since national interests and corporate interests were almost perfectly aligned. "What was good for our country was good for General Motors and vice versa. The difference did not exist. Our company is too big. It goes with the welfare of the country."

What we had arrived at, it seemed, was a kind of equilibrium between social and individual power, one in which individuals' growing capabilities were balanced by strong social structures. The result would be characterized as a golden age in which individuals enjoyed the benefits of a wealthy, fully industrialized economy with far fewer of the insecurities that had plagued the economy before the war. By the 1960s, the average American—at least the average white male American—was earning more than twice what his grandfather had. He worked a third fewer hours each week and enjoyed a paternalistic corporate culture that offered benefits, lifetime employment, and a pension.[20] He lived in a house nearly twice as large as that of his grandparents (even though his own family was probably half as big), in a suburb far from the crush of the city, equipped with air-conditioning and labor saving appliances, with excellent schools and retail opportunities nearby. He had access to the best medical care and public health in the world, which, coupled with his better diet, meant he could also look forward to living six years longer than his grandfather had.[21] Those extra years, compounded by shorter work weeks, meant he had time not only for entertainment and leisure but also to improve himself—to read, travel, appreciate art, take night classes, and, generally, create a richer life and a more satisfying sense of self. As psychiatrist Paul Haun, chair of the American Psychiatric Association's committee for the study of leisure,[22] told *Life* in 1964, "We have the opportunity now for the development of all our human potentialities, whatever they may be."

Naturally, much of that potential would come through consumption. More and more, the act of consuming was seen as inseparable from the process of emotional growth and self-discovery—of uncovering, over successive model years and seasons and product cycles, our real selves. Everywhere we turned, it seemed, we were being invited to find ourselves through our consumption choices. "Virtually everything is motivated by subtle reference to the person's self-ideal—the kind of character ideal he wants to become," declared Pierre Martineau, one of the leading consumer marketing experts of the postwar era.[23] "In this yearning for self-expression, we reach for products, for brands, for institutions which will be compatible with our schemes of what we are or want to be." Even traditional social roles, such as work, parenting, and marriage, were being subtly transformed into modes of self-expression. As sociologist Robert Bellah has shown, by the late postwar period, many middle-class Americans had come to view love itself as an opportunity for "the mutual exploration of infinitely rich, complex and exciting selves."[24]

Granted, this constant search for self could be exhausting and stressful and even guilt inducing. There was the clear sense that despite the broad-based postwar prosperity, certain groups (women, say, or anyone of color) had not achieved *quite* the same level of personal power. There was the worry that our search for self was normalizing overconsumption—that we had entered the "age of the slob," as *New York Post* editorialist William Shannon put it, where the "loudest sound in the land has been the oink and grunt of private hoggishness."[25] And there was the nagging certainty that no matter how far we rose, no matter how much we spent or how grandly we redefined ourselves, there was always another level, another upgrade.

But here, too, industrial progress had given our average citizen the means to overcome. Each year brought a proliferation of new diversions on television and in theaters. We had a growing spectrum of pharmaceutical miracles such as Miltown and Librium. And by the 1960s, we had the beginnings of a personal technology boom—wave upon wave of transistor radios, televisions, hi-fis, and other consumer electronics—that was giving us the power to shape our leisure time to the exact specifications of personal taste. For the average postwar American (at least, the white middle-class ones), each year brought only more capacity to choose one's life—a capacity that seemed likely to grow larger, as our various treadmills continued to spin faster and more efficiently. We might not be "making" a living anymore, but increasingly, we had the power to make our lives. Or as *Life* magazine noted in 1964, "mankind now possesses for the first time the tools and knowledge to create whatever kind of world he wants."

And what kind of world did we want? Not such a bad one, it turned out. Despite the oink of private hoggishness and our growing fascination with our inner lives, the average American was still "willing to sacrifice for the good of a common discipline" when necessary. When John Kennedy exhorted his fellow Americans to ask what they could do for their country, a great many of us found the request more than reasonable. In fact, contrary to the cynics, our growing prosperity and personal power only seemed to make us want to engage more deeply in the wider society. We were becoming more politically active: voter turnout in the early 1960s was higher than it had been in half a century. We were also getting more involved in our communities: We volunteered and attended church in record numbers. We joined service groups like the Lions Club and the Rotary at an unprecedented rate and turned the Parent-Teacher Association into one of the nation's largest organizations. Americans, as one commentator noted in 1964, "are satisfying their gregarious urges in countless neighborhood committees to improve the local roads and garbage collections and to hound their public servants into doing what the name implies." Nor was ours an easy do-goodism: by the early 1960s, more and more of us were taking substantial social and personal risks to join in organized protests against racism, sexism, and other inequalities. And what we couldn't do ourselves we were more than ready to let the state do on our behalf: a majority of Americans supported a much larger and more expensive role for government than we have today.[26]

For all our hunger for personal power and capability, and for all the marketplace's willingness to sell us more of it, we remained surprisingly ready to give up some of that power in return for public goods—and in particular, for the social relationships that formed the bedrock of our communities and our private lives. As Alan Ehrenhalt, chronicler of twentieth-century American civic life, notes, postwar America was a nation of loyalties. Americans "stayed married to their spouses, to their political machines, to their baseball teams. Corporations also stayed married to the communities they grew up with." If that loyalty came at the expense of individual freedom, Ehrenhalt writes, it brought us a critical sense of personal security, by way of "communities that were, for the most part, familiar and secure; stable jobs and relationships whose survival we did not need to worry about in bed at night; rules that we could live by, or, when we were old enough, rebel against; and people known as leaders who were trusted with the task of seeing that the rules were enforced."[27]

None of which would have surprised social scientists of the time, particularly the "humanist" scholars such as psychologist Abraham Maslow. In the 1940s and 1950s, Maslow had developed a theory of human motivation dubbed the "hierarchy of needs," which posited a critical link between material progress and enlightened social behavior. Maslow's argument was simple: as individuals become more able to satisfy basic needs, such as food or shelter or physical security, their ambitions turn naturally and ineluctably toward higher aspirations, such as love and community standing, until eventually they reach their full human potential. These "self-actualized" individuals, Maslow argued, are not only happy and exceedingly functional; they also exhibit what he called the "democratic character structure"—that is, they tend to be independent and freethinking, yet also highly ethical, and tolerant. And, importantly, they are deeply inclined to engage with the world and in vital social and political processes. In short, these self-actualized types become just the sort of people you'd want as neighbors or teachers or voters.

The catch is that before this ascent up the hierarchy can begin, the proper material conditions must be met: individuals need the material capacity to satisfy not only lower needs, but successively higher and more complex ones. They need the wherewithal to keep moving up the ladder. But once these conditions are present, the individual's desire to seek out his or her higher potential becomes a nearly irresistible inner force, as fundamental and natural as any other drive. "What a man can be, he must be," Maslow wrote. Just as "a musician must make music, an artist must paint, a poet must write, if he is to be ultimately happy," so, too, the rest of us are driven to find whatever it is we "are fitted for."[28] We might not all reach self-actualization, but the closer we get to it, the more pronounced our democratic character structure becomes. As far as Maslow was concerned, the pathway to a humane democracy is as much a psychological, individual process as it is a political, collective process. And yet, the net effect of so much individual actualization is a collective transformation: entire societies, Maslow argued, can move up the hierarchy of needs and become more enlightened and democratic: "There is now a hierarchy of societies paralleling the hierarchy of basic needs."[29]

Maslow's optimistic vision of mass self-actualization was just that, a vision. But in the late 1960s, a University of Michigan political scientist named Ronald Inglehart was able to measure this connection between affluence and a more socially engaged, democratic personality. While studying postwar political movements in Europe, Inglehart had observed what was essentially the Maslowian hierarchy in action. Whereas people born before the Second World War, who had grown up insecure, gave priority to economic stability, political order, and other traditional "materialist" values (even if it meant sacrificing some individual liberties), those born after the war had quite different concerns. Raised in a time of economic growth, baby boomers had been relatively free to focus on less urgent objectives: entertainment and leisure, but also education, cultural enrichment, travel, political activism, and other more elevated pursuits. In short, boomers had been allowed to discover not simply what they needed, but what they *wanted*. And the more accustomed they—that is, *we*—became to such "self-expressive" autonomy, the more they sought to protect and *extend* that autonomy by supporting liberal social institutions, such as democracy, freedom of speech, gender equality, workers' rights, and environmental regulations. This was not merely a theory. Drawing on extensive survey data, Inglehart was able to show that this shift to self-expressive, "postmaterialist" values occurred anywhere material conditions improved.[30]

Inglehart's "silent revolution" helped explain many of the developments in the second half of the twentieth century. We could see it in the massive political conflicts in the 1960s, as the postwar generation battled its parents' generation over everything from racial injustice to the war in Vietnam. We could see it in such things as the environmental movement, the emergence of new tolerance for cultural diversity, and the constant pressure for democracy by oppressed peoples across the globe. Further, postmaterialism showed us where civilization was headed. As economic growth continued, and as the older, more materialist generations died off, Inglehart argued, entire societies would gradually adopt postmaterialist values. The "tipping point," Inglehart later predicted, would occur around the end of the century, when postmaterialists would outnumber materialists. From then on, momentum would build toward a global postmaterialist revolution, when all of society would be configured to help the individual reach his or her highest potential.

For all its appeal, Inglehart's silent revolution seemed to carry a number of potential risks. Most obviously, if our social evolution depended on steady gains in prosperity, what would happen if those gains slowed, or stopped altogether? Would we slip back down the hierarchy and become more materialist once again—and perhaps undergo a different, much less silent revolution? Certainly by the late 1960s and early 1970s one could see the warning signs of an economy struggling to maintain a growth rate high enough to keep adding more jobs and higher wages. Inflation was creeping up. American dominance over the global marketplace was slipping. Most alarmingly, productivity at U.S. companies was slowing—our workers were no longer producing as much new wealth each year as they once had—and crucially, this slowdown occurred just as new competition was appearing in the rebuilt economies of Asia and Europe. And to top it all off, in the Middle East, exporters of oil, the single most critical raw material for an industrial, highly mobile society, were raising prices. If the economy tanked, would our social evolution tank as well?

And what of the opposite scenario? Suppose, instead, that our economic and technological advances continued to provide individuals with so much autonomy and self-expressive freedom that we no longer felt the need to support those high-minded postmaterialist, collective values? In fact, Inglehart would later warn of just such a pattern: as societies become more postmaterialist, he found, citizens tend to become steadily more individualistic in outlook, and to be less inclined, for instance, to support traditional, collective values and institutions. Inglehart and his colleagues insisted that any such surge in individualism wouldn't lead to "asocial egoism." His postmaterialists, he argued, would remain as committed to their communities and their societies as any of their predecessors had been.[31] Yet there were plenty of examples where consumers were exploiting their soaring individual capabilities in ways that were decidedly unenlightened and asocial. A case in point involved the automobile, which had become so large and powerful that it was creating a safety crisis on the nation's highways and, by the late 1960s, was contributing to serious air pollution, the overreliance on imported oil, and other reductions in "public" goods. And cars, surely, were just the start. As personal technologies made it easier and easier to pursue our aspirations without the acquiescence of those around us—or even at their expense—where would our postmaterialist society be then?

Or suppose it were possible to move both ways at once. For, as it happened, as the optimism of the postwar economic boom gave way to the much different, and difficult, circumstances of the 1970s, we had the opportunity to watch both scenarios unfold simultaneously.

CHAPTER 2

No Confidence

Twelve times a year, staff members at the University of Michigan's Survey Research Center dial up five hundred consumers and ask them how they are feeling about the American economy. Callers work from a list of fifty questions covering the full range of the consumer experience. There are questions about the consumer's expectations for the overall economy. (For example: "Do you think now is a good time or a bad time to buy a house?"[1]) There are personal queries. ("During the next 12 months, do you expect your income to be higher or lower than during the past year?") The answers, an amalgam of opinion, observation, aspiration, and anxiety—the self as seen by economists—are crunched into a single number, the University of Michigan Index of Consumer Sentiment, which is released mid-month and is one of the most closely watched of all economic indicators. Although the citizens surveyed are rarely experts in economics, their aggregated answers reliably foretell what will happen, three to twelve months hence, on everything from inflation and unemployment to home purchases, retail sales, and overall growth. An index of 85 or above almost always indicates that good times are coming. A drop of fifteen points, by contrast, nearly always predicts a recession. In recent years, the index has languished between 70 and 80—well below the numbers we put up in the postwar period, but a reasonable reflection of our ongoing anxiety over an anemic recovery.

The acuity of the index isn't surprising when you think about it. When 70 percent of the economy comes from consumer spending, much of it discretionary, the sentiments of those consumers can't help but be predictive. In any case, the University of Michigan index (along with its archrival, the New York–based Consumer Confidence Index) is embraced by the marketplace as if it were God's truth. Retailers and manufacturers dutifully build the indexes into their holiday forecasts and production schedules. The Federal Reserve and other central banks use them to set interest rates and other economic policy. And of course Wall Street treats the indexes as potentially lucrative "market-moving" data. Within milliseconds of the indexes' release, millions of shares of "consumer-facing" companies are purchased or dumped as traders—or, more precisely, their fast computers—race to convert our aspirations and anxieties directly into capital gains.* If consumer sentiment truly represents the essence of the consumer mind, then the gap between self and marketplace is now measured in fractions of seconds.

Sentiment indexes also provide an interesting way to track the evolving relationship between the self and the marketplace. The Michigan survey was created just after the Second World War, and for the first quarter century, the index hovered between 90 and 100 in an echo of our postwar prosperity and optimism. But in the 1970s the line abruptly turned jagged. The index plunged into the low fifties, recovered briefly, and then plunged even further. In part, our seesawing mood reflected a string of economic shocks, starting with the rise of competition from Europe and Asia and ending with oil price spikes, and the most severe recessions (in 1974 and again in 1980) since the

---

* In 2012, the University of Michigan came under fire after it was revealed that, since 2009, the index had been quietly released to a select group of high-frequency traders two seconds before the rest of the market saw it.

Great Depression. Almost overnight, our postwar prosperity vanished. Incomes stagnated. Joblessness was epidemic. The confidence we'd enjoyed in American economic dominance had been replaced by the insecurity and unfamiliarity of a more global economy.

But our wavering sentiment reflected another, deeper change. In the 1980s, conservative politicians such as Ronald Reagan had embarked on a series of bold new economic and social policies. Where governments since Roosevelt's New Deal had played a heavy role in the economy, we now shifted to a free-market, or "laissez-faire," policy that granted the maximum degree of economic freedom for businesses and individuals alike. This return to a more unfettered economic policy (*laissez-faire* means, literally, "let us do") marked an abrupt end to decades of government strategy, but it was probably inevitable. The economic crises of the 1970s had shaken Americans' faith in government's ability to manage the economy. According to conservative economists, it was precisely that New Deal–style attempt at economic management, via heavy regulations, high taxes, and strong support for labor unions, that kept U.S. companies from answering foreign competition. For Reagan and other conservatives (most notably, Margaret Thatcher in the United Kingdom), the solution was obvious: only by turning loose economic actors, businesses and consumers alike, to look after their own self-interest could one hope to lift society back into the light.

But that wasn't quite how things would turn out. Liberated by a new political philosophy and energized by new technologies, American companies would undergo a second revolution in efficiency that stripped away any operation or asset that didn't add directly to the bottom line. After decades of social restraints, American business was finally allowed to do what business does best—cut costs and maximize profits—and by the 1990s, this purified form of capitalism had pulled the U.S. business sector back to the top of the global economy. For many U.S. workers, however, it was a different story entirely. Simply put, our newly efficient business sector no longer produced the public goods that had fueled so much of our collective prosperity. As this second efficiency revolution hit its stride, we saw not only the declining fortunes for tens of millions of Americans, but also a disturbing shift in the relationship between the self and the marketplace. It's at this turning point that the story of the Impulse Society resumes.

If this unsettled new era of free markets and bold new theories could be distilled to a single character type, it would be that of the corporate raider. Where the dominant figure of the postwar business world was the empire builder (the CEO methodically assembling vast armies of workers and arsenals of products), the new figure on the scene was more like a demolitions expert or a hit man. The raiders' m.o. was simple: they looked for struggling companies whose sagging share price made them a bargain, quietly bought up a controlling stake (usually with high-interest loans, known as "junk bonds"), and then began what was euphemistically referred to as "restructuring." In some cases, the raiders—epitomized by flashy characters such as bond trader Carl Icahn and real estate mogul Victor Posner—would go on a downsizing tear. They shut down underperforming divisions and laid off hundreds and even thousands of employees before selling the restructured firm at a substantial profit. In other cases, the target would simply be liquidated: broken up into separate entities and sold off piecemeal. Through the 1980s, hundreds of companies were taken over and reorganized or eliminated entirely. The business pages were filled with gory details of economic violence done to venerable firms and to the employees and communities who had depended on them. There was Posner, who drained the pension funds from his takeover targets to bankroll a royal lifestyle of yachting and horses. There was Icahn, who, after raiding TWA, directed the struggling airline to borrow half a billion dollars (most of which he paid to himself), then sold off the airline's most profitable routes (a practice known as asset stripping) to service the debt. There was even a raiders' gala—a posh annual conference hosted by the deal-making firm Drexel Burnham Lambert for all the big names in restructuring, known as the "Predators' Ball."

For many critics, and a great many more traumatized former employees, the corporate raider perfectly captured the "greed is good" zeitgeist that overran American corporate culture in the 1980s. But to an emerging school of conservative economists, the raider was nothing less than an economic savior. Raiders had appeared because share prices were falling, and share prices had fallen in part because the companies were being mismanaged. After thirty years of postwar prosperity, many American firms had become complacent and inefficient. They had hired too many employees, expanded into too many side businesses. They had lost the religion of cost control. As a result, many American firms had been beaten by foreign competitors and were entirely unprepared for the recession. Share prices had plunged—the New York Stock Exchange fell by 50 percent in the early 1970s—and shareholders had watched, powerless, as their investments were nearly halved. For, in those days, shareholders had almost no say in the running of a company: decisions were made largely by corporate executives who treated shareholders (and share price) as a secondary concern, well behind factors such as labor or suppliers. As far as Wall Street was concerned, corporate raiders were the market's way of correcting years of bad management.

That correction was surprisingly swift. As one company after another was taken over and taken apart, corporate America panicked. Even unraided firms scrambled to fend off raiders by keeping their share prices high. Companies cut costs ruthlessly. As important, they began compensating their executives in company stock, thus transforming executives' priorities and strategies. CEOs who had once regarded shareholders as interfering busybodies now became shareholders themselves, embracing shareholder's obsession with share price and working to keep share as high as possible. This new fixation on share prices alarmed many traditional management experts—but it delighted the new shareholder advocates. In their view, a high share price meant the stock market was pleased, and the stock market, it was now argued, was rarely wrong. Under a concept known as the "efficient markets hypothesis," the market—or, more precisely, the hundreds of thousands of investors who carefully studied publicly traded companies—constituted a vast, virtually omniscient intelligence. This intelligence constantly assessed companies' strengths and weaknesses and then signaled which firms were hot and which were not by either buying or selling shares. Buying shares sent share prices up; selling shares sent prices down—in either case, the efficient market had spoken. The way forward was clear. Companies that embraced the wisdom of the efficient market, and aligned themselves with it—and thus kept their share prices high—would thrive. Those that did not would be destroyed. And so was born what came to be called, with the lack of irony possible only on Wall Street, a shareholder revolution.

This more Darwinian view of business represented a dramatic departure from the postwar philosophy. In that era, corporations had been seen as obligated not just to shareholders, but to all "stakeholders," not least workers and their communities. But the stakeholder idea, conservative theorists now argued, was simply wrong. A corporation is not some social entity with dependent constituencies. It is merely a legal contrivance, a "nexus of a set of contracting relationships,"[2] as economist Michael Jensen put it, whose sole purpose is maximizing "shareholder value." This nexus is no more obligated to anyone else (employees, say) than you or I am obligated to shop at a particular grocery store.* For advocates of "shareholder value" theory, it was this

---

* As economists Armen Alchian and Harold Demsetz famously put it, "I have no contract to continue to purchase from the grocer, and neither the employer nor the employee is bound by any contractual obligations to continue their relationship."

very idea of social obligations (that business somehow *owed* workers, or any other part of society, anything beyond efficient operations) that led so many firms to fail in their *real* social obligation: maximizing the wealth upon which all social progress depends. As economist Milton Friedman argued in a much-quoted article in *The New York Times*, "There is one and only one social responsibility of business—to use its resources and engage in activities designed to increase its profits." Here was the corporate variation on Adam Smith's "invisible hand." Companies turned loose to maximize their own wealth would improve society's fortunes far more efficiently than would any government-induced strategy based on an ideal of social responsibility.

By the 1980s the logic of efficient markets and shareholder value had expanded into a political philosophy. The market was not only the most efficient arbiter of corporate strategy, but also the most efficient means to organize a free society. The shift away from the managed economy of the postwar and the embrace of an unfettered, "efficient" marketplace was paralleled by a rightward swing in American political culture. For Reagan, Thatcher, and other conservatives had been successful not only in removing many business regulations (such as those impeding corporate takeovers), but also in discrediting the idea that government had any positive role to play in the economy. As Reagan famously quipped, "The most terrifying words in the English language are: I'm from the government and I'm here to help."

This new faith in free markets trickled down into every social sector. At many law schools and business schools, shareholder value became the new orthodoxy for future business leaders—despite some glaring inconsistencies. Damon Silvers, a labor lobbyist in Washington, DC, who graduated from both Harvard Business and Law Schools shortly after the shareholder revolution, recalls how shareholder value theory clashed with some of the more traditional management ideas. "You would hear a professor saying, 'A firm is a nexus of contracts; what matters is incentives'; and then literally ten minutes later, they would talk about the importance of teamwork. And you'd say, 'Well, hold on, you can't believe these two things at the same time. They're completely inconsistent.'"[3] Yet by the time this new generation of managers and corporate lawyers was rising through the ranks of the business world, most such concerns had faded. Companies had quickly become accustomed not only to less regulation and weaker unions (which had lost most government backing and a lot of membership), but also to the relaxing of traditional norms that had guided corporate management. Where postwar businesses had been satisfied with steady, long-term growth, managers were now expected to pursue strategies that could deliver much higher earnings and share prices—and were richly rewarded when they succeeded, since more and more of their compensation was in the form of stock. Inevitably, corporate strategy gravitated toward techniques that could lift share prices by boosting company earnings. And since one of the fastest ways to boost earnings is to cut costs, cost cutting now emerged as corporate America's go-to strategy. In fact, during the 1980s, it became an article of faith in the corporate world that the fastest way to please Wall Street and boost share price was simply to announce a major layoff. The days of the Company Man were over.

But this was only the opening round. For just as the revolutionaries were starting to remake the business world in the image of the efficient market, they got a powerful new tool—this one invented not on Wall Street but in Silicon Valley—that would push the shareholder revolution into hyperdrive and push the marketplace so deeply into the self that the two would seem permanently joined. The Impulse Society was about to be born.

Although business had used computers since the 1950s, the technology was so costly that its revolutionary potential was largely muted. But in 1972 this began to change with the arrival of the microprocessor, a tiny silicon chip etched with thousands of data-storing transistors that did what the big mainframe computers did, but faster, and at a fraction of the cost. The first microprocessor, Intel's 4004, had barely enough power to run a desk calculator. But fierce competition between Intel and its rivals[4] soon produced chips that were doubling in power, and halving in cost, every eighteen months. By the early 1980s, this twin curve of exponentially rising power and declining cost, known as Moore's Law (after Intel cofounder Gordon Moore), was enabling companies to flood the marketplace with ever-cheaper computing power.

For most of us, the most familiar consequence of the digital revolution was the personal computer and all its primitive, floppy-disk, green-text glory. In the context of the Impulse Society, however, the more immediate effect of this cheap computing power was an acceleration in the realignment of the business world with the will of the shareholder. Wall Street would now become an even more ruthless enforcer of corporate efficiency. With computers and computer-aided data lines, brokers and investment bankers could monitor company performance in near-real time, analyze company data rapidly, and then, thanks to computerized trading, act on that data almost instantly. By the 1980s a company reporting unsatisfactory quarterly earnings might see its stock price fall within minutes, and soon, seconds.

But computers also allowed companies to exploit more quickly the profit-making opportunities that Wall Street was demanding. With computer-assisted design and manufacturing, for example, companies could get a new product to market, and a return to investors, much more quickly. (In Detroit, the time needed to move a new car from drawing board to showroom fell from four years to just eighteen months.[5]) But the computer's real contribution was in cost cutting. Manufacturers could automate steadily more, and more complex, operations, allowing production volumes to climb rapidly while labor costs fell. Offshoring became much easier. An engineer in

San Francisco or New York (or Berlin or Tokyo) could create a new product on-screen and then flash the design to a factory in Mexico or China or wherever labor costs were lowest. With computers, the modern corporation truly could be a nexus, a shape-shifting entity that rapidly reconfigured capital, labor, and raw materials in whatever forms and locations brought the fastest return at any given moment.

And those returns were impressive. By the 1990s, corporate profits were soaring. The stock market was on fire. Shareholder returns (that is, share price appreciation plus dividends*) for the five hundred companies on the Standard & Poor's 500 were more than twice the level of the 1960s and nearly as high as the boom times of the 1950s.[6] With each quarterly report, the shareholder revolution and the logic of efficient markets were looking more and more right-eous—so much so that many firms granted senior managers steadily larger blocks of company stock in order to "incentivize" them to create even more value. By then, rapid increases in computing power had unleashed the Internet and the surge in technology stocks. For many experts, the dot-com boom was final confirmation of a new economic order, a double helix of digital power and market efficiency that, in theory, was capable of generating even more wealth than the postwar economy. America was back on top.

What was becoming clear, however, was that this massive new pros-perity wasn't anywhere near as broadly shared as its postwar prede-cessor had been—and this was hardly accidental. No longer hobbled by government intervention or expectations of social duties, American businesses were free to focus on a much more efficient and narrowly defined prosperity—one that gratified the interests of shareholders and executives, but left other parties to fend largely for themselves. Here was the logical outcome of our new, efficient markets—the

---

* A dividend is the portion of a firm's profits paid to shareholders periodically.

distillation of business into a pure, almost abstract form of capitalism, one that moved directly from investment to return with few inefficiencies left in between. Here, too, was the other, less expected part of the Impulse Society and its merger of self and marketplace: the corporation, free now to focus entirely on its own narrow gratification, could behave less like a social, collective institution and more like a self—an individual ego obsessed with its own agenda and utterly unmoved by the interests of others.

You could see this rising industrial egoism most clearly in the wave after wave of cutbacks, whose severity and duration went well beyond the traditional pattern of the business cycle. In previous recessions, there were layoffs, but they were always followed by surges in job growth during the recoveries. That wasn't the pattern now. Many of the eliminated jobs never came back, especially in the manufacturing sector, traditionally the biggest source of stable, mid-wage middle-class jobs. Between 1979 and 1983, more than 2 million American factory jobs were cut.[7] Yet even as the economy boomed in the late 1980s, not only did those lost jobs stay lost, but another 4.6 million manufacturing jobs disappeared permanently.[8] Certainly, the economy was creating lots of new jobs, including many in the new information technology sector, but not enough to offset the wages lost in manufacturing. Median incomes, which had risen swiftly and steadily in the postwar period, began to taper.

By the early 1990s, as the economy was undergoing its first "jobless" recovery, it was increasingly apparent that the postwar prosperity wasn't coming back—or at least, not for a large chunk of the workforce. In place of stable employment, we now had routine layoffs. Many remaining employees were turned into "contractors," a status with lower, or no, benefits, less security, and less chance for advancement. Wage growth now stalled out completely. From 1973 to 1993 the income for the median American family, adjusted for inflation, grew just 7 percent[9]—a far cry from the doubling in incomes that had occurred in the preceding quarter century. For middle-class workers, the shift in fortunes was stark. In 1973 a thirty-year-old man in a middle-wage job was making 60 percent more than his father had twenty years before. By 1993 the man's son was making 25 percent *less* than the man was in 1973. For the first time since the Second World War, wage growth, the centerpiece of postwar prosperity, and the mainspring behind our generous postmaterialist aspirations, could no longer be assumed.

The reasons for this downward income shift are still heatedly debated. Part of it, clearly, reflected the decline of the labor movement. As manufacturing jobs were eliminated, unions became not only smaller but less effective: in the 1950s and 1960s the United States saw around three hundred major labor strikes a year as unions pushed management for higher wages; by the 1980s, there were barely eighty strikes a year and just thirty-four in the 1990s.[10] Likewise, the computer-driven step change in manufacturing efficiency also undermined labor: manufacturers could produce far more output with far fewer workers. In fact, because computers were becoming so much cheaper and more capable by the year,[11] companies found it more profitable to invest in computers and computer-related machinery while reducing their investments in labor. Simply put, the return on technology was better than the return on people.

But workers' falling fortunes also reflected the degree to which the shareholder revolution had been internalized by a corporate management obsessed with cost cutting. True, there had been costs to cut: postwar corporate America had grown fat and lazy. Both management and labor had become accustomed to a business model that operated, in many cases, like a private welfare state. Unions in particular had failed to respond to the new economic realities, such as foreign competition—or to deal with their own complacency and corruption: many continued to demand regular, large wage increases even as worker productivity fell off. But that was only half of the story. From the start, it had been clear that the shareholder revolution wasn't solely about making business efficient. Thanks to the new model of stock-based executive compensation, the incentive for managers to create personal fortunes through ever-deeper cuts was becoming overwhelming. And since labor is always one of the top expenses, employees bore the brunt, not only through layoffs, outsourcing, and automation, but also in dramatic reductions in other benefits, including worker training—a loss that all but guaranteed that employees' value to the company would continue to decline.

The result, argues William Lazonick, an economist at the University of Massachusetts, was a complete reversal of what had become a bedrock of American business. Where postwar managers had followed what Lazonick calls a "retain and reinvest" strategy— they automatically plowed a large share of corporate profits back into the company in the form of new plants and higher wages—their postrevolutionary counterparts hewed to a strategy of "downsize-and-distribute."[12] That is, managers cut everything possible and passed along the savings to shareholders (and themselves) in the form of higher dividends and faster stock price appreciation. Cutbacks, once seen as temporary responses to recessions and other specific economic events, now became a routine, perpetual operational measure that required no crisis and certainly no justification. Management now cut all the time, in good times or bad. The shareholder revolution may have begun as an effort to squeeze out corporate waste and inefficiency, Lazonick told me. But it quickly became a socially acceptable rationalization for giving senior managers "totally free rein to get rid of the labor force and make other changes that [previously] would have been politically difficult—and get paid handsomely for doing it."[13] In the 1970s a CEO salary of one million dollars would have been rare. By the 1990s, thanks to stock options, a CEO could come away with a compensation package worth tens of millions and, in some cases, hundreds of millions of dollars.

What's more, thanks to the broad political acceptance of free-market theory, such massive compensation was widely regarded by policymakers as entirely just. By the 1980s and 1990s, mainstream society accepted the idea that whatever salary the efficient market was willing to tolerate was, by definition, entirely reasonable. And the market was in a tolerant mood, in large part because, in a self-perpetuating pattern, a new crop of stock "incentivized" executives had proven so willing to do whatever it took to keep share prices high. It is telling that one of the most lauded chief executives in modern American history is Jack Welch, who, as CEO of General Electric, earned the nickname Neutron Jack for eliminating more than one hundred thousand jobs between 1981 and 1985.[14]

This marked a profound change in corporate culture, to say the least. The typical postwar corporation had operated almost like a sovereign nation, complete with its own "nationalist" customs and norms that promoted employee pride and unity as a means to beat competitors. Even in industries where management and labor fought constantly, there was a grudging acceptance that neither side could prosper without the other. But the new corporate culture was far less familial. Employees increasingly saw management as ruthless and entirely self-serving, willing to cut loose anyone or anything in order to maximize its own compensation. This was not far from the mark. Under a corporate strategy centered increasingly on quick cost reductions and share price appreciation, management had every reason to treat its workforce like a balloonist treats ballast—the more he throws over the side, the higher he goes.

What is perhaps most curious about this steadily escalating disruption of economic security during the 1980s is the virtual lack of a sustained political backlash. Richard Curtin, longtime director of the University of Michigan consumer survey, says that when economic calamity first struck in the early 1970s, it provoked substantial political and social protest. After decades of postwar prosperity, Americans "were reluctant to give up their aspirations,"[15] Curtin told me. "And ultimately, they blamed government." And, indeed, Reagan's landslide victory over Democrat Jimmy Carter was unquestionably a protest. Americans were noisily rejecting New Deal postwar economic policies in favor of an ideal, however problematic, of unfettered capitalism and individual economic freedom. And yet, by the late 1980s, as laissez-faire and efficient markets failed to restore postwar prosperity, and even appeared to have eroded it even further, voters were curiously quiet.

Part of what this quiet reflected was the shrinking labor movement, which no longer had the political heft to support New Deal policies. But there were other story lines here. One, certainly, is that a great many Americans were enjoying the fruits of Reaganomics. Those in the upper income quintiles saw incomes and wealth increase steadily during the 1980s, thanks in no small part to declining taxes and a booming stock market. For the first time since the 1920s, the upper classes began to pull away from the rest of the population.

Yet even among Americans being left behind, support for free-market ideas remained surprisingly strong. Why? To understand that, we need to return to the ideas of Maslow and Inglehart, who argued that postwar prosperity allowed us to aspire to our better selves, and to a better society. As prosperity faltered, we now found ourselves in a paradoxical position. Most Americans were still much wealthier than their grandparents had been. But our ascent had stopped: we could no longer count on advancing economically as rapidly as those earlier generations had. Many of us had entered what Ted Nordhaus and Michael Shellenberger have called a state of "insecure affluence," where our material needs were still largely met, but our desires for better status, or more self-esteem, or other post-material aspirations, were being thwarted, which left us angry, anxious, and ready to blame someone. And yet, while such anger and anxiety, twenty years earlier, might have motivated us to take political action, the current culture pushed us in another direction. For many, the failures and excesses of the 1960s had tarnished the tradition of collective action. Even many Democratic voters had come to feel that the Great Society expansion of the New Deal welfare state had ultimately weakened the country.* Instead, many of us embraced the ideal of economic individualism, resurrected in all its Gilded Age grandeur, under which a person's fortunes were seen largely as a matter of individual initiative. Granted, in a globalizing, digitalizing, shareholder-dominated economy, individual initiative often fell painfully short. But this paradox failed to dislodge the potent message of unfettered economic opportunity: sooner or later, it really would be morning in America.

In the meantime, another factor was diluting our anger and anxiety. Many Americans might have found their fortunes derailed in the efficient marketplace, but that same marketplace was allowing us to gratify our aspirations in other ways. Thanks to remarkable efficiencies in computing, nearly every kind of product or service could be produced and delivered for a fraction of what preceding generations had paid. Between 1970 and 1989, real prices for durable goods in the United States tumbled by 26 percent. Food costs as a share of household expenses plummeted. The price of a pound of chicken dropped by half. A McDonald's cheeseburger cost 40 percent less. Consumption was becoming so cheap that the very idea of limits began to change. The ethic of frugality that had defined the American character before the Second World War, and that had briefly resurfaced during the 1970s recession, was finally put to rest as marketers used low prices and relentless abundance to teach us, as technology writer Chris

* Similarly, the obvious decay of the Soviet Union and the struggles of many socialist governments eroded the optimism, even on the American left, of a viable alternative to capitalism.

Anderson has noted, "how to waste newly abundant resources [and] to ignore our instincts about costs and scarcity."[16]

Computers made consumption cheaper, but also a lot more interesting. Computerized assembly lines meant companies could more rapidly shift between products—a single factory could generate many different models, and could upgrade those models more frequently. Computerized supply chains and inventory meant retailers such as Walmart and Target could more easily carry a much wider variety of products. And since greater variety tends to stimulate more purchases, businesses were encouraged to offer still more variety, and so on. Where a 1950s-era supermarket might have sold three thousand different products, or "stock keeping units" (SKUs),[17] by 1990 the number was ten times as high.[18] (Walmart stores would eventually carry more than one hundred thousand SKUs.) In everything from cars and clothing to interior decoration and music, Moore's Law of exponentially increasing computing power was leading to exponential increases in product choices. We had so many choices that consumption was becoming an exercise in customization—of being able to choose from among a nearly infinite menu of products and services to craft a consumption experience that perfectly suited our individual tastes. A case in point: Thanks to the miracle of the videocassette recorder, we no longer had to watch what everyone else was watching. If we wanted art films, we could rent art films. Romantic comedies. Japanese anime. Horror. Gore. Porn.* By the late 1980s, thousands of video titles were available, and video sales and rentals surpassed movie ticket sales.[20] The story was the same across the consumer spectrum. Jeff Madrick, with the New School's Schwartz Center for Economic Policy Analysis, estimates that between 1970 and 1995, the total number of consumer product SKUs available in the United States in any given year jumped by a

---

* Video technology was so much cheaper and easier to process than film that, by the mid-1980s, a revived porn industry was putting out 150 new "titles" every *week*.[19]

factor of as much as ten. Across most of the postindustrial West, notes Madrick, we had entered "the age of consumer choice."

The feedback loop between marketplace and consumer, between the economy and the self, was shifting into much higher gear. Even if we could no longer reliably improve our economic conditions, we could continue the postwar project of self-improvement and self-discovery. What had begun as crude quests for identity and self-actualization was now industrialized and professionalized into full-scale social agenda. We renovated our homes to match our emotional interiors. We pursued inner perfection through Scientology, Transcendental Meditation, and est. Physical fitness, for decades a specialty of athletes and drill sergeants, became the centerpiece of a secular religion. Between 1970 and 1990, the number of joggers in the United States jumped from perhaps one hundred thousand[21] to thirty million.[22] Gyms appeared by the thousands, and stores and catalogues burst with a new set of "productivity" tools (running shoes and spandex; stationary bikes and treadmills; the Universal gym and the aerobics routine; protein powders and carbo-loading; heart rate monitors and training diaries) that let us attend to the project of the self with ever-greater efficiency.

As important, even as computers were energizing our self-discovery, the technology also made it easier for us to finance the effort. With computerized credit scoring, banks could make loan decisions and approve credit cards in minutes, not days or weeks, as had once been the case. Further, because computers let banks more easily categorize borrowers by credit score, income, and other personal data, our multiplying debts could now be "bundled" into securities and sold to Wall Street investors for a tidy profit. Banks now had not only extra incentive to lend us credit, but also extra capital to lend, since cash from the sale of the "securitized" loans could be re-lent, and these new loans could also be securitized, and on and on. As the rising supply of credit helped push down interest rates, bankers' traditional source of profits narrowed. To compensate—and thus maintain the returns that Wall Street was demanding—bankers adopted a volume model. Credit would now be marketed as creatively and as aggressively as any other consumer product. Banks began lending for pretty much anything you could think of: home mortgages and car loans, but also home improvement, college education, vacations, boats, debt consolidation, even cosmetic surgery. And the more credit we were offered, the more we used. Our incomes might have been flattening as globalization, technology, and new business tactics remade the economy. But our spending power was, thanks in part to those same revolutionary forces, still climbing so rapidly that, from a certain angle, it was as if postwar prosperity really had returned.

By the mid-1990s the intertwined forces of computerization and finance had pushed the economy into another boom, and we resumed our self-discovery and identity creation with a renewed intensity. Ralph Brown, a sociologist at Brigham Young University who specializes in the sociology of commerce, suggests that for all but the very poorest of Americans, the process of acquiring an identity via consumption had become so efficient that it was almost second nature. "If we had a hankering for something new in our lives, we could just go out and get it," Brown told me. "We could buy an identity in a heartbeat. And the more easily we could do that, the more efficiently we can buy an identity, the more the efficiency itself becomes part of the identity."[23]

Certainly, there were concerns about how long this new efficiency could be sustained. In 1987 a lending bubble, fueled by too-easy computerized credit, burst, leading to a stock market crash that was made all the worse when computerized stock trading went out of control. Clearly, all the risks of a high-tech marketplace had yet to be uncovered. As one veteran broker complained, "We have made so many changes . . . we simply don't know what they add up to. We don't know where the technology is taking us."[24] For consumers, meanwhile, the new economy, despite all its new enticements, hadn't actually restored our economic security. Although incomes had kicked up toward the end of the 1990s, the overall growth rate (2.3 percent a year) was a third less than during the postwar period.[25]

Our capacity to self-gratify, meanwhile, was becoming so prodigious that we were running up all sorts of debts: financial, but also social, psychological, and even physical. We grew fat, despite our fitness obsession. We consumed oceans of tranquilizers and antidepressants. Our intensifying focus on self-improvement had grown so pervasive that many of us had little time or energy or thought for anything *not* related to the self. For many critics, the once-promising drive toward self-actualization, social engagement, and the "democratic character" had now become another brand of self-help—and justification for social withdrawal. Self-improvement, complained writer Peter Marin, had become the means for "a retreat from the worlds of morality and history, an unembarrassed denial of human reciprocity and community."[26]

Retreat was becoming the norm. The urban flight of the 1950s and 1960s had turned into a broad-based disengagement from society. Intellectuals, academics, and the rest of the "creative class," so central to the Progressive movement and the emergence of New Deal liberalism earlier in the century, were now abandoning those grand projects and cloistering themselves in trendy neighborhoods, private schools, and even strategic marriages: it was becoming less and less common to "marry down" or interact socially with those on a lower socioeconomic rung. "In effect, they have removed themselves from the common life,"[27] grumbled Christopher Lasch. And even among those still living the "common life," the older notions of solidarity and community were under pressure as the focus on the self, and rising expectations of personal freedom, made collective, communal action seem less and less relevant. It was a change many social critics found troubling. As Alan Ehrenhalt, a keen observer of our evolving urban society, warned in the mid-1990s, "Privacy, individualism, and choice are not free goods, and the society that places no restrictions on them will pay a high price for that decision."[28]

By the 1990s our aloofness had become endemic. In a widely read book, *Bowling Alone*, Harvard political scientist Robert Putnam bemoaned the loss of "social capital" as American citizens disengaged from social and community activities. We were voting less than in the past. We signed fewer petitions, wrote fewer letters to our congressmen, kept up less with political news. We volunteered less frequently, joined fewer clubs and organizations, went to church less often, served less often on local committees. We even visited our neighbors less frequently and had fewer close confidants. About the only thing that was increasing was our materialism: between 1965 and 1995, the percentage of college freshman who listed "getting rich" as a top life goal jumped from under half to just over three-quarters.[29]

And little wonder: at every turn, we were now surrounded by unapologetic materialism. Sports stars were now free-agent multimillionaires. Rock musicians and authors rocketed overnight from obscurity to affluence and celebrity. In the business world, even the pretense of corporate high-mindedness had been usurped entirely by the open pursuit of maximum rewards. Raiders and arbitrage specialists made hundreds of millions of dollars. The average CEO now outearned the median employee by a factor of one hundred to one—up from twenty to one two decades earlier.[30] The Gilded Age was back, but with none of the reformers.

Yet even before we could seriously question the durability of our new strategies and the sustainability of our new consumer culture, our attention was diverted by yet another surge of personal power that would push the self-centered economy to an even more commanding height.

The iconic image of this next wave is that of a baby-faced Steve Jobs, dapper in his Beatles haircut and black tux, unveiling his Apple

Macintosh before a hushed crowd of Apple shareholders in January 1984. Personal computers had been around since the late 1970s, but the Macintosh was the first machine that actually catered to the dimensions and desires of the average person, and its success would change everything. Watching the Macintosh event now (on YouTube, of course) you can still feel the shock of the new: the Macintosh is small, with a tiny, flickering black-and-white display, but the effect on the crowd is electrifying. Few outside the industry had ever seen graphical images, or a point-and-click, drag-and-drop "user interface"—we were all still typing in commands via DOS. Nor had anyone seen software that let you draw or paint or change fonts. The Macintosh even spoke to Jobs and the shareholders via a prerecorded monologue that, despite its tinny electronic accent (and perhaps because of it), drew wild applause. Here was a technology that, even in its preliminary form, hinted at a kind of magical potency, a level of individual power that no one, even at the height of our postwar glory, could have imagined. The gap between wanting and having, between who we are and what we love, was rapidly approaching zero.

Indeed, the gap *did* hit zero, in the online world. By the mid-1990s, the point-and-click splendors of Jobs's gadget had grown into an entire platform. Search engines, bulletin boards, and chat rooms were offering us near-instant access to a virtually infinite, infinitely diverse supply of information, interactions, and experiences, from esoteric hobbies and every conceivable shade of pornography to politically incorrect discussion groups and endless digests of news, sports, and weather.

Here, finally, was an answer to our aspirational anxieties: a new economic "paradigm" that seemed to transcend the limits and the inequalities of the old one. With the speed and scale that the Internet made possible, the entire process of consumption was being compressed and accelerated. The economy might still be volatile and uncertain—indeed, for many, the confidence and stability of the postwar period was only a memory. Yet the individual consumer had never seemed more capable of acting out his or her aspirations. You could buy from anywhere, work from anywhere, communicate from anywhere, with less and less reliance on traditional systems of production and less deference to professionals and experts. Under the digital wave, entire layers of previously essential intermediaries, from travel agents and telephone operators to editors and publishers, were being swept away. Even the financial markets were opening up. By the turn of the century, more than seven million of us were trading online, using digital power—and the sage advice of finance gurus such as Maria Bartiromo and Jim Cramer—to smash still more barriers to personal empowerment. "It's not a professional's game anymore," Bartiromo, CNBC's "Money Honey," assured her viewers in 2000. "The reason why individuals are becoming more powerful has to do with their access to information."[31]

And even if such rhetoric was a bit ripe, it still captured the strange optimism of the moment—and the belief, the *relief*, that our campaign for more personal power and affirmation could resume, despite our growing economic unease. Indeed, as each new surge in bandwidth and efficiency brought another iteration of faster gratification, our expectations and attitudes began to accelerate as well. Where once we had accepted the delays and inconveniences of the purely physical marketplace—in fact, we had once made a virtue of that acceptance—we now began to expect, and to feel entitled to, ever-faster gratification, not simply in the online world, but everywhere. Our entire sense of what was possible was being transformed by the rapid pace of technological change: if we were dissatisfied with the present, we could rest assured that some new product or experience or interaction—some new opportunity to narrow the gap between wanting and having, between desire and being—was only seconds away. The cheering for Steve Jobs and his toylike creation was utterly genuine and entirely understandable. We'd all been given a glimpse of the sort of power and freedom that would soon be available to the individual, and we could hardly wait to get started.

CHAPTER 3

Power Corrupts

In the early 1990s, just as the second wave of digital technologies was shoving the market into high gear, an aspiring behavioral scientist at the University of Chicago named Dilip Soman set out to study the effects of one of those technologies, consumer credit, on the human brain. Soman, an Indian-born engineer who had moved to Chicago to study consumer behavior, had become curious about credit after watching how casual Americans were about credit card debt. Not only did consumers here use credit cards for everyday purchases (something almost unheard of in India), but many of us also carried large balances and thus paid high interest. Such behavior was clearly irrational and even risky. Yet it was the norm in the United States. Soman had even seen it among his colleagues in the university's economics department—an extraordinary irony, given the department's fame for economic theories that treated consumers as hyperrational decision makers. But when the decision involved their own use of credit, Soman says, even the experts seemed guided not by rationality but by "something much more primal."

Soman suspected that something in the brain must actually perceive credit differently from cash, and he created a series of clever experiments to get at this difference. In one study, Soman had subjects pay a large number of fictitious household bills using either credit or a check, after which he offered each of them the chance to spend $450 on a vacation. Those who had paid the bills with credit, Soman found, were nearly twice as likely to splurge on the vacation as those who'd paid with a check, even though all subjects had paid the same bills. An even more intriguing finding emerged in a later study. Over a three-day period, Soman waited outside the university bookstore and asked exiting shoppers if they could recall the amount of their recent purchases. He then compared their answers to their receipts. The results were almost comical. Of those who paid with cash, check, or debit card, fully two-thirds could recall the purchase amount to the penny, while the remaining third came within three dollars. But those who bought on credit? Even though they'd made the purchases less than ten minutes earlier, only a third of the subjects could get within a dollar of the actual purchase amount. A third were between 15 and 20 percent too low. A third had no recollection whatsoever. "It was a real 'aha' moment," Soman, now at the Rotman School of Management in Toronto, told me. "People who routinely use credit cards simply don't have a good memory for how much they had paid."[1]

Exactly why we struggle to remember credit purchases isn't clear. Some researchers speculate that because the "pain" of a credit purchase is delayed, purchase details don't register as strongly in memory. Whatever the mechanism, the result is a sort of recurring error: something about credit throws us off. Other studies have found that people who used credit cards generally spend more than those who use cash. They leave larger tips. They offer higher bids at auctions. In one study, merely *seeing* the logo for a MasterCard or Visa was enough to stimulate larger-than-normal purchases. When it comes to credit, we have a bug in our mental software. And while we can override this bug, it's clear that as the "tool" of consumer credit has grown more powerful and available in recent decades our override switch has, for us collectively, become more likely to fail. Even by the time Soman began his research in the 1990s, credit overload had become routine. Average credit card balances had more than tripled since 1980.[2] Household debt was rising 25 percent faster than incomes. (The two had been evenly matched just fifteen years before.[3]) The rate of personal bankruptcies had tripled.[4] You could blame other factors, such as a decline in financial literacy and increasingly predatory creditors. But looking at the research, one could also ask whether we'd crossed some sort of neuro-economic threshold where our high-tech consumer economy was supplying more individual "capability" than many of us could comfortably handle.

This awkward possibility is part of a broader paradox at the center of the Impulse Society. In the last chapter, we watched as postindustrial economies, juiced up by technology, globalization, a more mercenary business model, and a less engaged government, offered consumers what amounted to a grand bargain: we would surrender much of our postwar economic security, but in return, we would receive some extraordinary new capabilities—manifest in everything from cheaper, faster food and more powerful cars to round-the-clock entertainment and, of course, ubiquitous, easy credit—that would let us continue our search for self-discovery and identity.

It wasn't long, however, before that bargain acquired a distinctly Faustian look and feel. Across much of modern life, self-discovery had turned into an orgy of self-centered gratification. Our spending was surreal. Obesity was soaring. (Between 1970 and 1995, the fraction of overweight American adults jumped from three in twenty to three in ten.) Drug use, sexual promiscuity, and infidelity were on the rise. Nor were our excesses confined to consumption. Patience, civility, and self-control generally seemed to be in short supply. We drove faster and much more aggressively. Our politics were becoming more sharply partisan and openly hostile. We positively annihilated each other online. The very fabric of community and neighborhood and society seemed to give way under our increasingly determined pursuit of individual fulfillment. It was as if the selves we'd been empowered to discover had turned out to be obnoxious, spoiled children, unwilling or unable to consider the consequences of their actions.

What, exactly, was happening to us? Partly, this is the story of cultural erosion: traditions that once constrained our id-like inner children have slowly dissolved under an acidic consumer culture that has made rapid self-gratification into both science and religion. But as a steady accumulation of research data suggests, there is another story playing out here, a quickening of the narrative of the empowered self. In blunt terms, the consumer economy now supplies so much raw individual capability that, when it comes to the pursuit of the perfect self, it's almost impossible *not* to go too far.

That we might struggle under the weight of our modern powers isn't exactly a radical proposition. A brain adapted for a prehistoric world of scarcity and uncertainty will, by definition, be challenged by the relative abundance and predictability of postindustrial, post*material* society. Yet one can still be impressed by the scale of the mismatch between our ancient physiology and contemporary realities, and also by its implications.

Take the way we make "intertemporal" choices, or choices between something now and something later. Should I spend my money today or save for retirement? Should I endure a workout now or die prematurely from a heart attack later? Should I make a pass at my co-worker at the Christmas party or relish the many documented benefits of an intact marriage thirty years hence? Intertemporal choices are among the most frequent kind of decisions we make, and also among the most important, determining everything from personal health and finance to collective outcomes such as national indebtedness, health care reform, and climate change. Alas, intertemporal choices are also among our most fraught. Time and again, we get them wrong, opting to enjoy an immediate reward (or to defer an immediate cost), even when we *know*, with utter clarity, that any short-term pleasure will be dwarfed by long-term pain. Human history is littered with the carnage of bad intertemporal choices.

Why are intertemporal decisions so difficult? In 1980 an economist at Cornell University named Richard Thaler came up with an explanation. The only rational way to understand our intertemporal irrationality, Thaler argued, was to imagine the human mind not as a single decision-making entity, but as a fractious joint venture between "two semiautonomous selves." One of these selves Thaler dubbed the "myopic Doer," concerned only with fast, efficient gratification. The other was a farsighted "Planner," tasked with managing, or trying to manage, the Doer. At the time, Thaler wasn't arguing that these two entities actually existed, physically, in the brain. His point was only that our decision-making process behaved "as if" it were made up of two systems that could come into "conflict at a single point in time"— conflict that ended in some pretty lame decisions.[5]

Thaler's "two-self model" landed him in hot water. Although the idea wasn't exactly new—Freud had posited an id-versus-superego struggle and even the proto-economist, Adam Smith, had described an internal contest between the "passions" and an "impartial spectator"[6]—by Thaler's time, such a notion was apostasy among mainstream economists. The field was still ruled by a "neoclassical" theory, known as "rational choice," which assumes that individuals will always strive to maximize personal utility by carefully weighing the costs and benefits of any action. In such a rational world, the suggestion of an internally conflicted individual actor was blasphemy. The whole argument for efficient markets—that they represent the sum of all human intelligence—requires the actors in those markets to be reasoned decision-makers, and not the sort who knowingly do the wrong thing. The two-self model was sharply criticized. Michael Jensen, the advocate of efficient markets and a former colleague of Thaler's, "was totally dismissive," Thaler told me.[7] And when Thaler later took a job in the economics department at the University of Chicago, one of the faculty, a Nobel laureate with deep affinities for rational markets, refused to speak to him.[8]

Yet Thaler was on the right track. By the late 1980s, new medical technologies, including the brain scan, had begun to confirm that our decision-making process is, in fact, something of a contest between two very different mental processes. In one figurative corner we have the higher cognitive processes, notably those of the prefrontal cortex, a relatively modern part of the brain that handles complex problem solving and abstract thought. In the other corner are the older processes, primarily those of the limbic system, a.k.a. the "lizard" brain, which governs our instinctive approach to danger, sex, and other survival-related activities. The original odd couple, the prefrontal cortex and the limbic system differ in everything from how they make decisions to, importantly, the sorts of things they can and can't perceive: where the prefrontal cortex can imagine how a shopping spree or an extramarital fling today might have downsides a month from now, the limbic system is utterly unconcerned with future consequences. Adapted to deal with immediate, fight-or-flight situations, the limbic system is literally blind to anything beyond the present moment. In a famous 2004 brain scan study at Princeton University, subjects who were offered immediate rewards showed flashes of intense activity in their limbic regions. But when those immediate rewards were replaced with mere promises of later rewards, the subjects' limbic regions stayed dark; to the lizard brain, the future simply doesn't exist.

This future blindness is important—and a central piece of the self/marketplace dance—because the limbic system plays such a dominant role in motivation. When it sees something it wants, the limbic system calls on a host of powerful mechanisms to provoke us to take quick action. It can unleash neurotransmitters, such as norepinephrine, which stimulates arousal, and dopamine, which brings us pleasure.[9] (That's one reason cocaine, which causes the release of dopamine, makes us so impulsive.) As significant, the limbic system bolsters its demands with emotional tugs: within milliseconds of a provocation—say, the sight of a crème-filled donut—the limbic system floods our brain with flashes of "affect," such as desire, which prime our entire body to act. Even the "rational" prefrontal cortex gets caught up in the limbic's campaign for instant gratification. When the limbic calls for action, the prefrontal cortex responds with an involuntary stream of related, and usually supportive, thoughts ("I *deserve* that donut"), which we typically experience as an intuition or a gut feeling.* In other words, within seconds, the limbic system can reorient our mental and physiological systems toward any number of short-term goals, from eating the donut to screaming at an errant motorist, even though those goals may be completely outside our normal mode of behavior. Or as George Loewenstein, a behavioral economist at Carnegie Mellon University, puts it, the limbic can "reprogram us into effectively different people."[10]

The prefrontal cortex, our rational planner, isn't without its own skills. It can generate counterarguments and recruit emotions, such as shame, to block the limbic system. But the prefrontal cortex is at a huge disadvantage against its fast, efficient rival. To counter an impulsive demand for immediate gratification, the conscious mind

---

* "Just look at your stream of consciousness when you are thinking about a politician you dislike, or when you have just had a minor disagreement with your spouse," writes Jonathan Haidt, a social psychologist at the University of Virginia and an expert in the neurology of motivation. "It's as though you are preparing for a court appearance. Your reasoning abilities are pressed into service generating arguments to defend your side and attack the other." In Haidt, "Moral Psychology and the Misunderstanding of Religion" Edge.org, Sept. 21, 2007.

must not only develop a compelling counternarrative ("donuts will make us fat"), but must pair this argument with its own flash of affect, which then competes with the limbic's emotional argument in a contest for our conscious attention. The problem, says Loewenstein, is that things in the future (the pain of receiving a credit card bill, say, or the pleasure derived from having a fit body) don't always translate into powerful emotions in the here and now. We may not have complete information about those future scenarios. Or they may be too complex to visualize, or they may simply be beyond our experience, and thus impossible to contemplate. As a result, future prospects are often so "intangible," Loewenstein says, that they fail to elicit an emotional response with enough power to blunt the limbic region's always-potent call of the wild.

What emerges from this lopsided neural wrestling match is a sort of perceptual myopia. Because the limbic system is so dominant in expressing its desires, we experience immediate options, whether pleasures or costs, much more intensely, while future options (and risks) feel smaller and less substantial. As nineteenth-century economist Arthur Pigou once put it, it's as if we're always looking at the future through the wrong end of a telescope and so see it "on a diminished scale." In modern economic terms, we "discount" the future— so steeply, in fact, that a reward that requires some waiting must be quite large before we'll voluntarily choose it over something available right now. In studies, subjects who are offered even comparatively large delayed rewards (say, an Amazon gift certificate to be delivered several weeks later) will consistently reject those rewards in favor of a much smaller immediate reward. In the Princeton brain scan study, most subjects wouldn't defer gratification even when doing so would have netted them a "return" equivalent to 5 percent a week, or 250 percent a year. "It was ridiculous," Sam McClure, the Princeton study's lead author, told me. "If you were making even *one* percent a week on your bank account, you'd be *rich*." Yet this "ridiculous" discount is, in effect, built into our heads, and this helps explain why we constantly make extraordinary intertemporal errors.

Credit is the obvious example. To the limbic system's Doer, a credit purchase represents only the pleasure of immediate gratification.* There will be pain when the bill arrives thirty days hence, and even more pain when unpaid balances begin accruing interest and penalties. But all that is invisible to the Doer. And while the prefrontal cortex *can* see that future pain, the "Planner" often lacks the capacity to make that prospective pain sufficiently vivid in the present moment—to "immediatize" it, as Loewenstein puts it—to override the limbic system. So we come home with the three-thousand-dollar flat-screen television or the forty-thousand-dollar pickup even when we can't actually afford them. And credit abuse is only one symptom of our myopia. Even when future costs are really high and readily apparent, the appeal of an immediate pleasure (the Burger King Triple Whopper with cheese, the fourth glass of cabernet, the come-hither look from someone who is not our spouse) is frequently just too vivid to resist. If the Impulse Society were a country, its flag would bear the picture of someone looking through the wrong end of a telescope.

Clearly, at one point in our history, discounting the future made a lot of sense. Our distant ancestors lived, literally, in the moment, or at least moment to moment, moving constantly after game and forage (which was eaten quickly, with minimal processing) and competing intensely for territory and mates. In such circumstances, focusing entirely on the present was how we lived long enough to *have* a future.

Yet, just as clearly, our ancestors had the capacity to override this natural short-termism when necessary. And as it became more and

---

* By contrast, the limbic system hates cash purchases, since cash is perceived as an asset to be guarded, and spending it registers as a loss, which the limbic system resists by flooding the brain with disgust-inducing neurotransmitters.

more necessary (as a changing climate forced us to adopt food strategies, such as farming, that required patience and long-term thinking), we found external, social means to correct our inherent impulsiveness. These corrections emerged gradually, in the form of what anthropologists Robert Boyd and Peter Richerson call "social workarounds": everything from taboos and laws, which harshly penalized impulsiveness, to institutions such as marriage, property rights, and contracts, which encouraged long-term investments and commitments. By alternately punishing short-termism and rewarding patience, society was able to embrace more sophisticated survival strategies (such as trade, irrigated farming, and manufacturing) with longer time frames, bigger operating scales, and better efficiencies. And with the greater wealth that these more efficient strategies generated, society could develop even more finely tuned forms of impulse control. The story of civilization is arguably the story of societies getting better and better at persuading, coercing, or otherwise inducing individuals to repress their impulsiveness and myopia, or repress them sufficiently, to keep civilization moving forward.

That story became much more complex in the sixteenth century, with institutions such as capitalism, liberal democracy, and Protestantism. Each in its own way added to individual power—through commercial freedom, the political protection of individual rights, and the "right" of individuals to commune directly with the Divine. Yet each simultaneously tempered that power by making it conditional on cooperation. In return for democratic freedoms, for example, we agreed to moderate our self-interest by entering a web of mutual civic obligations. In return for commercial opportunities, we promised to trade fairly and honestly. In return for direct access to the Divine, we submitted to a religious culture that frowned on excess. As Rousseau argued in his theory of a "social contract," liberal society "takes man's own forces away from him in order to give him [social] forces . . . which he cannot use without the help of others."

Here was society's new offer to the individual: show us a modicum of patience and cooperation and we'll use our collective scale and leverage and intelligence to guarantee you more long-term stability and security and even happiness than you could ever hope to achieve on your own.

In this context, civilization's high point (at least, in the industrializing West) may run from either Victorian England or early twentieth-century America. The unprecedented wealth and imperial reach of the Victorians arose directly from an extremely conservative, and highly effective, culture of personal restraint. Likewise in early twentieth-century America, a new bureaucratic order (composed of governments, schools, corporations, and other hierarchical organizations, and guided by the new behavioral sciences) deployed everything from sin taxes and calming architecture to time-management studies and "career ladders"[11] to systematically control impulsiveness and short-termism (and much else).

Yet society's triumph over individual myopia and impetuosity was never complete, nor anything but provisional. Rather, our success was conditioned on the fact that most of us had no alternative but to self-repress. So long as our lives were characterized by scarcity and insecurity, the best survival strategy for the average individual was to surrender to social norms of patience and cooperation. But it was always the case that once a more efficient individual strategy came along, one that let citizens get more satisfaction faster and more independently (as began to happen with industrialization in Western societies by the nineteenth century), we were obliged, as members of an efficiency-seeking species, to upgrade. And one could argue that at this point, many tens of thousands of years of social controls began to unwind and our old myopic impulsiveness began to reassert itself.

Today, of course, there are far fewer natural limits to curb the dictates of the limbic system. Even as our incomes stagnate, our digitally accelerated efficiencies continue to drive down prices for the basic gratifications. Food is so cheap that restaurants use cartoonish excess as a marketing tool: the half-gallon cups of soda, the bottomless shrimp basket, the infinite buffet. ("All-you-can-eat" is the fastest growing format in the world.) Information and entertainment, meanwhile, are almost free and virtually endless, leaving us to rely entirely on our own suspect capacity to self-limit.

But it's not simply that a brain designed for scarcity must now cope with superabundance. It must also cope with superabundance marketed explicitly to exploit our ancient wiring. The huge push by manufacturers into the youth market, for example, was driven in no small part by the understanding that kids and adolescents have not yet developed much in the way of patience or the capacity to imagine the future—they are the perfect customers for a market programmed to excess. Or consider our old friend consumer credit. Not only is credit cheap and ubiquitous, but the credit industry now uses the very same neuroscience to design marketing strategies (such as very low minimum monthly payments and very high credit limits) that feed off our neural flaws.

What's more, thanks to the accelerant of cheap computing power, the very essence of credit (the separation of immediate benefits from future costs, of pleasure from pain) has been embedded across the consumer economy. Virtually every consumer proposition today, from fast food and entertainment to social interactions, is deliberately crafted so that rewards are immediate while costs are deferred, and deferred so seamlessly that they almost disappear. Speed of gratification is now the standard against which all consumer experiences are judged. Each season, marketers pour huge resources into shaving a few more minutes or seconds off of fulfillment times. Retailers such as Amazon and eBay are experimenting with same-day delivery. Delis bring meals to your car.[12] (Soon it will be done by remote-control drones.) Online movie companies such as Netflix now release an entire season of a new TV show on a single day so that viewers can enjoy marathon sessions, or "binges." Car companies make financing so easy that even consumers defaulting on their home mortgages can afford a brand-new pickup.* Smartphone apps let you scan desirable objects anywhere you find them (on the train, in a friend's apartment, in a picture in a magazine) and have one delivered to your home.[13]

And to judge by the accelerating advances in consumer technologies (3D printing machines that can transmit products in real time; wearable smartphones; robots so lifelike they can serve as sex workers) the future will be only more challenging for a brain programmed to look through the wrong end of the telescope. We are fast approaching a tipping point in the already problematic relationship between the self and the marketplace—between an economy programmed to issue ever-larger increments of consumer capability and a consumer who is, to some degree, neurologically predisposed to abuse those capabilities.

The more we learn about our mental biases, and the sophisticated ways they are being exploited (or "mined," in the current lexicon), the more clearly we see how challenging it will be to make this self-centered economy of ours more sustainable, or simply saner. Previous attempts to control impulsivity with old-fashioned repression, via top-down regulation and prohibition, have mainly ended in spectacular failure. (See, for example, Prohibition or, more recently, former New York City mayor Bloomberg's risible effort to ban garbage-can-size soft drinks—or, for that matter, any effort to restrict even the most absurd manifestations of the right to bear arms.) Likewise doomed, it seems, are efforts to revive a puritanical "shame culture" as a means to encourage self-restraint. (Witness the inability to kill off the politically and environmentally incorrect sport-utility vehicle.) Subtler efforts, drawing on

* In fact, no sooner are you granted a bankruptcy than you are *inundated* with offers from dealerships and credit card companies to allow you to "start rebuilding your credit!!"

behavioral science to help us compensate for our obsolete neural wiring, show some promise. Walter Mischel, the researcher behind the famous "marshmallow study" from the 1970s, has developed effective strategies to train impatient children to be patient—an important success, given that impatient children have a high likelihood of growing up to be impatient adults.[14] There are other potentially fruitful ventures, such as what Richard Thaler (of the two-self model) and coauthor Cass Sunstein call "choice architecture." The term refers to carefully designed technologies, infrastructure, and other pieces of the built environment that subtly "nudge" us to act with more patience and long-term thought. An example: smartphone apps that automatically track our daily expenses and warn us when we're exceeding our budget.

But such efforts are swimming upstream against a current of world-historic proportions. Consider our political culture, which more and more encourages a rapid, visceral response to policy or events. Consider the relentless ideology of personal liberation that, in conjunction with the consumer marketplace, continues to reject anything hindering our all-important, all-justifying self-knowledge and self-discovery. (As Yippie activist Jerry Rubin boasted in 1970, "Whenever we see a rule we must break it. Only by breaking rules do we discover who we are."[15]) Or consider the growing research showing that myopia and short-termism actually increase when we're uncertain about the future—something our new economic model seems to have made more likely.

Further, some of the most troubling myopia occurs not at the consumer level, where "choice architecture" or nudges might have some positive effect, but at the institutional level, in government and especially in business. In many industries, today's senior managers wield an increasingly impressive set of tools, technologies, and other capabilities that can deliver ever-faster returns. Yet not only do these managers face the same inclination to discount future costs, but they also operate in a corporate culture that itself is increasingly limbic and shortsighted. In most firms, managers are under massive competitive pressure to exploit any and all capabilities as soon as they become available—and further, to exploit those capabilities even when mistakes will clearly have long-term consequences for society at large. You can see this tension as corporate managers use deep layoffs in an attempt to quickly restore share prices and protect personal bonuses—even when it brings a great deal of pain to many others. It is evident in the financial realm, too, especially as increasingly sophisticated technologies have given banks and traders the power to rapidly accumulate unprecedented fortunes, but also to put entire markets at risk. In fact, using technology to not only separate risk from reward, but to "reallocate" that risk onto others, and society at large, is now all but standard procedure in the financial sector. Some of this is the result of our intertemporal bugs. But the willingness by individuals to both maximize immediate personal and organizational gain and also to push future costs onto other parties actually points to a second category of bug—one that interferes, not with our capacity to *see* future consequences, but with our capacity to *care* about them.

In the early 1970s, a psychologist at Temple University named David Kipnis wanted to know how power affects individual ethics and, in particular, whether power really does corrupt. In a series of experiments, Kipnis had subjects assume the role of "manager" over a group of "employees" in a fictitious work situation. In some cases, Kipnis gave the managers very little power: they were told to use persuasion to get their employees to complete a task. In other cases, the managers had considerable power: they decided whether employees were fired, transferred, or promoted. As the experiments progressed, Kipnis observed how each boss's behavior changed, and the effects were striking. Whereas bosses without power tended to use what Kipnis called "rational tactics," such as discussing goals with employees, those with power began to exploit it. They were more likely to use coercive or "strong tactics," such as criticizing employees, making demands, and displaying anger.[16] They were more dismissive of employees' performance, and tended to credit themselves for their employees' success. Powerful bosses were also more likely to keep a psychological distance between themselves and their employees. The results led Kipnis to argue, under his "metamorphic" model of power, that having power so inflates our sense of self that we're less able to empathize with those lacking power.[17]

Kipnis's findings focused on the workplace of nearly forty years ago, but he might as well have been describing the culture of aggressive self-promotion that seems so pervasive today. Since Kipnis's study, research has only bolstered the notion that power can alter our behavior toward others. In dozens of studies, people in possession of some form of power (managerial authority, say, or social status or just plain old wealth) are measurably more likely to violate social norms in the pursuit of self-interest. We're more apt to be rude, to invade personal space, to use stereotypes, to cheat, and even to break the law. In one now-classic study, University of California–Berkeley psychologist Paul Piff found that "high-status" drivers (those in really nice cars) were nearly four times as likely as low-status drivers to cut off other drivers at an uncontrolled intersection and nearly three times as likely to drive through a crosswalk while a pedestrian was crossing.

One could argue that power doesn't necessarily lead to antisocial behavior, but rather, that naturally aggressive and self-centered people are simply more likely to become financially and socially powerful. However, researchers have been able to show what strongly looks like a causal effect. Simply by causing a person to feel rich or powerful even temporarily produces more self-centered or aggressive behavior. In 2012, Piff had subjects play a two-person game of Monopoly in which power was intentionally skewed: one player was given a large allotment of cash and the use of both dice, while the other player received only half the cash and could use just one die. Within moments of starting the game, the subjects with more cash and dice (the high-status players) began acting noticeably different. They took up measurably more space at the table than did the low-status subjects. They made less eye contact with the low-status players and took more liberties, such as moving the low-status players' game pieces for them. When moving their own pieces, high-status players did so far more forcefully, making three times as much noise as low-status subjects. (The testing room was equipped with a decibel meter.) In other words, these temporarily empowered subjects exhibited the same sorts of behavior that researchers observe in people who actually do have power and social status. "We're putting people in this low-stakes game where we've manipulated things—it's pretty clear to them, pretty transparent what we've done," Piff told me. "And yet, within a few minutes, it crystallizes these roles between people, and gets them to exhibit these patterns of behavior that you normally see in people who actually have high status in everyday life."[18]

How and why power leads to self-centered behavior involves a complex process, but the basic outlines are fairly well understood. According to psychologist Dacher Keltner, a pioneer in power research, the experience of power and status activates our "approach system," a neural mechanism motivating our efforts to gratify basic needs, such as sex, social approval, and attention, along with learned needs, such as money. Once triggered, the approach system "moves you forward," Keltner says. "You just go after things." What's more, even as power is making us more aggressive, it is also reducing our sensitivity to other people or to social norms. This mix of more "approach" and less sensitivity, Keltner told me, is quite potent: "Anything that seems rewarding and good, if you're feeling power-ful; you just go after it. If it's a little bit more of the pie of public goods, or your secretary, or whatever."[19]

o   o   o

Granted, few of us need a study to tell us that the rich and powerful often act like assholes. But what makes this link between power and solipsism so compelling—and so fundamental to the larger idea of the Impulse Society—is that it helps explain why the aggressive promotion of self-interest has become a hallmark at *all* levels of society, even instances where our real power is actually declining. For the truth is, for more and more of us, the tangible, durable, authentic kind of personal power that characterized life in the postwar period (rising incomes, an engaged government, a more secure sense of community) is seriously lacking today. But the patterns of the Impulse Society compensate for that lack in many ways. Culturally, the support for the pursuit of individual self-interest that surged in the 1980s seems even stronger today, which means that whatever tangible powers we do retain can be applied, guilt free, toward aggressive self-promotion. Meanwhile, the consumer marketplace has continued to crank out tools to make aggressive self-promotion not only easier and more efficient, but more likely. Think of the growing profusion of products and services that explicitly target our hunger for aggressive power: car stereo subwoofers designed and marketed for their capacity to piss off the entire neighborhood, for instance; or retina-searing high beams engineered, according to the ads, to fit "your aggressive driving style" (that is, to blind oncoming drivers).

For that matter, think of the quarter-century trend toward cars and trucks engineered unambiguously, shrewdly, and shamelessly to combine power and its abuse in the same package. During the 1990s, as journalist and author Keith Bradsher has documented, Detroit designed cars that were not only larger and more powerful than their predecessors, but even styled to look intimidating and mean. The front ends of Chrysler's Ram pickup and Durango SUVs, for example, were fashioned intentionally to resemble predatory animals. Into the 2000s, the Big Three introduced models that were larger, more powerful, and more openly intimidating, with wider, more heavily clad bodies (as if fortified) raised higher above the street, for a better "command" position. And fearsome they have turned out to be. Not only do SUV drivers tend to drive faster and experience above-average accident rates, but their vehicles' size, weight, and configuration mean those accidents wreak more damage. Studies show that although driving an SUV substantially lowers your own chances of injury in an accident, it doubles the likelihood that the people you hit will be injured or killed.[20] Yet this collision inequality is arguably part of the appeal. The aggressive mien of the SUV is all part of the industry's efforts to reach what Clotaire Rapaille, a marketing specialist who worked closely with Detroit, calls "the reptilian brain," the set of ancient neural programs that seek to maximize each individual's "survival and reproduction." The reptilian brain doesn't care about the so-called external costs of a big SUV, such as poor fuel economy or extra emissions, and it certainly doesn't care about the safety of other motorists. Rather, to the reptilian brain, every stranger is a potential criminal and every other motorist a potential adversary. As Rapaille told Bradsher in a moment of appalling candor, "The reptilian mind says, 'If there's a crash, I want the other guy to die.'"

The reptilian aura of the SUV is an extreme illustration of the way our appetite for personal power is being exploited to the detriment of the fraying social fabric. But much of what the consumer economy offers us is the power to, if not crush our fellow citizens, then at least to avoid having much to do with them. This freedom is the explicit promise of convenience: goods and services that let us consume with steadily greater independence —that is, with less reliance on, contact with, or even awareness of those around us. Many of our most successful food innovations, from TV dinners to self-browning microwavable entrees to the fully digitized fast-food drive-through window, were engineered to let us maximize our gustatory pleasure quickly and at any time or place, while avoiding such "inefficiencies" as

cooking or gathering for a group meal. And yet such personal empowerment has come at a social cost, not least the decline in the art of
cooking and the socializing power of the sit-down family meal.

This incremental erosion of our traditional attachments is no
accident. It is the implicit objective of the consumer economy, which
strives to replace those attachments with a product or service. The
genius of the big-box retail stores, for example, wasn't just their low,
low prices, but the depersonalized, one-stop format that let us mini-
mize shopping's social obligations. When Walmart, back in the
1970s, introduced rural residents to its formulaic customer service
and its titanic product array (everything from groceries and clothing
to housewares and auto supplies to appliances and a pharmacy, all
under one downtown-size roof), it was essentially liberating us from
many irritating inefficiencies of small-town life: no longer did shopping mean having to schlep from shop to shop or endure the implicit
obligations that come with small-scale vendors who are also our
neighbors. That freedom may not seem revolutionary. But as Ralph
Brown, the Brigham Young sociologist, notes, it marked a radical
break with tradition. For most of history, Brown says, economic
activity has been fundamentally inseparable from social relationships. It simply wasn't possible to be just a "consumer." Buying
something meant becoming a *customer*, a socially constructed,
socially constrained role that required us to engage in an often
complicated and time-consuming social interaction every time we
made a purchase. When modern retailers offered the customer the
efficiency of becoming a "consumer," a more purely economic actor
with few social obligations, most of us gladly took it. Or as one busi-
nessman in a newly Walmarted Iowa town complained to *The New
York Times* back in 1989, "Wal-Mart has replaced the need for Main
Street."[21]

For many conservative economists, this shift from customer to
consumer, harsh though it might be, marked a positive, necessary

change. Businesses were now being forced to square up to yet another fundamental reality of the efficient marketplace: the self-interested consumer. A consumer might tolerate social obligations when forced to by obsolete commercial arrangements (much as investors had tolerated corporate mismanagement in the days before the shareholder revolution), but beneath that veneer of sociality there was always coldly calculating self-interest. "For [consumers] nothing counts other than their own satisfaction," warned Ludwig von Mises, a member of the conservative "Austrian School" of economics, back in 1949. "They do not care a whit for past merit and vested interests. If something is offered to them that they like better or that is cheaper, they desert their old purveyors. In their capacity as buyers and consumers they are hard-hearted and callous, without consideration for other people."[22] Vendors who failed to accept these truths, and who continued to rely on social obligations and other nonmarket inefficiencies, were not only dooming themselves; they were also holding back the overall efficiency of the marketplace. As Adam Smith, patron saint of efficient markets, proposed two centuries earlier, the best outcome was achieved when individuals pursued self-interest. The shift from *customer* to *consumer*, conservative economists now argued, was merely a manifestation of Smith's great insight. It might be devastating to older, inefficient vendors and a few small towns. But in the long term, it would bring the social benefits of a more efficient economy.

Yet in viewing the social side of commerce through such a purely economic, Darwinian lens, we lose a lot of important detail. Adam Smith himself insisted that markets will not yield their famous optimality without a strong moral dimension: absent trust and empathy between buyer and seller, markets quickly lose their efficiencies and fail—as numerous scandals and scams and bubbles and busts have demonstrated. But you didn't have to wait for a full-blown collapse to see the costs of our mass migration from social customers to more purely economic consumers. You only had to look as far as the big-box phenomenon. Although these mega-stores with their mega-efficiencies meant lower prices and larger selections, they also brought a new set of costs for those same empowered small-town consumers. Kenneth Stone, a rural economist at Iowa State University, found that within two years of a new Walmart coming to town, local shops within a twenty-mile radius could expect sales declines of anywhere from a quarter to nearly two-thirds. Such heavy losses often led to the gradual unraveling of small-town downtowns, failures that tore at the community fabric while often, paradoxically, leaving residents fewer shopping options. Louisiana State University sociologist Troy Blanchard has found that in some smaller rural areas, the success of a new big-box retailer nearby can substantially increase the distance residents must drive for groceries. The loss of local business is even more damaging in light of new research showing that, in comparison to out-of-town retailers, local merchants provide more stable work environments—Walmart's staff turnover runs about 50 percent a year—and are more supportive of local social programs, political initiatives, and other pieces of a community's quality of life. Here, again, is the central paradox of the Impulse Society: an economic model that empowers us to destroy the very things that sustain us.

In 1953, decades before we had begun to quantify the challenges of personal power, the libertarian scholar Robert Nisbet offered a fore-taste of where that power might lead us. In his classic work *The Quest for Community*, Nisbet warns that by emancipating the individual from often-repressive traditional social structures, modern liberal society effectively severed and isolated him from "the subtle, infinitely complex lines of habit, tradition, and social relationship" that make individual freedom possible in the first place. Humans are inherently social, and it is only when individual freedom is mediated through social structures such as family, church, locality, neighborhood, or voluntary association that such freedom becomes meaningful or sustainable. Yet under the relentless advance of modern political institutions, Nisbet feared, these very social structures were being degraded, retired, and "almost uniformly reduced to their individual atoms"—and were thus relegating individuals into merely singular beings, "isolated and unattached."[23]

For Nisbet, one of the most articulate advocates of libertarian thought, the primary atomizer was the liberal nation-state and its steady penetration, through bureaucracies, subsidies, and expertise, into every cranny of social life. But Nisbet was as concerned over the erosion of social ties by the marketplace, and the way the "rationalization and impersonalization of the economic world" was undermining the capacity of family, village, and other "intermediate institutions" to function as "centers of security and allegiance." Nearly a century after Henry Ford let rural Americans begin to loosen their social ties, the atomization of all social attachments had become an industry aim. Year after year, we had stripped consumption of its social obligations, norms, and other inefficiencies as we aimed to reduce it to its essence—an individual act carried out totally for, by, and about the self. What's more, as unencumbered consumption has become the dominant mode, and a huge source of income for producers, that unencumbered mode has become more and more celebrated in, and legitimized by, our culture and our ideologies. First, it was the Me Generation's relentless emphasis on self-fulfillment and disengagement from tradition. A decade later, it was the economic individualism of efficient markets. Whatever the ideological flavor, the underlying cultural message was the same: as individuals, we were to be encouraged, both subtly and overtly, to see our interests as distinct from those of the larger society—and, increasingly, to put our interests above those of the larger society.

The move from customer to consumer was merely the most

outward sign of the emergence of a citizen who, explicitly or implicitly, regards himself or herself as being above it all. Yet as we have moved closer to this perfect consumption, we've found the ground beneath our feet giving way. By so completely privatizing consumption, we've also stripped away some of the last social structures that were helping keep our limbic, reptilian impulses in check. Where home cooking once curbed how much we ate, for example, that now disappeared with convenience food and fast food. Where fear of pregnancy once constrained premarital sex, the Pill made that fear obsolete. Even the long-standing concept of "character," which had once required individuals to submit to "the unity of moral codes and disciplined purpose," as Daniel Bell puts it, was suspended. In place of "character," we were now encouraged to pursue "personality," or the "enhancement of self through the compulsive search for individual differentiation," usually through serial consumption.[24] Such complaints were often voiced by social conservatives and prudes—and the social norms they mourned were frequently repressive, unfair, discriminatory, or medieval. But those moral codes had served a purpose: impulse control—and now they were being eradicated as impediments to efficient consumption. And where it might have been conceivable to replace those old-fashioned norms with something less medieval, we never got the chance. In many cases, those old constraints had been removed without any conscious deliberation, or any careful weighing of costs and benefits, but automatically, reflexively—because the market happened to be offering yet another increment of efficient, and profitable, self-expressive power.

In short, consumers not only had more power, but also were increasingly alone with this power, with few of the old parameters to guide us—a position that, paradoxically, many of us found deeply unsettling. Even as popular culture in the 1980s and 1990s projected the image of the triumphant, all-powerful consumer, we ourselves often had a different story. Cases of anxiety and depression were on the rise—a shift that mental health experts attributed partly to the erosion of social connections. "Where once we could fall back on social capital—families, churches, friends—these no longer are strong enough to cushion our fall," wrote Robert Putnam, the Harvard sociologist. "In our personal lives as well as in our collective life . . . we are paying a significant price for a quarter century's disengagement from one another."[25]

And yet, our "solution" was even more unsettling. While Putnam and others pushed for a revival of community connections, many consumers sought support and guidance from other sources—including, in many cases, the very suppliers providing us with our new powers. Thus, we let food companies determine the ideal portion size (much larger today than forty years ago). We let automakers regulate the optimal amount of horsepower and acceleration.

And, of course, we let the banks determine how much credit we should use. Research by Dilip Soman, the behavioral scientist we met earlier, has shown that many of us base our credit card use, not on a calculation of our financial needs and resources, but on the credit limit set by the bank. And while such a strategy might have been remotely logical in the days of stingy credit, when it was a safe bet that a lender had actually scrutinized our ability to repay a debt, that logic vanished with the rise of a banking model geared for high volumes and quick returns. By 1990s, bankers were carefully targeting consumers with the worst credit histories, since these people could be counted on to generate steady streams of late fees. What's more, they were exploiting every one of our neurological glitches— raising credit limits and reducing minimum payments, for example, because these were shown to give consumers a false sense of wealth. For the financial sector, our faulty wiring would now be a critical source of profit. As Elizabeth Warren, then a Harvard law professor, noted in a scathing 1989 report, bank card companies "were willing to give out the fourth, sixth, or seventh bank card and to approve charges after debtors already showed short-term debt so large that they could not possibly pay the interest, much less the principal."

By the turn of the new century, the consumer was about to step into a perfect storm. Not only were many of us carrying around more power than we could easily manage, but in so many areas of life, this very same power had cut us off from the social and cultural arrangements that might have stayed, or at least steadied, our hand. Instead, bereft of traditional guideposts, we came to rely more and more on the market itself to determine how much power we should use. By the early 2000s, as a housing bubble pushed the economy back into overdrive, and as the financial sector prepared to unleash yet another round of consumer "tools," it would become clear that our entire culture had been, in effect, wired for disaster.

CHAPTER 4

Something for Nothing

In the summer of 2005, when the economy was in a vertical climb and the real estate market was minting cash, the place to be on Sunday afternoon was poolside at the Las Vegas Hard Rock Café. Each week, the café hosted the Rehab Party, a sort of canned spring break with booming DJ'd music, booze, and acres of tan. From noon on, the place would be wall to wall casino tourists, but also a lot of locals, including many in the Las Vegas real estate business, nursing hangovers and trading stories about the escalating madness of the market. Home prices in Las Vegas were rising by 50 percent a year, and every conceivable kind of player was now trying to get a piece of the action. There were the mega-developers building entire neighborhoods in the desert outside of town. There were cold-eyed investors from Hong Kong and Seoul snapping up units in the luxury high-rises going up along the Strip. Doctors and dentists from Orange County were buying and flipping homes as if they were day traders.

And then there was another category of player—a sort of amateur, Mr. Magoo type who hit the real estate jackpot by accident. The Magoos were locals who'd seen their home values double and had used the sudden wealth to jump on the real estate gravy train. They'd refinanced, put the cash on a second home, flipped it a few months later for thirty or forty grand in profit, and all at once, they could picture a real estate empire. "It's like, 'Hey, I doubled my money—I must be a fucking genius,'" recalls a mortgage lender who worked in Vegas during the Roaring Aughties. "So they buy two or three more houses and sell them, and now it's, 'I have a hundred thousand dollars in the bank, so why not keep doing it?'"[1] By 2005, some of the Magoos had five or six or even twenty properties. Collectively, perhaps half the home sales in Las Vegas involved amateur speculators, meaning that a large share of the region's new prosperity was in the hands of people with no idea what they were doing. "These weren't real investors," Todd Miller, a longtime realtor, told me. "A real investor buys a property and holds it for the cash flow from rent. Or looks for seriously undervalued properties and figures out exactly how much you're going to need to fix them up. These guys weren't doing that. They were just rolling the dice."[2]

And yet, there was little to stop them. Virtually anyone could become a realtor. More to the point, the entire credit system had been engineered expressly for the Magoo fantasy. By the early 2000s, you couldn't open your mailbox or turn on your TV without getting a refinance offer. Not only were banks expanding their mortgage operations, but the loan process itself was now fully automated and so efficient that getting a loan was as simple as getting a credit card. "You could state what your income was, state your assets and that was it—you didn't even have to show us your bank statements," a former loan officer from Las Vegas told me. "Or you could do a 'NINA' 'no income, no assets.' You put in the person's name, address, and Social Security number, and that was all you needed. We wouldn't even call their employers, because we wouldn't have known who to call; there wasn't a place for it on the application. And you could finance one hundred percent. Looking back on it, it was a little insane."[3]

Indeed, if you had wanted to see the Impulse Society at its starkest and most fully developed, the housing bubble was the perfect case study. To watch the antics in places such as Vegas, or Orange County, or Miami, or Phoenix (or, for that matter, Madrid or Dublin[4]), or any of hundreds of other hot markets, was to erase any doubt about the triumph of the self-centered economy. It was here, in the housing boom, that every unsettling, impulsive trend from the past half century converged in a toxic brew of socioeconomics, technology, and neurochemistry. Here was the manic drive for self-expression and the blatant manipulation of ancient reflexes. Here was the desperate campaign to recover postwar living standards. Here was the blind acceptance of the efficient market, and trust in whatever personal power that efficient market might bestow, no matter how implausible or socially irresponsible.

It was here, too, on the front lines of the financial bubble, where self and marketplace, psychology and economy, could be seen feeding off one another with the greatest efficiency and naturalness. For, in many respects, the financial sector is the most psychological part of the market—the "self" of the modern economy. It is the market's id, its lizard-brained Doer—creative, resourceful, tireless, and efficient, yet so ruthlessly self-serving, myopic, and shameless that it will happily drag the Planners and the rest of society off the fiscal cliff. It's no accident that we once kept our financial sector locked up, repressed, sedated with regulations and norms (much as we once did the self), because we had learned to fear what happens when the financial id gets loose.

But by the 1970s, of course, we had conquered those fears. We had new technologies and new theories that let us harness finance's creative, productive energies, just as we had harnessed the self to the consumer economy. Slowly, tentatively, we released the financial sector and hitched our fortunes to it—and they were fortunes indeed. By allowing us to borrow from the future, the financial sector enabled the economy to expand beyond the material constraints of the here and now. But in making us richer, the financial sector gradually overwhelmed us. Just as the liberated self reshaped consumer culture to fit its own insatiable criteria, our financial sector restructured and reoriented the broader economy (along with most of our political and social institutions and much of our culture) to serve its own very limbic imperatives. By the early 2000s, as the Magoos were piling into the real estate market, the financial system had remade much of the economy in its own id-like image—impulsive, wholly devoted to short-term gratification, and blithely untroubled by the thought of consequences.

The financial sector, we should point out, was not always quite so reckless. After the crash of 1929, a chastened (and tightly regulated) financial industry resigned itself to the role of adjunct to the manufacturing economy. Bankers and other financial players pursued conservative, low-risk strategies—"patient capital" was a motto—that delivered steady modest returns: through the postwar era, the financial sector (banking, insurance, and real estate) accounted for less than 10 percent of all corporate profits. But all pretense of patience and modesty was swept aside by the chaos of the 1970s. As double-digit inflation and competition from foreign banks eroded profits on traditional investments, bankers, investors, and other financial players went looking for new strategies to generate higher, faster returns. Almost overnight, patient capital gave way to a frenetic "hunt for yield." Fueled by computer technologies and restive shareholders, that hunt would take financial players around the world in search of any "vehicle" with a high return: leveraged buyouts, precious metals, food commodities, oil futures, and Third World government debt.

But the most lucrative hunting grounds would be the big consumer economies of North America and Western Europe. Here, the finance sector gradually worked its way into every sphere of public and private life. It became massive—by the early 2000s, the American financial sector was generating nearly 25 percent of all corporate profits—and with size and ubiquity came influence. The more we relied on finance, the more we came to share the sector's new imperative for faster, higher returns. That was clearly the case in the ballooning world of consumer credit, where credit's guiding logic of immediate rewards and deferred costs became the consumer's logic as well. But the deeper effects of this "financialization" of the economy were felt elsewhere. For instance, as governments began borrowing more heavily—it was Ronald Reagan, that free-market conservative, who discovered it was easier to finance a budget than balance one—policymakers grew increasingly beholden to the desires and agendas of the debt markets. When President Clinton tried to fulfill a campaign promise for more infrastructure and schools, bond traders, anxious about more government spending causing inflation,[5] bid up long-term interest rates, which threatened the housing market and, by extension, Clinton's chances for a second term. ("You mean to tell me," Clinton reportedly griped to aides, "that the success of . . . my reelection hinges on a bunch of fucking bond traders?"[6]) Government, too, would embrace the short-termism of the financial markets.

Where the shortsightedness of the financial sector has had its most lasting effect, however, has been on corporate strategy. Since the shareholder revolution of the 1980s, not only have corporate managers become more eager to please financial markets—fully two-thirds of the average senior executive's compensation is now in stocks and options[7]—but those markets are much harder to satisfy. The stock market today is ruled by so-called institutional investors—pensions, mutual funds, hedge funds, and, especially, hedge fund "activists"— investors who buy up large stakes in companies and then seek to influence share price. For these big institutional players, which collectively control around three-quarters of the shares of big, publicly traded companies,[8] the hunt for yield is life's overriding goal. To prosper— indeed, to survive—the institutional investors must please their own clients (everyone from retirees to billionaires), and this they do by setting aggressive quarterly "return targets" for their portfolios—targets that, as economists Eric Tymoigne and Randall Wray have pointed out, are generally well above the growth rates projected for the American economy as a whole. To deliver such high returns, fund managers must constantly "churn" their portfolios, buying shares in whatever companies are "outperforming" the market and dumping those that aren't. Because institutional investors are such large players, their constant buying and selling has a disproportionate effect on share prices. In other words, fund managers are essentially reacting to their own trades—a feedback loop that has gradually increased the pace at which shares are bought and sold. Indeed, churn is the market's new rhythm. In the 1970s, institutional investors held shares for an average of seven years before selling. Today, it's less than a year.[9] The biggest players on the market are now like the lovers all the relationship books warn about: impulsive, short-term, and wholly unwilling to commit.

For a publicly traded company, the significance of this quickening of financial markets is hard to overstate. Because the stock market's most important players are now hypersensitive to even small changes in a company's share price, and because these large players can instantly signal their dissatisfaction by pushing down share prices, corporate management is increasingly about managing the factors that impact share price, factors that don't always have much to do with the sensible management of a company. Because share price is heavily influenced by a company's quarterly earnings report, managers go to extreme lengths to protect the next quarter's earnings—even to the point of hurting earnings in future quarters. In a startling 2005 survey of more than four hundred chief financial officers, researchers found that half the executives would readily delay investing in a profitable long-term project if doing so would help meet the current quarter's earnings target. Likewise, nearly four of five said they would cut current spending on research and development, maintenance, advertising, and hiring—"assets" that are essential to long-term profitability—if doing so protected the next quarter's earnings. Companies have also become more reluctant to defer any income—even when doing so might mean forgoing a chance to make more money later. In another survey, this time of executives of British firms, most said they would choose a project delivering a £250,000 return tomorrow over a project delivering £450,000 three years from now.[10] These are exactly the sorts of intertemporal mistakes that behavioral economists chide consumers for—and yet, at the corporate level, they are becoming standard operating procedure. The idea that corporate managers are thinking long-term is "baloney," writes economist Shiva Rajgopal, an expert in corporate accounting and coauthor of the 2005 survey. "These guys don't have a long horizon; they're just thinking about maybe the next two or three quarters."[11] And this sort of corporate myopia is infectious. Because firms are, in effect, competing for investors' affections, any management technique that is effective at boosting earnings and share price is quickly copied by other firms, argue corporate strategy experts Gregg Polsky and Andrew Lund at the Brookings Institution: "Once one firm sacrifices the future to boost current earnings, executives at other firms will be compelled to follow suit lest their share price and, correspondingly, their career prospects suffer."[12]

This isn't how "efficient markets" are supposed to work. The efficient market is supposed to encourage long-term thinking, because share price is supposed to reflect a company's long-term profitability. Share price, in theory, represents the "net present value" of all future profits—that is, the sum of everything the company will ever earn, in current, inflation-adjusted dollars. Anything that threatens future earnings—say, management's failure to invest today in long-term research—*should* worry investors today. The worry should cause many to sell their shares, which depresses share price and thus punishes such managerial shortsightedness. In other words, in a world of truly efficient markets, if managers "indulge in value-destroying actions," Rajgopal says, "the market finds out eventually and their future wages get cut."[13] But in the bizarro world of contemporary corporate finance, the opposite is true. The stock market today is so focused on short-term performance, says Judy Samuelson, an expert in corporate short-termism at the Aspen Institute, that even big, successful companies—the pillars of the global economy, and the traditional font of most of our technology—must tread carefully when investing in the long term. Samuelson notes that when Google announced plans to hire nineteen hundred employees in 2011, the company's share price went into a massive swoon, eventually tumbling more than 20 percent,[14] as investors scorned "merely the *idea* that the company would be spending money."[15]

The market's distaste for long-term investment can be painfully explicit. Once, during the late 1990s, executives with aerospace giant Lockheed Martin met with Wall Street stock analysts to show off the cutting-edge technologies the firm was preparing to invest in. No sooner was the presentation finished, recalls Norman Augustine, then CEO, than the analysts "literally ran out of the room . . . and sold our stock." Over the next four days Lockheed Martin's share price fell 11 percent. Stunned, Augustine phoned an analyst friend who had attended the presentation and asked him why the market had punished a technology company for investing in new technology. Augustine recounted the analyst's answer. "He said, 'First of all, it takes fifteen years for research to pay off, if it pays off at all. Second, your average shareholder owns your stock for eighteen months. Fifteen years from now, they'll probably own Boeing's stock, and they don't want you to have any good ideas. Furthermore, they don't want to pay for it.' And then he gave me the *coup de grace*. 'Our firm just doesn't invest in companies with such short-sighted management.' Those were his words."[16]

This isn't to say that large, publicly traded companies have stopped spending money. But more and more, those expenditures are designed explicitly with short-term, share-price goals in mind. Take the example of share "buybacks." In the 1980s, companies discovered that the quickest way to boost share price (other than announcing a layoff) was to use their profits to buy up a large block of their own shares. By taking shares out of circulation, the company was artificially restricting the supply of remaining shares and thus driving up the price. With buybacks, managers found they could boost share price (and their own compensation) quickly and efficiently, without any of the risks involved in investing in new business activities, such as building a new factory, developing a new product, or, certainly, hiring new workers. For most of the last century, share buybacks were regarded as an illegal manipulation of the market. But in 1982, as part of the free-market revolution, the strategy was legalized by the Reagan administration. And while there are occasions where buybacks are entirely appropriate—as, for example, when firms are trying to fend off hostile takeovers—this isn't how they were mainly used. By the late 1990s, when buybacks were consuming some two hundred billion dollars a year, or a quarter of all corporate earnings[17]—it was clear the technique had become an end in itself. In fact, what we were seeing was an entirely new corporate business model, one in which actual output, such as cars or cotton or coal, was secondary to share price—or rather, where output *was* share price. Here was the final step in the evolution of industrial efficiency: capital efficiency, or the conversion of capital directly into shareholder value, and executive compensation, as quickly as possible.

The success of this new corporate model has been bittersweet, to say the least. Over the last two decades, soaring share prices have brought great wealth to large numbers of American investors, both large and small, and, in particular, have turned a small elite of corporate managers into billionaires. But that prosperity has masked, and even encouraged, some truly egregious problems. It was, clearly, the obsession with share price that encouraged many companies to start inflating quarterly earnings. From 1992 to 2005 the number of firms issuing earnings "restatements"—essentially, admissions that previously reported earnings were bogus—jumped from six a year[18] to nearly a hundred a month.[19] And the term *earnings fraud* doesn't do justice to creative accounting undertaken at firms such as WorldCom, which padded earnings by nine billion dollars, or Enron, which concealed twenty-three billion dollars in liabilities in "special purpose entities." In hindsight, however, it's plain that these scandals were only a prologue. The real catastrophe would come as Wall Street's new mentality of capital efficiency—of delivering high returns by whatever means necessary—made the jump, like a virus, into the mind of the consumer.

It was spring 2002 when realtors in Las Vegas noticed the market was behaving strangely. At open houses, buyers were showing up with unusual bank loans—loans with high interest rates and a low down payment. Or loans with no down payment. Ordinarily, such loans were reserved for borrowers with ample income and assets. But now banks were issuing them to first-time buyers, including people who clearly weren't ready to own a home. "All of a sudden, it's like everyone is qualifying for zero down," Adam Fenn, a realtor in Las Vegas at the time, told me. "And we're all thinking, 'What is going on?'"[20]

What was "going on" was that Goldman Sachs,[21] Merrill Lynch, and other big investment banks had discovered new territory in the hunt for yield: the manic, limbic realm of consumer real estate. By the early 2000s, investment banks were buying up tens of thousands of home mortgages and bundling them into securities called collateralized debt obligations, or CDOs, and selling these to pensions and other institutional investors. Demand for these new "financial technologies" was strong: with the CDO, the investor got a high return, the stream of interest and principal payments from each mortgage, but with the supposedly low risk associated with a collateral-backed asset: a house. In the context of capital efficiency, the CDO provided an effective means to convert a long-term physical asset into a quick return.

Demand for this new efficiency was so strong, in fact, that investment banks were running out of mortgages, and they pushed lenders to make more loans. But since the fundamental conditions of the housing market hadn't really changed—there weren't, suddenly, more people who could afford a house (quite the reverse, given stagnating incomes)—the only way to increase the supply of mortgages was to lower lending standards. And that, as we all know now, is precisely what Wall Street began pressuring lenders to do. Wall Street's bankers didn't put it in those terms. "They never told us to make bad loans," lender Bill Dallas later told *Vanity Fair* in an article about Merrill Lynch, one of the biggest mortgage bundlers. "They would say, 'You need to increase your coupon'"—bank jargon for CDOs with higher yields. But as Dallas explained, "The only way to do that was to make crappier loans."[22]

Although some banking and real estate veterans were uneasy about this more relaxed loan regimen, their anxiety was no match for the gold rush mentality that ensued. Everyone with any connection to real estate began making money, and some people were making fortunes. Wall Street banks were earning billions of dollars in commissions. Developers were building tens of thousands of units using high-speed methods that cut costs (and often hurt quality) but generated massive returns. And those on the front lines of the real estate boom were positively floating in cash. In booming Las Vegas, a realtor with hustle could make a half million dollars a year. A mortgage broker could make a million. "It was unreal," a former broker told me. "I went from making fifty thousand dollars a year to making that much in a month. We went out every night. We went to strip clubs. We partied.

You'd wake up in the morning and a porn star is walking around your kitchen. And then you go the office and do it all over again." Like the song says, it was money for nothing and the chicks for free.

What was so compelling about the real estate boom was that you didn't have to be a professional to get in on it. Simply owning a home was your ticket to vast streams of money for nothing. In hot markets such as Vegas, where home prices were doubling every few years, bankers began seeing "serial" refinancers, who would refinance every six months, cashing out forty or fifty thousand dollars at a time and using it not for investments, but for vacation, groceries, mortgage payments. Serial refinancers were, in effect, using financial technology to sell their house . . . to themselves, over and over again. It was like something from an Escher drawing, a perpetual-motion machine that violated the basic laws of supply and demand, of labor and reward—yet somehow was working. "Basically, it meant you could keep on being a receptionist or whatever and still have this amazing lifestyle," a banker told me. "Or you didn't even need to work to make a living; refinancing *was* your living." And, of course, this wasn't simply a Vegas thing. Serial refinance was the new form of employment— and the new engine of the consumer economy and of identity maintenance. Of the nearly $1.3 trillion in equity that Americans extracted from their homes between 2003 and 2005, a third of it was spent on cars, boats, vacations, plasma screen TVs, and other items of personal consumption.[23]

Even government policymakers caught the virus. At the Federal Reserve, chairman Alan Greenspan, another champion of unfettered, efficient markets, saw rapidly appreciating housing prices and equity withdrawals as an easy way to help offset consumers' flattening incomes. In this Panglossian scenario, by keeping interest rates low, the government hoped to harness financial markets to do what traditional economic activity no longer seemed capable of doing: maintain rising living standards. Government, too, had gone myopic. As

Greenspan explained in a 2004 speech, the "surge in mortgage refinancings" had "likely improved rather than worsened the financial condition of the average homeowner . . . and has very likely been a supportive factor for the general economy." Meanwhile, on suburban tracts no more than forty-five minutes from Greenspan's office at the Fed, new housing developments were selling out before crews had broken ground, and units were flipping once or twice or even three times before they were finished. In this new, financially supercharged, self-centered economy, the free lunch was now a legitimate business model.

In hindsight, of course, it clearly wasn't a legitimate business model. Finance was, in effect, attempting to fill in the gap in consumer incomes that followed the end of the postwar economy and the rise of the shareholder revolution. By definition, it was prosperity that couldn't last. Yet there was no one to say "no." The financial sector was too busy making a mint. Policymakers were too busy congratulating themselves for "saving" the economy. Consumers, clearly, weren't interested in any sort of self-regulation. Not only were our limbic brains in full party mode, but the traditional social institutions, such as norms against credit or the chaperoning affects of close community ties, had all been weakened by the relentless efficiencies of the self-centered economy. This lack of traditional social restraints was particularly evident in hot real estate markets, such as Las Vegas, where many who had come to cash in on the property bonanza found themselves immersed in a provocative environment with few familiar structures to moderate their enthusiasms. Many newcomers to Vegas "don't have much of a support network," Michele Johnson, a veteran credit counselor in Las Vegas, told me. "You don't come with your [extended] family. You don't know your neighbors. You don't have the strong sense of community . . . of someone overseeing what it is you're doing and saying, 'Hey, don't be such a chump.'"[24]

o   o   o

Sigmund Freud, when he was describing the process of emotional development nearly a century ago, coined the term *reality principle* to describe how the healthy individual must learn to defer gratification. To fail to submit to reality—to remain guided instead by the "pleasure principle"—Freud argued, was to lock oneself in an infantile, stunted stage, forever unfulfilled and unsociable. For Freud, the forces of reality were mainly social, such as family and institutional authority. But he could just as well have been talking about market forces, since, generally speaking, a person or organization unable to defer economic gratification is soon ostracized by the efficient market.

But with the rise of modern finance in the last years of the twentieth century, it was as if we'd all agreed to suspend the reality principle—and with it, the idea that returns can't happen without patience and effort and actual productivity. For, in the world of finance, clearly miracles were possible. A person or company with the right connections or technology or timing could reap an enormous return in a fraction of the time and for a fraction of the effort necessary in the real world. You saw the miracle on Wall Street, where raiders flipped entire companies for imperial sums. You saw it in the consumer culture, with serial refinancers and the part-time speculators. You saw it in the policy world, with low interest rates and the Greenspanian hope that a real estate bubble would restore postwar prosperity. By the early 2000s, the entire society had embraced the idea that instant returns were not only possible, but, by definition, preferable to returns that required effort or patience or hard choices. In this, financialization is the very essence of the Impulse Society, which is all about cutting to the largest return as quickly as possible, while avoiding any inefficiency (work, social obligations, norms) that might slow things down.

Ultimately, of course, financialization's rejection of the reality principle isn't sustainable. Throughout history, every society that has institutionalized the pleasure principle through its financial sector—and it has happened repeatedly—eventually implodes. But to focus as we do on the crashes and busts and other corrections is to miss the subtler, deeper damage that occurs in an economy that lets itself be dominated by finance. As the financial sector comes to occupy a larger share of economic activity, it pulls away resources from other, more essential sectors, such as manufacturing or infrastructure or education. In the United States especially, home to the largest financial sector in the world, an increasing share of our capital now flows not into material improvements such as roads or energy research or classrooms, but into purely speculative assets such CDOs and credit swaps. And while some of this increased flow reflects the financing needs of a much larger, more complex economy, the real driver is simpler: modern finance offers people and companies much larger returns than you can find nearly anywhere else.

Capital isn't the only asset being diverted into the financial sector. The promise of sweet returns also lures many of our best and brightest away from fields where their talents might be put to better use. Since the 1990s, when financial sector salaries kicked up sharply from those in other professions (they're now 50 percent higher),[25] there has been an equally sharp increase in the proportion of college graduates heading to Wall Street. The trend is particularly noteworthy in the case of graduates in the so-called STEM fields—science, technology, engineering, and math. Bright young women and men who traditionally took positions in essential fields such as engineering or medicine or research are increasingly likely to opt for the faster returns of the financial sector.[26] "Finance literally bids rocket scientists away from the satellite industry," write Stephen Cecchetti and Enisse Kharroubi, economists at the Bank of International Settlements and experts in the effects of financial sector expansion.[27] "People who might have become scientists, who in another age dreamt of curing cancer or flying to Mars, today dream of becoming hedge fund managers." Even many conservative economists who are generally content to let markets allocate talent worry about the financial sector's warping effects on the job market. "The last thing we need is for the next Steve Jobs to forgo Silicon Valley in order to join the high-frequency traders on Wall Street," writes Harvard economist Greg Mankiw. "That is, we shouldn't be concerned about the next Steve Jobs striking it rich, but we want to make sure he strikes it rich in a socially productive way."[28]

Mankiw's point about striking it rich in "a socially productive way" is central here. In a truly efficient market, people and companies earn only as much as is necessary to induce them to deliver a particular service or product. So a brain surgeon commands a high salary because it takes lots of skill, nerve, and college loans to be a good brain surgeon. If the job paid any less, no one would undertake the effort or risk. And if it overpaid, so many med school graduates would decide to be brain surgeons that the field would be glutted, salaries would fall, and the job would lose its attractiveness. In other words, the job market, like any market, corrects itself, and this capacity to self-correct, to efficiently allocate talent (or any resource), is why we're generally comfortable with a market-based economy. But finance's outsize effects on the labor market, and the economy generally, underscore why most of us aren't quite ready to trust the market for everything. Simply put, the financial sector is able to sidestep that natural corrective mechanism and reap a larger reward than can be justified by the service it provides—or the risk it poses.

Finance isn't alone here. In any economy, there are players able to exploit certain advantages (a monopoly position, say, or insider information) to extract a much larger wage or profit than the market would otherwise bear. Economists refer to this unearned surplus as "rent." But no other sector exhibits the "rentier" tendency as dramatically as finance. For centuries, financiers have found ways—lobbying for a regulatory loophole, say, or devising a technology so complex, or a technique so arcane, that no one else understands it—to extract a larger profit than would otherwise be necessary to persuade the financiers to perform the socially essential function of finance. (It's hardly coincidental that during the 1990s, as financial deregulation and financial technologies were just ramping up, the median compensation for investment bank executives, which until then had been on par with compensation at other companies, leapt ahead by a factor of between seven and ten.[29]) And like some black hole, as finance's surplus has grown, so, too, has the distortion of the economy as steadily more resources are pulled away from sectors that are arguably more socially productive yet don't offer returns that are as competitive.

The problem with rent, of course, is that it defends itself. The massive flow of talent and resources into the financial sector keeps the sector so well stocked with innovators and entrepreneurs and lobbyists that it is always able to find or create new advantages and thus maintain its large rents. This is one reason the finance sector continues to balloon in size and employment and profits, while nonfinancial sectors struggle. In the United States, the manufacturing sector accounts for around 12 percent of the total economy, down from nearly 25 percent in 1970,[30] while finance now accounts for 8.4 percent,[31] or nearly triple its historic share. (In the United Kingdom, where the financial business has also ballooned, manufacturing contributes just 12 percent of the national economy, half of what it did thirty years ago,[32] while the financial sector has grown at roughly triple the rate of the rest of the economy.[33])

This shift in the relative sizes of sectors matters immensely for many reasons. Manufacturing has historically provided far more middle-wage jobs than finance does. Technologies developed in a healthy manufacturing sector "spill over" into the rest of the economy and spur broader growth, while the financial sector, as we've seen, tends to have a reverse spillover effect, siphoning off talent and resources from other sectors. What's more, manufacturing also tends to be less volatile—that is, where failure in the manufacturing sector leads to job losses, failure in the financial sector can utterly destroy an economy. And because finance can offer such massive rewards, it is far more prone to the sort of speculation and mega-risk taking that leads to booms and busts. Thus it's no surprise that researchers such as Cecchetti and Kharroubi, the economists at the Bank of International Settlements, have found that once an economy's financial sector exceeds a certain size, it may actually begin undercutting economic growth. [34]

In short, we should be doing everything we can to expand our manufacturing sector and shrink our financial sector. Instead, in the United States, we do the opposite—allowing the manufacturing sector to wither while directly and indirectly encouraging the financial sector to grow. (As we'll see in later chapters, the financial sector is the most politically connected and protected sector in the economy.) And note: many of our global competitors have maintained much larger manufacturing bases. In Germany, manufacturing generates 21 percent of total economic output, while finance contributes just 4 percent. In Korea, manufacturing is 31 percent and finance just 7 percent. Even in Italy, manufacturing is a larger piece of the economy: 17 percent, while finance is just 5 percent.[35]

Ultimately, the real risk of a hypertrophied financial sector isn't the misallocation of resources and talent or greater volatility. It's the way the mind-set of the financial sector becomes the mind-set of the culture at large. Even in nonfinancial businesses, executive attention is increasingly fixated on finance. Nearly all companies have a chief financial officer—the role barely existed before 1980—whose duties include "investor relations" (that is, managing the company's image among financial analysts, institutional investors, and other emissaries of the market). Nearly all companies tie their management directly to the financial markets with stock-based compensation. (By 2000, stock options had lifted the average CEO's compensation to more than four hundred times that of the median employee, up from a ratio of twenty to one in the 1970s.[36])

Likewise, "financial engineering," or the use of financial techniques, such as share buybacks, to raise share prices, is now a standard part of the corporate strategic repertoire. During the 1990s stock market boom, hundreds of companies used their own rapidly appreciating shares as a kind of übercurrency to go on acquisition sprees. America Online, a dot-com upstart with revenues of barely five billion dollars, leveraged its steroidal stock valuation—one hundred and seventy-five billion dollars at the time—to buy Time Warner, a vastly larger firm with revenues of twenty-seven billion but only half of AOL's market value.[37] By the turn of the century, more than half the mergers involving large companies were stock-only, up from almost zero a decade before.[38] And of course companies with massive market valuations were being created virtually out of nothing: during the 1990s dot-com boom, many start-ups with no product or profits were sold, with ample help from Wall Street banks, to eager investors for hundreds of millions and eventually billions of dollars in shrewdly pitched public offerings. Every year, more of the economy—more of the compensation, more of the purchases, more of the total value— was based not on the production of something real, but on an abstraction engineered in financial markets.

By the early 2000s, as the real estate bubble began inflating, much of the economy was in full Escher mode. Consumers were funding elaborate identities with equity that did not exist. (In fact, thanks to a neurological glitch known as the "wealth effect," merely knowing that our home values were increasing was enough to make us spend more—to the tune of four hundred billion dollars a year.[39]) Corporations were manipulating share prices with massive buybacks. (Between 2003 and 2007, buybacks by the five hundred firms listed on the Standard & Poor's 500 quadrupled.[40]) On Wall Street, meanwhile, the rocket scientists turned investment bankers were devising ever-more baroque ways to multiply that nonexistent wealth. There was, for example, the "CDO-squared"—essentially a CDO built from two or more other mortgage-backed CDOs, which let investors "expose" themselves to more lending risk, and thus earn commensurately greater returns. More innovative still was the "synthetic" CDO, by which investors bet on other CDOs without actually owning them. With synthetic CDOs, any number of investors could bet on the same security and, by extension, the same physical house securing the original mortgage. Wall Street was now manufacturing "housing" wealth many times the size of the physical housing market. The financial sector itself was now financialized. As the late economist Hyman Minksy pointed out, where an earlier generation of financiers got rich investing in the "capital development of the economy"—railroads, oil pipelines, factories, and other pieces of the industrializing system—during the industrial boom in the late nineteenth century, the current emphasis, Minsky noted, was no longer on "the capital development of the economy but rather upon the quick turn of the speculator, upon trading profits."[41] Finance was investing in itself. The pleasure principle was now a science. The Impulse Society was just hitting its stride.

But here, too, the illusion was wavering. The flaw of the Impulse Society and its primary engine, the self-centered economy, is that the more robust it seems, the less sustainable it actually is. Well before the actual collapse of the housing bubble, the prime players knew the entire edifice was tottering. At Goldman Sachs, Morgan Stanley, and other investment banks, traders routinely referred to the new securities as "shitty deals," "monstrosities," "Nuclear Holocaust," "Mike Tyson's Punchout," and, fittingly, "Subprime Meltdown." Still, the banks continued not only to sell the now-toxic securities, but also to devise ways to profit when the toxic securities failed. Yet this, too, was hardly surprising, given the financial market's obsession with efficient returns. The very nature of the new financial tools meant any failure or breakdown would happen somewhere else, in time or space, and well outside Wall Street's increasingly myopic field of vision. Or, to quote the acronym that traders and executives repeated whenever anyone raised concerns about the deals being done, "IBG YBG"—as in "I'll Be Gone, You'll Be Gone."[42]

Gamblers, when their luck turns sour, often exhibit a behavioral tic known as loss aversion. It's a survival thing—because we were adapted for scarcity, we're predisposed to hate losing any sort of asset. In studies involving gambling, subjects perceive losses to be twice as large as wins even though the losses and wins involve the same amount of money.[43] Loss aversion is why blackjack players will double-down repeatedly after a bad hand, and why stock traders will ride a losing stock into the ground. It's also why homeowners often refuse to lower their selling price even when the market is collapsing, which is what began to happen in 2006. "It stopped on a dime," Florence Shapiro, a forty-year veteran of the Las Vegas real estate scene, told me recently. "One day, it was just over. We couldn't sell the houses."[44] Adding to the misery, however, realtors now had to get clients to understand that the massive wealth they'd possessed only months before was now gone. "You had to counsel people. I had one client come to me. He had twelve houses. He had been buying them and flipping them, and he got stuck with twelve houses. I said to him, 'The market has stopped.'"

Loss aversion is also an apt description of how the entire market, and especially the financial market, reacted to the collapse—with increasingly desperate moves that made the final damage so much worse. As the economy stalled and corporate earnings flattened, panicked CEOs initiated massive share buybacks. In 2007, companies on the Standard & Poor's 500 spent 62 percent of their net profits on buybacks. The following year, they spent 89 percent.[45] The buybacks helped preserve share prices and executive compensation, but they also left the companies less able to weather the downturn. Research by William Lazonick, the economist we met in chapter 2, shows that many of the companies that ultimately needed federal bailouts or that were "rescued" by foreign investors had, just before the meltdown, drained their cash reserves through epic share buybacks. Lehman Brothers, whose 2007 bankruptcy tipped the market into free fall, had just spent more than five billion dollars on share repurchases that year and the year before. Fannie Mae and Freddie Mac, the failed government-backed mortgage companies, together had ten billion dollars in buybacks since 2003.[46]

Share buybacks were just one of the strategies deployed by the finance sector to escape the ruin they'd helped create. Many investment banks sought to offset their housing market losses by speculating heavily on the price of commodities, such as oil and grain. These "hedging" moves let the banks cushion some of their losses, but they also helped run up the prices for the commodities, thus ensuring that the millions of workers who would be losing their jobs in the financial collapse would now also be paying more for food and gas. And, finally, when banks could no longer outrun the crisis, they played their trump card: arguing that they were too large and important to the economy to be allowed to fail, Wall Street's big players turned to the government for bailouts—a move that, in effect, shielded the banks (and their executives' careers) from the purifying market discipline that was supposed to discourage such risk taking in first place. The entire economy, it seemed, had been turned into an experiment into the effects of power and loss on human behavior—and the results were pretty much what we've come to expect. Across the board, the reptilian brain was now in charge.

Just over a century ago, the British learned a similarly painful lesson about the risks of a financialized economy. Not only was public and private debt soaring, but vast amounts of capital were moving out of manufacturing and other "hard industries" and into financial activities, notably investments offshore. This shift had worked out nicely for British capitalists. But it was starving the home economy of resources, financial and intellectual, just as Britain's global economic supremacy was being challenged by the United States. In a 1904 speech to British bankers, Joseph Chamberlain, England's former colonial secretary, summarized the dilemma in harsh terms. "Banking is not the creator of our prosperity but the creation of it. It is not the cause of our wealth, but it is the consequence of our wealth." England could not survive merely as the "hoarder of invested securities" if that capital were not being employed as the "creator of new wealth."[47]

More than a century later, the leading postindustrial economies still seem determined not to learn that lesson. Not only has finance remained the dominant sector in the U.S. economy, but the players are more firmly entrenched than ever. The finance sector is even more concentrated today, with just twelve megabanks, including JPMorgan Chase, Bank of America, Citigroup, and Wells Fargo, holding more than two-thirds of all U.S. bank assets.[48] Meanwhile, the limbic attributes of the sector continue to shape the culture at large. The "hunt for yield" has become part of the national character. Sports-team coaches and university presidents all now flit from post to post in search of the best package. Marriage continues to decline as partners now hold out the possibility for a better romantic return elsewhere. And of course the business world remains locked in the finance mind-set. The tenure of the average company CEO has fallen to five years, from nine two decades ago.[49] Stock-based pay remains the norm, as does the strategy of share buybacks and other financial engineering. Lazonick has calculated that between 2001 and 2012, buybacks by the five hundred companies of the S&P 500 sucked up a stunning three and a half trillion dollars—roughly three-quarters as much as the U.S. government spent to win World War II.[50] These are the classic symptoms of the Impulse Society—an economy so thoroughly reconfigured around the desire for rapid returns that it is increasingly incapable of producing what we need.

Perhaps most disturbing, consumers themselves have embraced, or absorbed, the character of the financial sector. Not only do many of us continue to seek the fastest return in every conceivable situation, but when those efforts go awry, we're also more likely to display an indifference to consequences that is as callous, as reptilian, as anything you'd find on Wall Street. Indeed, it's as if the real lesson of the financial crisis has been to teach us all the benefits of acting like an investment banker or a corporate raider. In the aftermath of the housing collapse, Todd Miller, the Las Vegas realtor we met earlier, began working as a liaison between banks and foreclosed homeowners. The job often had him delivering bad news from banks to the soon-to-be-evicted homeowners. When he started the job, Miller says, the homeowners he met were usually mortified and deeply distressed. "They would invite me in and tell me their whole story, and they would be in tears because they had gotten foreclosed on," Miller told me. "They were so ashamed." But these days, Miller says, he finds an entirely different scene. The homes he visits are often tricked out with improvements paid for by equity extractions. There is usually a new car or two in the driveway and various recreational toys around. And the homeowners are rarely upset. "Now they *brag* about it," says Miller. "I'm at the gym and the guy next to me is telling his buddy next to him, 'I'm at almost three years without making a payment, and they're going to foreclose, but I could care less. I've got fifty grand from a refi in the bank.'" As Miller relates this story, his voice tightens. "There's no shame in being foreclosed on anymore. It was 'not your fault.' 'It was the bank.' Blah blah blah. It used to be socially unacceptable—the worst thing that could happen to you. Now? It's no big deal. If something doesn't work out, you just walk away."

Part Two

Cracks in the Mirror

CHAPTER 5

Home Alone

Every Saturday from March through October, the Farmers' Market on the west side of Portland offers visitors a taste of what life might be like beyond the shortsighted, self-centered vortex of the Impulse Society. The vendors' stalls are packed with handcrafted, artisanal delicacies that have made Portland a capital for "slow food." The air thrums with strains of the city's famously noncorporate music scene—everything from a "green" choir and a didgeridoo to a unicyclist, in kilt and Darth Vader helmet, bagpiping the *Star Wars* theme. And the crowd itself is a cross section of the city's hyperengaged civic culture: the graying hippies and assertive cyclists; the earnest, thickly tattooed hipsters; and of course the activists, of every stripe, educating anyone who will listen about logging and homelessness, about bike lanes and gay marriage, about whether corporations should be treated like citizens and whether citizens should have to drink fluoridated water. Yes, Portland's civic self-consciousness is so intense that real life here can feel like an episode of *Portlandia*. (Where else will you find the official city bike map in Spanish, Somali, Nepali, Russian, Burmese, and Arabic as well as English?[1]) But it all comes across as sincere and purposeful and solid, as if Portland might be a place where people don't just "walk away" from their messes, but stick around and work them out.

In a sense, though, Portland is all about walking away. Although the city's alternative culture goes back decades, some of its most ardent *alternistas* are newcomers, transplants seeking reprieve from the imbalances of mainstream culture. At the Farmers' Market, I meet Ally, a gay woman who moved up from Los Angeles because Portland was the first place where she felt she "fit in." Back in LA, Ally tells me, "I didn't know what my next-door neighbors' politics were, and I wasn't going to assume that they're buying organic or support same-sex marriage." Nearby, Stephan, a schoolteacher, says he left the Midwest to escape the conservative, anti-environmental mind-set. Here, he says, "you just feel comfortable putting up a sign saying, 'I Have a Pesticide-Free Yard.' You feel comfortable talking about recycling at the grocery store." In a town teeming with recent arrivals, many seem to have similar tales of carefully considered flight. Coming to Portland "was a strategic decision," says thirtysomething Marin, who, with her boyfriend, Adam, chose the city after surveying half a dozen other locales. "We wanted to make sure we were going to a place where we would want to be every day."[2]

Portland is scarcely the only beacon for cultural refugees. As Bill Bishop observes in his prescient book *The Big Sort*, urban centers such as Austin, Boulder, and Madison have emerged as sanctuaries for left-of-center settlers. Conservatives, meanwhile, are flocking to communities such as Orange County, Colorado Springs, and the suburbs of Birmingham and Houston. Where geography was once shaped by employment, family connections, or other materialist factors, Bishop says, we now often relocate "for a whole set of 'life-style' reasons," such as politics or cultural amenities or proximity to shopping malls and sports stadiums. "People have become very calculating," Bishop told me. "In ways our parents never even thought of, people are parsing the choice of where to live as if they were going through a menu at a restaurant." To put this in the language of the Impulse Society, we now seek the place that can most efficiently deliver the highest aspirational return.

Our sorting isn't limited to cities and neighborhoods. More and more of our personal consumption is aimed at finding or creating "enclaves" of self-reflecting utility—places, products, experiences, networks, and people that reinforce our self-image and aspirations by emphasizing what we like and filtering out what we don't. For some of us, this process of personalization might mean a new neighborhood with just the right mix of prewar Craftsmen bungalows and recycling bins. For others, it might be a group of online friends whose likes and dislikes mirror our own. It could be a political movement that confirms our deepest hunches about humanity—or a cocoon of "self-tracking" technologies that lets us fixate on our physical state. It might be a brand, like Apple or Harley-Davidson, that offers us easy group identification. Or a cable channel offering a constant diet of cooking shows or politically incorrect news—or, for that matter, a 3D gaming environment where we can disintegrate anyone we don't like. These are very different "places," but all reflect the same basic desire for spaces and experiences that embody our personal preferences. As important, all are examples of the way our economic system has become steadily more efficient at delivering these personalized realities.

On one level, this is our triumph. To be able to shape our lives and lifestyles and interactions with the world to fit our personal agendas—it's exactly the sort of freedom that makes the consumer economy, and the American version in particular, so attractive and desirable. And yet this power to personalize is also turning out to be our Achilles' heel. The better the market gets at letting us gratify our preferences, while filtering out whatever we don't want to deal with, the more we seem to land ourselves in hot water. That was clearly the case in the housing bubble, where hyperefficient financial systems let us enjoy the look and feel of a "successful" lifestyle while evading all the irritating details—such as the fact that we couldn't afford it. True, most of our efforts at personalization don't cause the economy to melt down. But they often impose costs and consequences that we're just as happy not acknowledging.

Take our hunt for the ideal city. On the one hand, who could be blamed for wanting to live around people with similar views or values or, at the very least, fashion imperatives? At a time when community can be so hard to find, places such as Portland and Austin and Orange County may have figured out how to create a sense of shared purpose. On the other hand, thanks to that same success in finding communities that match our preferences, the country as a whole is gradually losing some of its social cohesion. Consider the way the political map of the United States has changed since the sorting trend began in the 1970s. Back then, just one in four Americans lived in a county that was bright red or bright blue—that is, where one political party regularly won presidential elections by a margin of 20 percent or more. Today, after four decades of sorting ourselves into like-minded communities, more than half of Americans live in so-called landslide counties.[3] (In Portland and surrounding Multnomah County, the political balance has shifted from dead even in the 1960s to Democratic victory margins of forty-five points.[4]) This gradual segregation by political preference is clearly a factor in the stalemate in national politics (an issue we'll return to in later chapters). But that segregation is also stripping local communities of the diversity and dissent that once forced us to practice the arts of compromise and moderation. In the suburbs of Houston or Kansas City or Birmingham, the liberal voice is now all but an endangered species—and likewise for conservatives in left-leaning places such as Madison, Austin, and Portland. This makes for a nice, easy place to live, but it may not be the recipe for a vigorous civil society. In being able to "select our neighbors," says Joe Cortright, a Portland economist who studies migration, "we're losing these cross-cutting opportunities to encounter people who have really different views from us."

Political polarization is merely one example of the unintended costs of this intensifying drive to craft lives in our own image. The bigger risks in our rush to personalize are subtler: the more we retreat into self-made experiences and lifestyles, the harder it becomes to engage in what is *not* familiar or personalized. And the brute fact is that some of the most important things in life, and certainly most of the biggest challenges we face as a society, are anything but personal or personalizable. Rather, they are generic, collective, and often unpleasant, requiring patience, a tolerance for the unfamiliar, and a willingness to compromise and even sacrifice. In short, the challenges we face require us to confront the very irritations and inefficiencies that our desire-driven, efficiency-obsessed Impulse Society has persuaded us we shouldn't have to deal with.

The financial meltdown is the most salient example. In the aftermath of that massive failure, we should all be working, collectively and individually, to change the financial system—and the corrupt political system that enables it. Instead, we've mostly done just the opposite: we've retreated deeper into our own lives and lifestyles and selves. Here is the trap created by a society that insists on delivering more life-shaping power to its citizens yet has largely stopped talking about how those powers might best be put to use. Indeed, we blithely defer to the wisdom of the market and assume that if some new increment of capability is being offered that allows us to disengage even further from the broader society and its irksome problems—it is, by definition, entirely acceptable and even desirable. It's the Impulse Society's signature move: every man, woman, and hipster for themselves.

In some respects, we've been moving toward this crisis of hyperpersonalization for well over a century. Nearly two hundred years ago,

Alexis de Tocqueville noted how Americans, having freed themselves from the tightly controlled European culture, were constantly tempted to leave "the greater society to look after itself" and focus entirely on individual pursuits. What kept us from flying apart, de Tocqueville argued, was what he called "self-interest properly understood." The average American, being highly pragmatic, saw that his individual interests couldn't be far advanced without the community; he remained engaged with those around him "because union with his fellows seems useful to him."[5] Here was the quality that allowed the New World to maintain such a vigorous, productive society and economy. "Each American," de Tocqueville wrote, "knows when to sacrifice some of his private interests to save the rest."

But de Tocqueville's optimism about enlightened self-interest always rested on the premise that individuals truly saw their own interests as inseparable from the community's. As we've already seen, however, as the consumer economy has brought steadily greater individual power, or, at least, the perception of greater power, "union with our fellows" hasn't felt quite as useful. Certainly there were countervailing forces that tempered our desire to cut the ties that bound us. Through much of the last century our values and institutions were shaped by people who had lived through war and depression, and who knew firsthand the utility of social cohesion and of the self-sacrifice necessary to maintain that cohesion. But by the 1970s that spirit of cohesion was under heavy assault. Ideologically, individual fulfillment was the order of day both for the left and especially for the right, where a rising strain of libertarianism chafed at the assumptions of self-sacrifice implicit in the New Deal's march-as-one communitarianism. (As libertarian economist Milton Friedman scornfully noted after Kennedy's "Ask Not" speech, "'What you can do for your country' implies that the government is the master or the deity, the citizen, the servant or the votary. To the free man, the country is the collection of individuals who compose it, not something over and above them.")

As important, the rapidly evolving consumer economy was supplying that citizen with steadily more opportunities to pursue self-interest without the assistance or approval of others—and, indeed, often in spite of others. Our cars had morphed from mobility tools to rolling fortresses. Our homes gave up their outward-facing structures, such as front porches and lawns, in favor of larger interior spaces, back patios, and enclosed garages. And even after the faltering economy stopped generating so much real individual prosperity, the ongoing digital revolution ensured that our campaign for personal liberation would become a permanent culture fixture, a lifestyle in its own right.

So while it's true that the Great Recession tempered some of our grander efforts at life personalization—we're not relocating to lifestyle cities with quite the same fervor as we were pre-2008—our personal technologies let us keep customizing on the cheap. With the ubiquitous smartphone and an all-but-omniscient Internet, even consumers like myself, with little technological skill, now sit effortlessly at the center of a data universe that is both vast and personalized. We can communicate constantly with colleagues, family, and friends. We can map out our entertainment options and shopping expeditions with a precision once confined to science fiction. (We can see which bars our friends, and "friends," are getting drunk at and summon turn-by-turn driving directions to reach them.) We can clean house to a song list tailored for us by a computer algorithm or click our way through a never-quite random series of YouTube videos, Vine shorts, or Chatroulette encounters. Moment to moment, we have the potential to make our leisure time (and a distressing fraction of our workday) into a sequence of personal, personalizing experiences in which various smart technologies filter out the stressful and the mundane so we can get on with our real job, which, apparently, is self-expression.

And these capabilities, inconceivable even a generation ago, pale in comparison to what will soon be available as smartphones become wearable and embeddable and as the Internet links us not merely to digital objects, but to anything in the physical environment. My car, my house, my appliances, my pets, the products on the grocery shelves, the stores I am walking past—all will constantly inform me about their potential to enhance my well-being—or, at the very least, will offer to sell me something I'm statistically likely to find appealing. At malls and airports, kiosks will detect my presence and flash specials tailored to my shopping history. At parties, virtual labels will reveal guests' relationship statuses and professional rank, so I'll know whom to hit on versus whom to suck up to.[6] And between conversations (or during, if they're dull), I'll answer texts, scan personalized news streams, and order kebabs from the corner deli (and probably have them delivered by a tiny drone). To read some of the more optimistic forecasts, it will be a life of relentlessly enlightened self-interest: at any given moment, no matter where I am or whom I'm with, I'll know precisely where my own self-interest lies and thus precisely how much, or how little, to engage with those around me, or with society generally, to maximize my own personal returns.

Or so we're constantly assured. But by this point in the narrative of the Impulse Society, we know better than to trust the promises of a marketplace that has steered us so disastrously wrong on previous outings. Although personal capabilities grow more miraculous by the week, there is mounting evidence that these greater levels of person-alization aren't necessarily making us any more enlightened—about our own self-interest or the interests of the broader society. At the outset of this book, we saw how software designers keep online gamers glued to their screens—and thus evermore detached from the real world. But that dynamic, it turns out, isn't confined to gaming. As journalist Nicholas Carr demonstrated in his sharp and depressing account *The Shallows*, everyone who regularly partakes of the digital realm is exposed to the same patterns. The problem, as Carr documents, lies in the very elements of the digital environment that so willingly conform to our preferences. The online environment is naturally organized like a gigantic game, with endless opportunities for what psychologists call positive reinforcement. Whenever we click, we're rewarded with something new—a text, picture, or some other digital object—and that novelty (and the associated neurotransmitters) soon becomes as important as the information content of the object itself. The digital environment, writes Carr, "turns us into lab rats constantly pressing levers to get tiny pellets of social or intellectual nourishment."[7]

On top of this, our hunger for more novelty interferes with our comprehension of the data we're consuming. Because the act of retrieving a new piece of information becomes as important as the information itself, Carr writes, our consciousness begins to bifurcate between the information we've already retrieved (say, a downloaded article we're now trying to read) and the thought of the next object we expect to retrieve. But because the act of anticipation and the act of deep comprehension are two very different mental processes, toggling between them interrupts our concentration and makes it harder to really dig into the thing we're supposed to be looking at and absorbing. We end up consuming much more information, but processing it in a more superficial way. Further, research suggests that because any routine eventually alters brain structure, this high-volume, low-comprehension mode becomes habit—and, in fact, it even alters the way we process information when we step outside the digital realm. Online or off, we become overly focused on finding new information, while our motivation to dig deeply into the content at hand diminishes. We become more distractible, less able to differentiate the meaningful from the merely stimulating. We're more likely to struggle with complex, challenging ideas and problems. As neuroscientist Jordan Grafman tells Carr, "The more you multitask, the less deliberative you become; the less able to think and reason out a problem."

And, presumably, the less able you are to "properly" understand your own self-interest—or to know when part of it ought to be sacrificed.

That our new tools might be making it harder, not easier, to assess and pursue our own self-interest shouldn't be too surprising. In a sense, the problems we're having with our digital capabilities are just the latest variant on the challenge we've faced since the consumer economy started handing out tools more than a century ago: whether we're talking about smartphones or barn-size SUVs or a Double Bacon Whopper with cheese, these tools weren't really designed for our benefit, but for the bottom lines of the companies selling them. The increments of self-expressive power we now exercise so imperiously are really just outputs from sophisticated companies whose ultimate goal isn't actually empowering anybody but their own managers and investors. No company can sell increments of power that consumers don't want. But in a postmaterialist, hyperconsumer society, "want" has as much to do with the financial dynamics of corporate treadmills as it does with any single consumer's burning desire for self-expression or freedom or personal preference. For all the emphasis we put on consumer demand, it's not demand alone that brings forth steadily more powerful consumer tools with every product cycle. How can it be, given that consumers often have no idea that we want a new gadget or feature or increment of power until we see it advertised or in the hands of a friend? Rather, the flood of so much personalizing power into the marketplace each year is primarily a reflection not of our own desires, but of the industrial imperative to keep treadmills turning, throughput flowing, and share prices rising.

Granted, this has been a reality since Albert Sloan began mass-producing obsolescence nearly a century ago. But given our accelerating digital efficiencies and intensifying corporate priorities, and given that more and more of our lives and selves now unfold entirely in the context of consumption, this coincidence of personal and corporate agendas is no longer merely *a* reality, but increasingly *the* reality. Our factory treadmills now overproduce increments of personal power as routinely as farmers overproduce grain—with the result that consumer markets are perpetually glutted with an excess of horsepower and megapixels, square footage and gigabytes, ready-to-eat calories, caffeine, and whatever other forms of personal capability companies have learned to mass-produce. The fact that individuals frequently don't need or want all that capability, or would be better off without it entirely, is no longer relevant. Once created, surplus capability must be moved through the supply chain and into our lives, and to ensure this, manufacturers resort to ever-more-creative and aggressive marketing techniques. These include coercive upgrades, naturally, but also increasingly intrusive methods, such as tracking the websites we visit, or mining our purchase histories and social media trails to predict where our potential desires might overlap with their quarterly earnings targets. Already cable TV firms can deliver "microtargeted" ads to individual households, directing, as one company executive boasted, "dog-food ads to dog owners, cat-food ads to cat owners and, to a home nearby with three kids, a minivan ad."[8] And before Target was infamous for massive data breaches, it was infamous for a marketing system so precise it predicted a teenage girl's pregnancy, based on her changing purchase patterns, before her parents even knew.[9] In such a carefully, creepily calculated consumer environment, our choices aren't really personal decisions at all. They are collaborations between us and a marketplace that often appears to know more about our inner lives than we do ourselves. How much longer before market and self actually merge—and our own desires for ever-more-efficient gratification synchronize perfectly with the corporate desire for capital efficiency—is hard to say. What matters is that with this synchronization of self and marketplace, we're becoming more accustomed to seeing ourselves at the center of our own private universes. With every upgrade and every product cycle, the act of self-expression feels more and more like second nature, or a lifestyle, a job, and we gauge the world around us less as citizens and more as gourmands. The quality of our lives, the health of our economy, the usefulness of our technology, the acceptability of our politics—increasingly these are assessed by their capacity to let us move from one moment of self-gratification and affirmation to the next.

This is the cultural end point of the Impulse Society: the self is at the center of everything, and everything is bent around the self. We see this in the flattering and obsequious consumer market, but it is the emerging reality for other sectors, too. Contemporary politics are becoming less about whether a policy or policymaker is effective or useful than about whether they affirm the voter's sense of self. (Would you have a beer with Ted Cruz? Is Hillary Clinton emasculating?) Our news is no longer a worldly survey of the issues that matter to us, collectively, as citizens, but a tailored feed created either by a person-alizing algorithm or by our random clicks on whatever headlines or images catch our eye—"the Daily Me," as technologist Nicholas Negroponte has dubbed it. Even art is less about transcendence, or argument, or important, universal questions, than about personal affirmation. As the sociologist Daniel Bell once observed, when a citizen of our self-centered culture encounters a painting, a poem, a book, his or her first question is "not whether it is good or meretri-cious, but 'What does it do for *me*?'" And Bell was writing before digital editing technologies had turned any piece of culture—a TV episode, a song, a film, a book—into just another aesthetic molecule to be pulled apart and reassembled in ever-more-elaborate mash-ups of self-expression. In the Impulse Society, all of culture becomes the stuff of the self, which grows larger with each act of cultural consump-tion and self-creation.

Given the ease with which we are allowed to concentrate on inner matters and to surround ourselves with the self-referential and the familiar, it's hardly surprising that we bristle at that which is not familiar or about us. Unfamiliarity and strangeness can be stressful. Disagreement is traumatic. For even the most civic-minded citizen, diversity takes effort, involves risk, and requires compromise—precisely the sort of inefficiencies our consumer culture and self-centered ideologies now demean. Yet these discomfiting inefficiencies are essential to the process of balancing personal interest and social interest. They are fundamental to democracy and to community, two institutions that are inefficient by definition. As Cass Sunstein (the University of Chicago legal scholar we met in chapter 3) argues,* a functioning democratic culture requires the messiness and awkward potentialities of "unplanned encounters" where citizens are "exposed to materials that they would not have chosen in advance [and to] topics and points of view that [they] have not sought out and perhaps find quite irritating."[10] But as we've seen, unplanned encounters, unexpected ideas, and irritating people are precisely the things we feel increasingly entitled to filter out of our customized lives and experiences.

This isn't to say that during the golden age of our democratic republic, we all embraced diversity; we didn't. Nonetheless, we found ways to cope with the differences we did have—by, for example, avoiding certain topics, such as politics and religion, in polite company—and in so doing preserved enough common ground to keep communities, and a society, intact and functional. Today, even these modest efforts at accommodation can feel like violations of our drive for self-expression. It's simply easier to interact with people like us, or consider ideas and viewpoints that fit in with the ones we already hold.

But this is a dangerous habit. Once we've stopped trying to tolerate difference and start putting distance, real or virtual, between us and those who differ from us, our separateness begins to harden. As

---

* In his book *Republic.com 2.0: Revenge of the Blogs*.

Sunstein and Bishop have documented, thanks to the power of group psychology, like-minded communities tend to become more extreme in their views and less tolerant of dissent. The reason: being in a like-minded group gives us more confidence in our own views. On most political and social issues, research suggests, the average person doesn't have a strong opinion. We generally haven't done the difficult work of parsing all the arguments and reaching a conclusion. As a result, we lack conviction in our own viewpoints. So we hedge our bets by adopting the average view of those around us—which, in a diverse, heterogeneous community, "inclines [us] toward the middle," Sunstein says. In other words, we naturally revert to the mean. But in a homogenous, like-minded, sorted community, an individual can quickly gain confidence simply by agreeing with everyone else: consensus lets you feel good about your views without having to do the work of deliberation. And, Sunstein notes, the more confident we become, the more intense our beliefs. "In many contexts, people's opinions become more extreme simply because their views have been corroborated, and because they become more confident after learning that others share their views."[11] This dynamic, adds Bishop, operates in virtually any homogenous group. Voters, students in a classroom, juries, federal judges—as diversity falls, all become more extreme in their views.[12] "The lesson for politics and culture is pretty clear," adds Bishop. "Mixed company moderates; like-minded company polarizes. Heterogeneous communities restrain group excesses; homogenous communities march toward the extremes."

This hardening of positions has huge implications for politics, a problem we'll return to in chapter 8. But paradoxically, the more fundamental danger may be to our capacity to sustain ourselves as individuals in a social world. Michael Lynch, a professor of philosophy at the University of Connecticut and an expert in theories of human knowledge, argues that in losing our willingness to tolerate diversity, we are losing the capacity for authentic self-knowledge. When we refuse to acknowledge those who differ from us, we reject not simply those particular people, but the very idea of the "other," of a reality that is beyond our own and that does not depend on us or refer to us. But we need "the other," Lynch says, not only to challenge our own ideas and opinions, refresh our thinking, and keep democracy vibrant, but also to *know* ourselves. It is only by acknowledging something truly larger than ourselves that we can really understand who we are and, importantly, who we *aren't*. In a consumer culture that increasingly reflects our preferences and desires, the line between us and the world begins to blur. "We need the other to determine . . . the bounds of our selves," Lynch says, "because, right now, the boundaries of our selves are expanding in bizarre ways. Our selves are getting bigger and bigger and extending out more and more, so that being interested in the world is becoming increasingly about being interested in your*self*, and there is something wrong with that. It's based on an illusion. Because the world *is* bigger than us, any of us, and the more that you think that you're in control of it, the less you're getting yourself out of the cave and the more you're being fooled by the shadows on the wall." Instead of being empowered by our steady self-expansion, we grow weaker. "We become massive and fragile," says Lynch. "You know, like a balloon filling up with hot air."[13] This is another paradox inherent in the Impulse Society. We are desperate for community, and yet, in our capacity to create communities that reflect our individual identities, are we eliminating what is most essential to actually *being* an individual?

The metaphor of the expanding fragile modern self is quite apt. To personalize is, in effect, to reject the world "as is," and instead to insist on bending it to our preferences, as if mastery and dominance were our only mode. But humans aren't meant only for mastery. We're also meant to adapt to something larger. Our large brains are specialized for cooperation and compromise and negotiation—with other individuals, but also with the broader world, which, for most of history, did not cater to our preferences or likes. For all our ancestors' tremendous skills at modifying and improving their environment, daily survival depended as much on their capacity to conform themselves and their expectations to the world as they found it. Indeed, it was only by enduring adversity and disappointment that we humans gained the strength and knowledge and perspective that are essential to sustainable mastery.

Virtually every traditional culture understood this and regarded adversity as inseparable from, and essential to, the formation of strong, self-sufficient individuals. Yet the modern conception of "character" now leaves little space for discomfort or real adversity. To the contrary, under the Impulse Society, consumer culture does everything in its considerable power to persuade us that adversity and difficulty and even awkwardness have no place in our lives (or belong only in discrete, self-enhancing moments, such as ropes courses or really hard ab workouts). Discomfort, difficulty, anxiety, suffering, depression, rejection, uncertainty, or ambiguity—in the Impulse Society, these aren't opportunities to mature and toughen or *become*. Rather, they represent errors and inefficiencies, and thus opportunities to correct—nearly always with more consumption and self-expression.

So rather than having to wait a few days for a package, we have it overnighted. Or we pay for same-day service. Or we pine for the moment when Amazon launches drone delivery and can get us our package in thirty minutes.* And as the system gets faster at gratifying our desires, the possibility that we might actually be *more* satisfied by waiting and enduring a delay never arises. Just as nature abhors a vacuum, the efficient consumer market abhors delay and adversity, and by extension, it cannot abide the strength of character that delay and adversity and inefficiency generally might produce. To the efficient market,

* But don't answer yet: Volvo's new "digital keys" technology will allow online shoppers to use their car as an address for pickups and deliveries.

"character" and "virtue" are themselves inefficiencies—impediments to the volume-based, share-price-maximizing economy. Once some new increment of self-expressive, self-gratifying, self-promoting capability is made available, the unstated but overriding assumption of contemporary consumer culture is that this capability can and should be put to use. Which means we now allow the efficient market and the treadmills and the relentless cycles of capital and innovation to determine how, and how far, we will take our self-expression and, by extension, our selves— even when doing so leaves us in a weaker state.

Consider the way our social relationships, and the larger processes of community, are changing under the relentless pressure of our new efficiencies. We know how important community is for individual development. It's in the context of community that we absorb the social rules and prerequisites for interaction and success. It's here that we come to understand and, ideally, to internalize, the need for limits and self-control, for patience and persistence and long-term commitments; the pressure of community is one way society persuades us to control our myopia and selfishness. (Or as economists Sam Bowles and Herbert Gintis have put it, community is the vehicle through which "society's 'oughts' become its members' 'wants.' ") But community's function isn't simply to say "no." It's in the context of our social relationships where we discover our capacities and strengths. It's here that we gain our sense of worth as individuals, as citizens and as social *producers*—active participants who don't merely consume social goods, but contribute something the community needs.

But community doesn't simply teach us to be productive citizens. People with strong social connections generally have a much better time. We enjoy better physical and mental health, recover faster from sickness or injury, and are less likely to suffer eating or sleeping disorders.[14] We report being happier and rank our quality of life as higher—and do so even when the community that we're connected to isn't particularly well off or educated.[15] Indeed, social connectedness is actually more important than affluence: regular social activities such as volunteering, church attendance, entertaining friends, or joining a club provide us with the same boost to happiness as does a doubling of personal income.[16] As Harvard's Robert Putnam notes, "The single most common finding from a half century's research on the correlates of life satisfaction, not only in the United States but around the world, is that happiness is best predicted by the breadth and depth of one's social connections."[17]

Unfortunately, for all the importance of social connectedness, we haven't done a terribly good job of preserving it under the Impulse Society. Under the steady pressure of commercial and technological efficiencies, many of the tight social structures of the past have been eliminated or replaced with entirely new social arrangements. True, many of these new arrangements are clearly superior—even in ostensibly free societies, traditional communities left little room for individual growth or experimentation or happiness. Yet our new arrangements, which invariably seek to give individuals substantially more control over how they connect, exact a price. More and more, social connection becomes just another form of consumption, one we expect to tailor to our personal preferences and schedules—almost as if community was no longer a necessity or an obligation, but a matter of personal style, something to engage as it suits our mood or preference. And while such freedom has its obvious attractions, it clearly has downsides. In gaining so much control over the process of social connection, we may be depriving ourselves of some of the robust give-and-take of traditional interaction that is essential to becoming a functional, fulfilled individual.

Consider our vaunted and increasing capacity to communicate and connect digitally. In theory, our smartphones and social media allow us the opportunity to be *more* social than at any time in history. And yet, because there are few natural limits to this format—we can, in effect, communicate incessantly, posting every conceivable life event, expressing every thought no matter how incompletely formed or inappropriate or mundane—we may be diluting the value of the connection.

Studies suggest, for example, that the efficiency with which we can respond to an online provocation routinely leads to escalations that can destroy offline relationships. "People seem aware that these kinds of crucial conversations should not take place on social media," notes Joseph Grenny, whose firm, VitalSmarts, surveys online behavior. "Yet there seems to be a compulsion to resolve emotions right now and via the convenience of these channels."[18]

Even when our online communications are entirely friendly, the ease with which we can reach out often undermines the very connection we seek to create. Sherry Turkle, a sociologist and clinical psychologist who has spent decades researching digital interactions, argues that because it is now possible to be in virtually constant contact with others, we tend to communicate so excessively that even a momentary lapse can leave us feeling isolated or abandoned. Where people in the pre-digital age did not think it alarming to go hours or days or even weeks without hearing from someone, the digital mind can become uncomfortable and anxious without instant feedback. In her book *Alone Together*, Turkle describes a social world of collapsing time horizons. College students text their parents daily, and even hourly, over the smallest matters—and feel anxious if they can't get a quick response. Lovers break up over the failure to reply instantly to a text; friendships sour when posts aren't "liked" fast enough. Parents call 911 if Junior doesn't respond immediately to a text or a phone call—a degree of panic that was simply unknown before constant digital contact. Here, too, is a world made increasingly insecure by its own capabilities and its own accelerating efficiencies.

This same efficiency-driven insecurity now lurks just below the surface in nearly all digital interactions. Whatever the relationship (romantic, familial, professional), the very nature of our technology inclines us to a constant state of emotional suspense. Thanks to the casual, abbreviated nature of digital communication, we converse in fragments of thoughts and feelings that can be completed only through more interaction—we are always waiting to know how the story ends. The result, Turkle says, is a communication style, and a relationship style, that allow us to "express emotions while they are being formed" and in which "feelings are not fully experienced until they are communicated." In other words, what was once primarily an *interior* process—thoughts were formed and feelings experienced *before* we expressed them—has now become a process that is external and iterative and public. Identity itself comes to depend on iterative interaction—giving rise to what Turkle calls the "collaborative self." Meanwhile, our skills as a private, self-contained person vanish. "What is not being cultivated here," Turkle writes, "is the ability to be alone and reflect on one's emotions in private." For all the emphasis on independence and individual freedom under the Impulse Society, we may be losing the capacity to truly be on our own.

In a culture obsessed with individual self-interest, such an incapacity is surely one of the greatest ironies of the Impulse Society. Yet in many ways it was inevitable. Herded along by a consumer culture that is both solicitous and manipulative, one that proposes absolute individual liberty while enforcing absolute material dependence—we rely completely on the machine of the marketplace—it is all too easy to emerge with a self-image, and a sense of self, that are both wildly inflated and fundamentally weak and insecure. Unable to fully experience the satisfactions of genuine independence and individuality, we compensate with more personalized self-expression and gratification, which only push us further from the real relationships that might have helped us to a stable, fulfilling existence.

It was this empty individualism that Christopher Lasch diagnosed in the 1970s as a kind of culturally induced narcissism. As industrialization turned us from producers to consumers, we lost many of the skills and the sense of competence and self-reliance that had fostered an identity that was confident, secure, and "innerdirected." Lacking that self-assured inner life, we turned increasingly to external substitutes. We became steadily hungrier for the approval of peers. We sought the opinions of experts, reveled in stories about celebrities and success generally. We pursued the quick pleasures of status and novelty. And, inevitably, our consumer culture, ever alert to opportunity and deficiency, responded by giving us ways to temporarily fulfill those appetites—and did so with such proficiency that we became addicted to this external sustenance. Our inner life and our outer life merged, and the result, Lasch declared, was a "culture of narcissism."

Lasch's diagnosis was social and cultural, not clinical. But by the 1980s and 1990s, psychologists and counselors were seeing an increase in the numbers of people—patients, but more important, members of the general population—with symptoms of clinical narcissism. The inflated self-importance, the tendency toward aggressive self-promotion, the paradoxical dependence on external sources of affirmation, the deep sense of entitlement that easily turns to anger— it was all becoming more common. Although the percentage of people with full-blown narcissistic personality disorder was fairly small, the number of people who exhibited one or more of the identifying traits was growing much more rapidly than with other disorders, such as obsessive-compulsive disorder. Today, according to social psychologists Jean Twenge and Keith Campbell, authors of *The Narcissism Epidemic*, symptoms of narcissism in the general population are growing as rapidly as other public health problems, such as obesity.

Why is narcissism on the rise? Standard explanations have focused on cultural and family factors, notably the heavy emphasis, beginning in the 1960s, on building self-esteem in children. By the 1990s many of us had spent decades being told we were special and different, and as a result, some of us emerged from childhood with an unrealistic, even fantasy-like sense of our place in the world. But there is likely an economic element at play here. Narcissism is fundamentally about a refusal to accept limits, and until fairly recently, the only people who could steadily make such a refusal were the wealthy elite. For most of the rest of us, life quickly imposed a more realistic self-conception—Freud's reality principle in action. But as Twenge and Campbell argue, over the last century, and in the last four decades in particular, soaring levels of personal power (technical, financial, and social) have allowed a narcissistic avoidance of reality to take root among a much broader population. Of particular interest to Twenge and Campbell is the rise of easy credit, which enabled the narcissistic personality to simultaneously avoid the reality of financial limits while using overconsumption to affirm his or her massively inflated sense of self-worth. By the 1980s and 1990s, Twenge and Campbell suggest, the financial revolution and narcissism were feeding off each other. "The availability of easy credit—in other words, the willingness and ability of some people to go into tremendous debt—has allowed people to present an inflated picture of their own success to themselves and to the world."

Credit isn't so easy anymore, of course. But with the meteoric rise of personal technologies, the narcissistic personality has an even cheaper and vastly more efficient way to present an inflated self-image to the world (and to itself). The "self-tracking" movement—the monitoring, analyzing, and even posting of everything from calorie intake to mood to home office productivity—provides us with an "objective" reflection of ourselves that is, almost by definition, encouraging the tendency toward self-focus. (Technology skeptic Evgeny Morozov calls self-trackers "data-sexuals.") And of course the growing practice of photographing and displaying everything we do only fuels the narcissistic love of celebrity. Forty years ago, Lasch observed that modern life was so "thoroughly mediated by electronic images that we cannot help responding to others as if their actions—and our own—were being recorded and simultaneously transmitted to an unseen audience or stored up for close scrutiny at some later time."[19] Today, that vaguely paranoid sentiment is standard operating procedure. "We film everything," says Campbell, who now runs the psychology department at the University of Georgia. "People will film themselves at the concert and that becomes the experience itself. Rather than 'being there,' it's 'showing people that you were there.' It's like, 'God, I've got to get a picture of this so I can post it and get all this feedback.'"

Indeed, to be seen by others is increasingly regarded as a requirement for personal and social advance. We are successful to the degree that our self-expression is consumed by others—whether via our do-it-yourself promotions on YouTube or Facebook or, better still, in the commercial realm of reality TV, whose entire premise is average people doing un-average things. We are, once again, producers—but the new output is extremity, outrageousness, egoism, and anything else that might look good on-screen. Reality TV (and the "on-camera" culture it arises from and feeds into) is the logical conclusion of our march for personalization, and a real-time chronicle of the Impulse Society. Everything is here: the narcissistic impulse of participants and would-be participants; the viewers' desire for a quick, smug thrill; and especially the relentless drive of technological and financial efficiency. Networks love reality TV programs because they are dirt-cheap: participants rarely get paid (they expect to turn their momentary fame into a career), and video technology makes it possible to quickly edit hundreds of hours of tape into drama-filled episodes. Once again, the efficiency of the business model drives the market further into the self and pushes the self more fully into the market.

More fundamentally, this wildly popular format essentially

legitimizes the conceit at the heart of the Impulse Society: that the self is the measure of all things, and that *any*thing that enlarges the self and draws more attention to the self (no matter how impulsive or antisocial or just plain stupid) is the mark of personal success. "The idea is that you can be a star if you're willing to be notorious or dysfunctional enough to get noticed," says Campbell, who is putting together a study on reality TV. "It's not fame based on ability or even birth—it's fame the easy way. I mean, Kim Kardashian is probably the most famous person in the world, and it's brilliant, sort of like Paris Hilton squared. But for *what*?"[20]

Reality TV also offers a glimpse of a central failing of the Impulse Society: the steady loss in the understanding of what it takes to create a resilient, independent self. Historically, Americans saw the self as the ultimate DIY project: from the republic's earliest days, we were "self-made" individuals, free to fashion our identities out of any and all cultural materials, from the deeply religious to the entirely commercial, and toward whatever end was individually most appealing. What's more, this project of self-creation necessitated a degree of stepping back from society: for nineteenth-century American writers such as Emerson, Thoreau, Melville, and Whitman, self-realization required individuals to break from "large societies and dead institutions," as Emerson put it, and to follow their own distinctly individual compass. Indeed, we were even encouraged to withhold our support from the political system when, as Thoreau argued in "Civil Disobedience," that system violated our individual principles and beliefs.

But this traditional view of American identity never confused self-absorption with self-realization; nor did it imagine the creation of the self as somehow authorizing us to disengage from society altogether. Indeed, for most nineteenth-century American intellectuals, sociality was an essential aspect of the American character. Melville and Whitman were intensely committed to the notion of a reciprocal, mutually empowering relationship between the individual and society. Even Thoreau's boycott of the American political system reflected the desire to change a system he was deeply devoted to. We Americans might have declared our independence from the Old World hierarchies that locked citizens in place and defined who they were. But in truth, with our immigrant heritage, we never truly rejected the Old World's explicitly social conceptions of character and identity. So, for example, you could find in our cultural DNA the European notion of the bildungs-roman, or "coming-of-age" story, where the act of self-creation is an overtly social process: the individual rejects society and strikes off alone, largely to become strong enough and wise enough to be able to rejoin society as a productive member. The goal of the individual is social. There was no such thing as self-realization simply for the sake of the self.[21] The entire point of self-creation was, as Hegel put it, to discover the "universal," the common ground between the individual and broader society. In such a venture, writes Yale University's Allen Wood, individual success came not through "cultivating or indulging arbitrari-ness, personal peculiarity and idiosyncrasy, but in developing a charac-ter which values itself for what it has in common with other people."[22]

Today, by contrast, it is precisely arbitrariness, personal peculiar-ity, and idiosyncrasy that we cultivate, in part because these "quali-ties" are seen as the only way to get ahead. There are depressingly few contemporary examples of celebrated, socially productive men and women working *quietly* toward the greater good. The very concept of work itself has been degraded. Not so long ago, we told our children that personal success required sustained effort, a willingness to delay gratification, and the capacity to control impulses. But today our chil-dren look around, and that's not what they see. They see their parents and grandparents working hard and being patient and keeping their passions in check and still being tossed aside like an old couch—while investment bankers and reality TV stars appear to make huge, easy dollars. Little wonder cheating is now endemic in high school and college. Or that college and high school kids now routinely film themselves in extraordinarily compromising situations in the hopes of converting millions of "views" into megabucks. "When you speak to kids, the number one thing they want to be is famous," Brian Robbins, whose company, Awesomeness TV, creates YouTube channels for teens and tweens, told *The New Yorker*. "They don't even know for what."[23] This really is an anything-goes, something-for-nothing culture. Ask a twenty-year-old how to get rich, says Campbell, and you'll probably get three answers: "'I can either be famous on reality TV, or I can go start a dot-com company and sell it to Google in about a week, or I can go work for Goldman Sachs and just steal money from old people,'" Campbell told me. "I mean, those are the three models of wealth. There just isn't a good model of hard work getting you somewhere anymore."

In a sense, the narcissistic personality could be seen as a logical response to the Impulse Society and to a world that no longer rewards long-term commitment or concern for someone other than ourselves. As Campbell notes, narcissistic business executives are ideally suited to a corporate world that prizes fast results. "With a lot of these CEOs, you end up with these high-risk, sometimes high-reward outcomes," Campbell says. Unfortunately, these kinds of high-risk personalities are also associated with "poor ethics—they kind of go together." Campbell says narcissists also have an advantage in situations of social churn, moving from job to job or to a new community, where it helps to be able to quickly ingratiate oneself into a new group or relationship. The narcissist's inflated sense of self-importance, Campbell says, projects a "confidence that helps you in interviews. It can help in some aspects of sales. It's like dating. Narcissism is great for starting relationships; it's lousy for keeping them." And of course the narcissistic personality is ideal for a consumer economy that thrives on perpetual insecurity, dissatisfaction, and possessiveness. As Campbell puts it, "If you want to build the perfect consumer society, what do you want? You want people who are anxious and arrogant and enti-tled. You want the bifurcation of the personality into anxiety and arro-gance. And that's what you end up with. Nobody ever made money from humility."

CHAPTER 6

Hard Labor

In late 2011, as Occupy Wall Street jumped from the United States to England, a young British attorney, newly admitted to the bar and identified only by a Twitter pseudonym, OccupyTheInns, launched what may have been the least likely political action in history: a protest over the lack of jobs for . . . new lawyers. "Through no fault of our own, a generation of [law school] graduates find ourselves with no jobs—or no jobs as lawyers anyway," the protestor wrote on a blog. "The lucky ones are paralegals. The unlucky ones work in bars (not the bar)."[1] The protest went nowhere, naturally—lawyers are about as popular in England as they are anywhere else. But the underlying complaint is still worth considering. In the postindustrial world, the market for attorneys is becoming glutted. In the United States, the ratio of graduates to job openings is currently running at about two to one,[2] and this despite the recovering economy. In the United Kingdom, the market is even tighter: in 2011 the number of applicants for "trainee" openings at London law firms exceeded actual openings sixty-five to one.[3] Nor is there much reason to expect the picture to improve substantially. Not only are law firms on a massive cost-cutting kick—many British and American firms offshore their "low-value" work, such as claims processing, to

Sri Lanka and the Philippines—but even the most tradition-bound firms are confronting a trend that, until recently, few attorneys thought much about: automation. With "semantically sensitive" search algorithms, labor-intensive tasks such as reading the thousands of documents in a complex case no longer mean weeks of work by small armies of well-paid attorneys, but can be done in days or even hours by machines.[4]

And that, say industry wags, is only a hint of what will happen as artificial intelligence and Big Data make possible something called quantitative legal prediction, or QLP, a process that does for lawyering what statistical analysis did for baseball in *Moneyball*.[5] The idea behind QLP is simple: Much of what we pay lawyers to do is to forecast the future. Given a certain set of facts, what is the likely outcome of a lawsuit? What are the chances a contract will be breached? How is a particular judge likely to rule? Attorneys normally base their predictions on past experience—cases they have tried, deals they've negotiated, lawsuits they've defended—a resource that, even for veteran attorneys, is necessarily limited. For any given case, "even a seasoned partner will only have tens of data points that are really relevant," says Mark Smith, an attorney and process-automation expert at the London office of LexisNexis. But with QLP, Smith says, "suddenly, you're able to analyze every contract your company has ever done." What's more, your analyses won't be tainted by the neurological biases that plague human decision making. Even now, experts say, computers can predict court decisions with 75 percent accuracy, compared with 59 percent for humans.[6] And as the new laborsaving technologies are rolled out, law firms will have little choice but to use them—the treadmill spares no profession. All told, the legal profession, once the go-to career for smart, ambitious men and women, is about to change radically—although, clearly the message has yet to fully be absorbed by law schools. "I lecture at universities to law students," Smith told me, "and few of them understand what's actually happening." He adds: "I wouldn't advise my kids to go into the law."

This sort of advice is likely to be heard more frequently in coming years. Out-of-work lawyers may not seem like a national tragedy. But even avowed lawyer haters shouldn't need a predictive algorithm to see how the innovations upending the legal profession will someday do the same thing to lots of other jobs, as companies large and small reach automatically for whatever cost-cutting capabilities roll off the treadmill—and as those capabilities become more and more impressive. Already, computers can drive cars and pilot jumbo jets from takeoff to landing. They can analyze X-rays, grade college essays, write sports briefs, and sift through news stories and tweets for market-moving data, then exploit it with perfectly timed stock trades. They can run "lights out" factories—that is, factories that don't need lights because no humans work in them. And these are only previews for the automation blockbusters said to be just around the corner, as the exponential rise in computing power, sensor technologies, and Big Data pushes the economy, and the job market, into entirely new territory.

This isn't supposed to worry us, though. As members of an educated, technologically savvy, postmaterialist society, we're supposed to understand that even truly disruptive innovations and the enormous new efficiencies they bring make us better off. And historically, that's been absolutely the case. Innovation has been very good for us and very good for the job market. By allowing us to increase our output and reduce our costs, each new increment of efficiency-enhancing innovation—our laborsaving machines, our higher-volume factories, our more meticulous management strategies—though they might bring temporary "dislocations," eventually meant more jobs and better jobs, with higher wages and safer conditions. Innovation, efficiency, and jobs—since the industrial revolution, these three have risen almost in lockstep.

Lately, however, as the financialized, quick-returns model has come to dominate the economy, it has been much harder to be so confident about where all this innovation and efficiency are taking us. In what is rapidly emerging as the economic signature of the Impulse Society, even as our companies become steadily more efficient at converting capital into more capital, the returns for most employees have flattened out. You've heard these statistics dozens of times, but stop to consider the implications. Despite a more or less full recovery in economic growth, in corporate profits, and in stock price appreciation, especially technology stocks, the hyperefficient economies of the big postindustrial societies are barely producing enough new jobs to replace the ones lost in the recession. In the United States, to use the most extreme example, new job growth has been so slow that economists don't expect to return to pre-crash employment levels until 2020, or roughly twelve years after the Great Recession.[7] What's more, the new mix of jobs is nowhere near as inviting as it was even a decade ago. Across the postindustrial world, most of the jobs that have come back are either high-end positions requiring a lot of specialized knowledge or, more often, low-skill, low-wage service jobs—the baristas and barkeeps. Notably absent are middle-skill, middle-wage jobs that were once the backbone of middle-class society. That's one reason why, in the United States, median household income is 7 percent *less* today than it was fifteen years ago,[8] and why the term *middle class* rarely appears in print these days without the modifiers *declining* or *hollowed-out*.

Why are we losing the middle? Although there are many social and political factors at play here, a lot of what is happening can be traced to changes in our approach to innovation under the Impulse Society. It is no surprise that the middle of the job market began to soften as computing technologies let companies cut costs through aggressive consolidation and downsizing. But the deeper story here is the rupture in the historic linkage between innovation and the broadly based prosperity that characterized the postwar economy. Simply put, although innovation continues to benefit all levels of society, more of the rewards now flow to a narrower population—while, in many cases, excluding whole sectors and social strata. We've seen this pattern as a small number of very large "winner-take-all" firms[9] such as Walmart and Amazon "leverage" data technologies and efficiencies of scale to crush local vendors in any market they enter. We saw it during the financial crisis, when a small group of bankers used the efficiencies of financial engineering to extract huge "rents" from an inflating housing market—while pushing the risk of those efficiencies onto taxpayers. And now, of course, we're seeing the same pattern in the job markets, as companies use the rapidly rising efficiencies of automation and other cost-cutting, output-enhancing innovation to shift a greater share of corporate profits from labor to management.

More and more, the *point* of innovation in the Impulse Society seems to be to create extraordinary new efficiencies that enable an enterprising elite to carve off ever-larger pieces of the pie—a share that is increasingly difficult to justify as benefiting the larger society. Efficiency itself now seems corrupt: the drive for ever-greater output at an ever-lower cost, once the engine of rising living standards and universal progress, now seems to work mainly for those who own the machines, factories, and other capital assets—as if we've somehow deleted much of the social progress achieved over the last century and slipped back to the Gilded Age. Such a development should be troubling to more than the members of Occupy Wall Street. Indeed, it should prompt even those in high places—attorneys, say, or stock traders, and certainly politicians—to ask not only where our efficient innovations are taking us, but what, and who, that innovation is really for.

We should pause here to remind ourselves that the whole innovation-prosperity process was never exactly smooth. Certainly few of the tens of millions of European and American farmers who were "de-labored" by mechanization a century ago regarded the experience as progress. What farmers couldn't see, however, was that this same disruptive force was rapidly making new jobs. The very innovations that were shrinking the farming sector were also creating entirely new sectors, such as railroads, manufacturing, road building, and utilities. These new sectors offered not only higher wages, but also entirely new kinds of employment. Making a car, for example, required steel workers and tire makers—plus a lot of engineers and designers and marketing experts and Freudian analysts—and the wages from these new jobs led to even more economic activity. This "gale of creative destruction," as economist Joseph Schumpeter called it, was the defining force of industrial capitalism, "incessantly destroying the old [economic order], incessantly creating a new one." And generally speaking, the new order was a definite improvement. In most industrial societies, this surge in new prosperity was broadly enjoyed. We got higher wages, lower prices, and a steady stream of innovations, such as jet engines and X-ray photography and color TV, which lifted everyone's living standards while creating still more avenues for growth and employment. When economists, historians, and your grandparents wax rhapsodic about the postwar economy, they are not being sentimental; it was a prosperity machine.

So what happened to the machine? Why has the age-old pattern of creative destruction become one that often seems mainly about destruction? Again, there are many parts to this story—cultural, political, and ideological. But an important one is that our innovation has, somewhat paradoxically, become less disruptive—at least, in the way Schumpeter meant. The industrial revolution of Ford's era was hugely disruptive because it involved multiple breakthroughs—automobiles and assembly lines, but also logistics, business administration, accounting, petrochemicals, pharmaceuticals, and communication, among others—all feeding off one another and creating an economic whole that was much larger than the sum of its parts. By contrast, our more recent disruptions have been less epochal. Computers have brought all sorts of transformative enhancements in personal power, but as an industrial catalyst, the computer's biggest impacts have often come by making existing industrial processes more efficient—that is, by making assembly lines faster, or allowing stores to carry more items, or empowering consumers to shop or communicate more easily. Important stuff, to be sure, but not quite enough to spark a third industrial revolution.

Some of this can be laid to historical timing: world-changing breakthroughs are a lot harder to come by these days in part because the easy ones have already been made. In times past, we were able to get massive increases in productivity by eliminating large and obvious inefficiencies—moving from animal-powered farming to mechanization, for instance, or switching from manure to synthetic fertilizers. But as George Mason University economist Tyler Cowen has argued, most of that "low-hanging fruit" has all been picked and eaten, and today it's simply much harder, and more costly, to achieve similarly epoch-defining breakthroughs.

But it's not just that innovation has gotten harder. One can also make the case that, under the financialized business models that emerged with the Impulse Society, the way we pursue innovation has gotten weaker. As we've already seen, the manic drive to cut costs and protect quarterly earnings led to steady reductions in research and development, and these cuts have added up. A half century ago, the amount of money that American industry invested in R&D was growing by 7 percent a year, according to the U.S. Bureau of Economic Analysis. Today, annual growth is just 1.1 percent.[10] What's more, when companies do spend on R&D, it's increasingly aimed at quick returns, and not long-term advances. American manufacturers were once famous for investing heavily in basic and applied research—that is, in making discoveries and then figuring out how to turn those discoveries into new technologies. Today, more of our R&D dollars go toward the *D*, development—that is, in turning already existing technologies into a steady stream of new products and applications that might be quite useful, but don't really break new ground.

This tilt toward "incremental innovation" is most familiar to us in the consumer-product space, where firms such as Microsoft have made a fortune converting older technologies into a steady stream of modest upgrades timed to deliver steady quarterly earnings and share price appreciation. But incremental innovation is even more evident at the structural level of the economy. As we saw in chapter 2, much of our innovation now focuses on making basic businesses processes, such as manufacturing and logistics, more efficient. So we automate assembly lines. We streamline the process for making a bank loan. We digitize the supply chain linking a retailer in the United States with a manufacturer in Asia. These innovative efficiencies have helped bring down prices for consumers. But in many cases, they have also affected the jobs those consumers once had. For instance, Walmart's pioneering use of inventory data (the company even launched its own fleet of communications satellites) eventually gave the retailer such a large market share and bargaining power over its suppliers that many suppliers had to accelerate their own cost cutting, which often meant automation and offshoring. That same pattern, in which process innovation drives cost cutting along the entire supply chain, played out across the economies of the industrialized world and was a major factor in the surge of manufacturing job losses that began in the 1990s. In Europe, Japan, and the United States, manufacturing sectors that had slowly been shrinking were now pushed into free fall. Between 1998 and 2004, Britain lost a quarter of its manufacturing jobs; Japan, a fifth. In the United States, another six million manufacturing jobs, or a third of the total, went away between 2000 and 2007.[11]

Granted, we should not sentimentalize manufacturing jobs, which are often monotonous, dangerous, and unpleasant; many a factory worker would likely be glad to upgrade to something better. Nor, obviously, is there anything inherently wrong with automation or even offshoring. They are simply instruments of Schumpeter's creative destruction: In "destroying" these older jobs in industrialized economies, automation and offshoring are, ideally, "creating" room for the next generation of jobs that will allow those displaced workers to step up the ladder to more productivity, better wages, and higher aspirations. Except that, under the Impulse Society, this is not what has happened. Displaced workers by and large have not stepped up to the next rung on the job ladder—or not in the numbers necessary to maintain the pattern of rising postwar prosperity. Instead, many workers have remained on the same rung or, often, have slipped down.

Here, too, there are multiple factors at play. By many accounts, Western workers aren't gaining new skills as rapidly as they need to or used to, in part because our education systems haven't kept up with a job market that, thanks to the computerization of the workplace, demands more and more skills. As Harvard economists Claudia Goldin and Lawrence Katz have argued, this gap means that each year, a steadily smaller fraction of the population can take advantage of, or even keep up with, so-called skill-biased technical change. Yet while revamping education is clearly a necessity (one we'll return to shortly), of equal importance is that companies themselves, under the financialized imperatives of the shareholder revolution, have dramatically reduced efforts to help their own workers lift their game. Where firms like AT&T and IBM and General Motors all once operated extensive employee training programs, such efforts have receded dramatically as all firms have slashed personnel costs to the bone. Many in-house training centers have been shuttered. Human resources departments have been outsourced, leaving employees and their supervisors to manage training and career development largely on their own. Indeed, employees are not only expected to manage their own careers; they are also expected to constantly "reinvent" themselves in order to maximize their appeal to a management that no longer feels obligated to help in the reinvention. As Cort Martin, a veteran IBM employee, told *The Washington Times* after leaving the company, "You've got constant churn. You'd have to sell yourself, have another skill set" to avoid being laid off. "You didn't want to be the guy who doesn't have a chair when the music stops."[12]

What's more, thanks to the success of our cost-focused, process-oriented innovation, there's often no place for "reinvented" employees to climb up to, since many of the higher-level jobs they might have aspired to have also been eliminated. Thanks to the arrival of high-speed data networks in the 1990s, companies were able to offshore not only manufacturing jobs, but "knowledge" jobs. From bookkeeping and customer support to engineering, financial analysis, and architecture[13]—all could be done for about a tenth the labor cost in India, Sri Lanka, the Philippines, Russia, Poland, and China.[14] Even in fields such as software development, chip design, or aeronautical engineering, where Western firms once held an unassailable advantage (and, thus, where job security seemed assured), jobs have flown offshore. Such "innovations" have allowed firms to quickly generate cost reductions—and therefore improvements in earnings and share price—that might have taken decades with more conventional methods, and CEOs embraced it as fervently as their predecessors had embraced the assembly line, the telephone, and other, more traditional innovations.

Here is the real crisis in innovation under the Impulse Society. Where innovation was once a tool to improve the productivity of the entire economy—companies and workers, capital and labor—it's more exclusive today. Increasingly, innovation improves the productivity of capital, via faster returns, while leaving labor's productivity largely unchanged, or even slowed. For instance, where early moves toward factory automation were generally associated with increased worker productivity—that is, each factory worker could now produce more output per hour and thus merit a higher wage—the "innovation" of offshoring has often yielded lower worker productivity. Chinese factory workers in the 1990s were substantially less productive than their U.S. counterparts,[15] which companies compensated for by piling on more workers. Offshoring "knowledge" jobs also turned out to have lots of hidden inefficiencies. "The promise of offshore, and the way it was sold to American executives, was that you would just take the IT jobs and throw them over the wall, where you're paying these great engineers in China and India five dollars an hour as opposed to fifty dollars an hour, so, wow, it's great," a former executive who managed offshore IT teams in Asia told me recently.[16] "But it was never about just throwing something over the wall. With engineering, there's always an intense interaction between the people creating the product and the business owners it is being created for. And that works most easily when everyone is in the same building and they can meet every day and have informal conversations in the hallway. It doesn't work nearly as well—or, sometimes, at all—when you're in a time zone twelve hours away." In a sense, we were fracturing the work community to improve costs—and suffering a poorer product. Yet because overall costs were lower, offshoring's efficiencies were deemed a huge win—at least by executives and investors.

But was there an alternative? Among business leaders, the conventional wisdom is globalization has simply changed the rules of business: there just isn't much a company can do when foreign labor costs a tenth as much. But this is by no means the whole story. If we compare the American response to globalization with that of Europe, it's clear there are other ways to manage the impacts of innovation and globalization on workers. Thanks in part to stronger unions, stricter labor regulation, and a different corporate culture, most European companies continue to invest heavily in worker training—and retraining: in many European Union countries, employees whose jobs have been permanently offshored are trained for a new job.[17] "It's not that the Germans don't offshore or that the Swedes don't offshore," says William Lazonick, the economist. "But [thanks to] the governance structures of their companies, there's reinvestment back in the countries where they're based—and so you have much better outcome."[18]

Granted, these outcomes represent larger investments: it costs more to protect your employees from the disruptions that result from innovations such as automation or offshoring. And in the Impulse Society, such costs are simply not acceptable. To the contrary, the objective of corporate strategy is to accept only the rewards of globalization, while carefully pushing all globalization's costs, or the costs of any other innovation, firmly onto labor. This was not always the American policy. When the U.S. economy contracted during the 1973 recession, cuts in wages accounted for just a third of the lost wealth; the rest of the losses from the recession were absorbed internally by companies, through reductions in output and by cutting returns to investors. In other words, companies made a deliberate effort to spare their workforces from some of the pain of the downturn by spreading that pain across other parts of the business and to other stakeholders. But as the shareholder revolution took hold, and as new technologies gave managers the ability to more precisely target cost cutting, and as unions gradually lost government backing, that earlier policy shifted as well. By the 1981 recession, according to a recent study by the consultancy Deloitte, cuts to labor accounted for half the overall reduction in economic output; and by the recession of 1990, labor absorbed three-quarters of total cutbacks. With each downturn, investors were getting much more of the gains from the cost savings while workers were absorbing most of the pain. The trend has only sharpened. In the last two recessions, in 2001 and 2007, labor absorbed 98 percent of total cutbacks. As the Deloitte study notes, "Where once companies were shielding workers and absorbing losses themselves, in this globally competitive economy, companies are seeking to preserve profits at the expense of employment."[19]

The significance of this shift is hard to overstate. Offshoring's massive cost savings[20] helps explain why corporate profits and share prices recovered so quickly after the past two recessions. But two decades of offshoring also help explain the "jobless" recoveries that followed those recessions. Here was the fundamental absurdity of the model of innovation that emerged with the Impulse Society—a model that, in effect, acknowledges no contradiction in innovations that increase profits while reducing wages. A century earlier, Henry Ford had argued that high wages were critical for a vibrant consumer economy in large part because they meant workers could actually afford the very products they were producing.[21] "The people who consume the bulk of goods are the people who make them," Ford declared. "That is a fact we must never forget—that is the secret of our prosperity."[22] By the end of the twentieth century, that idea had been tossed aside. Companies were happy to have customers with fat wallets (as long as someone else was paying them). But just as consumers had been enabled by innovation to pursue their interests independently from the larger society, companies, too, had discovered how to use innovation to separate their own fortunes from those of their workers. Whatever sense of common purpose or social duty corporate America had espoused in the postwar period was now largely gone. From here on out, the corporation would use its massive efficiencies and innovative power solely for its own narrow self-interest.

As the economist Herb Stein once argued, "If something cannot go on forever, it will stop," and although Stein was talking about the U.S. trade deficit, one could just as well apply that statement to today's approach to innovation. Sooner or later, markets correct themselves. Companies that spend too little on real innovation, for example, will run out of things to sell. Companies that demoralize their workforces will see performance lag. Companies that rely too heavily on the cheapness of foreign labor eventually get pushback over quality problems. And, in fact, in the aftermath of the Great Recession, some in the business world seemed unhappy with its chosen path. The offshoring miracle was losing some of its glow. There were continuing problems with quality and communication. Many foreign workers were demanding substantially higher wages. Slowly, some Western firms began bringing back some offshored jobs—a shift that was quickly dubbed reshoring, and has since spurred a lot of talk of an American manufacturing renaissance.

At the same time, the widening gap between job requirements and workers' skills was becoming so large and unsustainable that the education sector was under heavy pressure to reinvent itself. Of particular note have been efforts to upgrade education with the efficiencies to digital technology. In recent years, universities such as Harvard and MIT have rolled out ambitious new education programs centered on MOOCs, or "massive open online courses." Combining video lectures, online interaction, and automation, these programs will, in theory, allow name-brand universities to mass-produce a high-level educational experience and thus make it much more affordable and accessible. And the MOOC model, which has since spread internationally, is merely the opening move in what advocates promise will be an education revolution. With Big Data, the entire university experience—from admissions and course selection to studying and job placement—can be quantified and radically improved. Professors, students, counselors, and parents will now have hard data showing exactly what kinds of teaching or materials or housing or extracurricular activities produce the fastest learning. As Gary King, director of Harvard's Institute for Quantitative Social Science, told *The New Yorker's* Nathan Heller in 2013, "We could instrument every student, every classroom, every administrative office, every house, every recreational activity, every security officer, everything. We could basically get the information about everything that goes on here, and we could use it for the students."[23]

You can feel the excitement building around these initiatives. If such an education revolution takes hold, advocates say, the impact on employment and prosperity could be as great as anything that occurred in the past two centuries—not least because this revolution could help spur a return to a more progressive, future-oriented approach to innovation. Maybe all the low-hanging fruit of innovation has already been picked. But if an upgraded education system were producing more graduates skilled in today's technologies, and if companies and governments were willing to increase their investment in strategic sectors, such sectors as energy or biotechnology, we could very well see the sort of breakthroughs that spur entirely new industries—and job categories.

Developing a genuinely new energy technology—one that is carbon-free, economically viable, and decentralized—could be just such a game-changer. Likewise, biotech, after decades of failing to deliver on its promises, is also said to be poised for the sorts of breakthroughs that could create entirely new economic sectors. Michael Mandel, an economist with the Progressive Policy Institute, points to recent advances in biotechnology that could soon allow us to commercially "grow" replacement organs. Already, you can buy factory-made skin, and simple organs such as tracheas are now grown in laboratories and used in transplant operations. Mandel argues that once the process has extended to more complex organs, an entirely new and very large industrial sector, with its own manufacturing base, distribution system, and export market, will emerge with incredible speed. And with it, a vast number of new jobs, many of them quite well paying—think about the demand for people trained to do organ quality control. "We know these sorts of innovations are tantalizingly close, and that they could easily be very job productive," Mandel told me. "If I was to take a guess, I would say that ten years from now, we're much more likely to have labor shortages than job shortages."[24] For Mandel and others, our innovation-and-job machine hasn't stalled—rather, it has been delayed by the massive complexity of today's technical challenges, and a lot of unnecessary government regulation, and is now poised for a major breakout.

And yet, while it's clearly the case that the innovation-jobs machine is nowhere near tapped out, even positive trends such as reshoring and a biotech revolution will be hard-pressed to counter the larger trends now in motion without a much deeper shift in our impulsive approach to innovation. To quote another economist, John Maynard Keynes, "Markets can remain irrational a lot longer than you and I can remain solvent." And there have been many developments in our emerging, impulsive economy that will forestall any sort of market correction to our myopic innovation strategies.

One development, clearly, is the tendency at many of today's biggest technology firms to use financial engineering to effectively blunt the market's corrective discipline. Take the case of Microsoft. Like many "mature" technology companies, it has amassed a large market share based on earlier breakthroughs—notably, the Windows operating system—and it uses that market share to generate huge piles of cash. A rational strategy would be to reinvest a large part of that cash in developing the next generation of technology. And yet, while Microsoft does spend billions of dollars each year on research and development, Lazonick says, the company fails to invest sufficiently in improving how the organization itself functions so that its workers can fully exploit that R&D investment. Instead, cash that might have gone toward organizational upgrades is "invested" in share buybacks: from 2003 to 2012, Microsoft spent $114 billion buying its own shares—or nearly one and half times what it spent on R&D. The results are classic Impulse Society. Microsoft milks the Windows franchise with a steady stream of mediocre, buggy upgrades, while efforts to create genuinely new products have largely fallen flat. Yet through massive share buybacks, the firm has kept share prices high and investors mollified—and, thus, has avoided the discipline of the efficient marketplace. Microsoft, Lazonick says, is a company that is "run to keep share prices high rather than to keep people engaged."[25]

This myopic, financialized innovation strategy is endemic across American corporate culture. Many big American technology firms have found that when it comes to R&D spending and returns, it's much more capitally efficient to live off of past innovation, cut investment in the organizational capacities for future innovation (including worker skills), and spend the "savings" on their own shares. The dot-com sector is a classic example. Without decades of heavy investment by the likes of IBM, Hewlett-Packard, and Xerox—on top of massive public investments—the Internet wouldn't have happened as early or as spectacularly as it did.[26] Yet it is precisely in the dot-com space today where companies, under rising Wall Street pressure, have been most likely to reallocate R&D money into buybacks. From 2003 to 2012, Intel, the inventor of the microprocessor, spent $59.7 billion on share buybacks, or just a few billion dollars less than it spent on R&D, according to Lazonick. Cisco, a key early creator of Internet architecture, spent nearly $75 billion, more than one and a half times its R&D budget, on buybacks. More and more, the innovative energies of corporate America are being focused not on discovery or creating new products or technologies that add real value to the economy, but on compensating for the *absence* of genuine discovery and value-creation.

The problem, argues Lazonick, is the myth at the heart of the shareholder revolution—namely, that shareholders are somehow responsible for a company's performance, including its innovation, and should be rewarded accordingly. But except in situations when companies are raising start up capital, or are selling new shares to fund a new expansion, shareholders have little real involvement in a company's ability to innovate. "Profits really are generated by the labor force," says Lazonick. "Shareholders have nothing to do with it."[27]

In a real sense, industry's reluctance to invest in its workforce reflects a broader indifference toward labor—one that, thirty years ago, also might have resulted in a market correction. Certainly, to have treated workers as callously and as expendably in, say, the 1950s or 1960s as is commonly done today would have led to a backlash. And yet, just as management now uses financial engineering to blunt a market correction for its strategic errors, management is also able to blunt the effects of a labor backlash. The simple fact is that, after decades of relentless, and often ruthless, layoffs, offshoring, and other "restructuring," the workforce isn't doing a lot of pushing back. In the United States, strikes and other labor actions are at an all-time low, thanks to a decline in union membership and increasing readiness by unions to compromise to save jobs. A few years ago, the United Autoworkers, once one of the biggest and most aggressive of all unions, agreed to a deal that let automakers pay new factory workers half of what veteran workers get.[28] And in 2013, Boeing machinists in Seattle were essentially blackmailed by the company to accept cuts in pension and medical benefits to keep the company from moving operations to nonunion South Carolina*—and this as Boeing was seeing record highs in share price.

And, of course, with each round of cuts and each new jobless recovery, labor's bargaining position grows weaker. As economist Hirsch Kasper showed back in the 1960s, the longer we go without work, the more willing we are to accept a lower wage simply to return to work—a self-feeding pattern that management has been more than

---

* And this on top of roughly eight billion dollars in tax breaks offered by state government.

willing to exploit.* With every extra year of unemployment, according to more recent studies, this so-called reservation wage falls 3 to 7 percent. This is one reason that workers, once they find a new job, suffer a 20 percent loss in average earnings.[29] Seeing such statistics, you begin to understand the new realities of long-term unemployment—and also the fear that now pervades the workplace. Across the labor market, there is a growing conviction that management feels largely free to treat the workforce as a tool to absorb the costs of ever-greater efficiencies—even though such a strategy is creating huge social harms. After the 2001 recession, it became clear that many Western companies were using the crisis as justification (and opportunity) for lowering wages, deeply cutting their workforces, and accelerating offshoring. What's more, as the economy recovered but the cuts continued, the tactics took on a meanness and arrogance—as if management were supremely confident of its position and totally unconcerned about a backlash. During the early 2000s some of the offshoring campaigns were conducted with astonishing, almost calculated coldness—for example, threatening to withhold severance packages from employees whose jobs had been offshored unless those same employees devoted their final weeks to training their foreign replacements.

Moreover, these strategies were undertaken despite the obvious damage being done to the firm's morale—and its capacity to function productively. This was an especially bitter irony given the emphasis many companies had placed, in the 1980s and 1990s, on team building and a new, more sensitive corporate culture. Suddenly there was no team and no sensitivity. "You'd have your senior managers telling everyone, 'We've got to be lean and mean and this means offshoring,' even when it was manifestly distressing your company, destroying the morale of everyone," the former IT executive told me. "And this after

---

* Albeit no more so than unions were willing to push for higher wages when the economy was booming and foreign labor was not yet accessible.

they'd spent the previous ten years talking about, 'Oh, our people are our best resource,' which, in a knowledge-worker industry, is completely true. And yet now you're prepared to gut this organism in pursuit of cost savings and quarterly bonuses?"

One could argue that this, too, is simply a correction for the excesses of a labor movement that, at its height in the 1960s, showed little sympathy for the challenges management faced in a newly globalizing economy. But that correction has now become an overcorrection. What we're seeing is not only the end of the belief that the fortunes of labor and management are linked; we're also seeing the end of the idea of *work* as a collective effort—one in which individuals come together for a common purpose. This loss is most evident in the specific decline of labor unions that once enabled individuals to bargain collectively for better wages and conditions. But the loss is also clear in the broader sense that the workplace is, or was, a community, a space where individuals could reasonably expect a modest sense of security and permanence, of shared norms and values, of friendship and mentoring; work was a community no less important than any found in other, more private parts of our life. But under the efficient market of the Impulse Society, that community has been steadily demolished. In its place is an atomized, impersonal, *efficient* environment where nothing is permanent and the sense of shared purpose has been replaced by a Darwinian competition to survive.

Here was the last gasp of the old producer economy, where workers could pride themselves as *producers* of labor who gained pleasure and identity and meaning through the act of creating something of value. From now on, as the sociologist Richard Sennett has suggested, the typical worker, to cope with constant churn and uncertainty of the workplace, would much more resemble the consumer, "ever avid for new things, discarding old if perfectly serviceable goods, rather than the owner who jealously guards what he or she already possesses."[30] In other words, where postwar employees saw themselves as part of a steady community of fellow workers, post-postwar employees see themselves much more as free agents who have learned to make and break personal connections easily, to let go of the past, to treat all circumstances as provisional and, above all, to focus on their own survival. It's a workplace version of the self-absorption and narcissism that has already infected much of the rest of life—and hardly the sort of attitude one imagines at the forefront of any industrial renaissance.

There is a more fundamental reason to be skeptical of any imminent turnaround in the current hollowing of the job market in the Impulse Society. So much of the current investment in innovation is actually intended to prevent a turnaround from happening. Even if the reshoring movement were to pick up steam, the reshored jobs would be nowhere nearly as numerous as the ones that left. That's because, in the two decades since the offshoring trend kicked in, multiple generations of automation technologies have continued to reduce labor demands. Consumer products firms are experimenting with sealed, fully automated assembly lines, where humans only supervise and fix things. Factory robots are growing much more sophisticated and far cheaper. McKinsey, the consultancy, found that since the 1990s, the cost of a factory robot has fallen by as much as 50 percent compared with the cost of human labor. Even in China, some factory workers are being replaced by robots, and in more advanced economies, such as Japan, the people-less factory is no longer simply a science fiction fantasy. For more than a decade, FANUC, a Japanese builder of robots for other manufacturers, has made those robots with . . . robots, at the rate of fifty units every twenty-four hours. The FANUC facility can run, without human supervision, for days—and stops only to allow shippers to remove the completed robots.[31]

In the United States, meanwhile, companies are now snapping up robot technology as rapidly as it comes onto the market. Rodney

Brooks, a robotics pioneer, has recently introduced a model, dubbed Baxter, that is designed to work on an assembly line. The model sells for around twenty-two thousand dollars[32]—less than the average factory worker's pay—and is so easy to program that line workers will be able to "teach" it how to do tasks. Baxter is meant to work alongside humans, but Brooks says some companies see Baxter as a way not simply to complement human workers, but to avoid the humans altogether. At a recent symposium on robotics in Boston, Brooks remarked that some companies were looking at Baxter as a way to expand factory output without the cost or administrative hassle of additional personnel—and especially additional low-wage personnel. "A lot of the small companies that we've talked to say there's more work that they could bid on, but they don't want to put on a second shift, because they don't want people who would do a second shift in their factory at night. So they like the idea of having Baxter as the second shift . . . Then they can be more competitive and win more contracts, rather than employ more people, which is an interesting perspective: they don't want to employ more people because it's too much effort to get someone they can trust."[33] In the Impulse Society, the future of manufacturing isn't blue collar: it is no collar.

It isn't just factory jobs that the robots are gunning for. As we saw earlier with our lawyer friends, computers are rapidly "delaboring" even complex and "creative" jobs. Many of the sports briefs you read today are written entirely by computers, and as artificial intelligence and Big Data advance, they will take over more and more of the "probability-based" work that people now spend years at college learning how to do. We'll still need lots and lots of professionals, but their job requirements will be quite different. Mark Smith, the London attorney and expert in high-level automation, told me that artificial intelligence and other automation will likely split the legal profession into two very different wings. One will be a fairly narrow cadre of highly talented, well-paid superattorneys hired for their intellect, their management talents, and their networking skills—chores computers won't likely be able to do for some time. The other, larger wing of the legal profession will be a sort of mass-production, Walmart model that digitally processes hundreds of thousands of simple cases, like uncontested divorce or mortgage contracts.

This two-tier market is the pattern that some economists foresee for the entire job market. The scenario is most graphically laid out by Tyler Cowen, the economist, in his recent book *Average Is Over*. In Cowen's version of the future, the top 15 percent of the workforce will be made up of what he calls "hyperproductives"—individuals who are extremely bright and who either know how to use the latest technologies or know how to manage other hyperproductives, and for whom each new generation of corporate efficiencies will mean an ever-larger slice of the pie. Just below the hyperproductives will be a narrow stratum of service providers—everyone from masseurs and trainers to decorators and personal assistants to tutors, artisans, and entertainers —who will cater, often quite lucratively, to the hyperproductives. Below them, however, things get tricky. In a job market that has been systematically and efficiently stripped of any task that can be automated or offshored, many of the remaining workers will have extremely slim pickings—mainly low-skill service-sector jobs such as food service, security, janitorial, lawn and garden, beauty shop, and home health care. On the plus side, such jobs are probably safe from offshoring or automation "because they often involve hands-on contact," explains David Autor, a job market expert at MIT, whose research informs Cowen's book. On the downside side, Autor told me, those jobs will always be low-wage "because the skills they use are generic and almost anyone can be productive at them within a couple of days."[34]

And, in fact, there will likely be far more downsides to these jobs than upsides. For example, because Big Data will allow companies to more easily and accurately measure worker productivity, workers will be under constant pressure to meet specific performance metrics and will be subject to constant ratings, just as restaurants and online products are today. Companies will assess every data point that might affect performance, so that every aspect of employment, from applying for a job to the actual performance of duties, will become much more closely scrutinized and assessed. "If you're a worker, there'll be, like, credit scores," Cowen told NPR.[35] "There already are, to some extent. How reliable are you? How many jobs have you had? Have there been lawsuits filed against you? How many traffic tickets?" Such assessments, Cowen says, will be part of a larger trend to measure *everything* more precisely. "But we as individuals will quite often find this oppressive."[36] Here is the darker side of the merger of self and market: workers studied and assessed and analyzed to help them fit more snugly and with more coglike efficiency into the machine. (Already, companies such as Bank of America are experimenting with digital badges that track employees' movements and interactions—right down to tone of voice—in order to assess productivity.[37]) Most oppressive, however, will be the economic conditions of this large lower half. If the upper 15 percent is far wealthier than today, Cowen suggests, most of the rest will be much poorer. There will be no middle class in the way we now understand the term: median income will be much lower than it is, and many of the poor will lack access to even basic public services, in part because the wealthy will resist tax increases. "Rather than balancing our budget with higher taxes or lower benefits," Cowen says, "we will allow the real wages of many workers to fall, and thus we will allow the creation of a new underclass."

Certain critics have found such dystopic visions far too grim. And yet, the signs of such a future are everywhere. Already, companies are using Big Data performance metrics to determine whom to cut—meaning that to be laid off is to be branded unemployable. In the ultimate corruption of innovation, a technology that might be used to help workers upgrade their skills and become more secure is instead being use to harass them. To be sure, Big Data will be put to more beneficial uses. Digital technologies will certainly remake the way we deliver education, for example. But the fraying of the social fabric under the Impulse Society is already so pronounced that we'll need more than a new education system, or even a new economic sector, to turn things around. The massive job losses and the extended joblessness from the Great Recession in particular have set in motion a cascade of corrosive social changes that have pushed entire swathes of the workforce onto a down escalator. Because many manufacturing workers, though they earned a mid-level wage, were often not particularly skilled, the collapse in manufacturing has left a large pool of unskilled workers, largely male, who are much more likely to remain unemployed or underemployed. This, in turn, has contributed to unstable family situations that lead to higher-than-normal rates of drug use, teen pregnancy, and school dropouts among the next generation, which is then even less likely to escape the lower classes, much less gain acceptance to college, no matter how improved by digital technologies. And even as the middle class sinks, the upper classes rise. In an economy that increasingly rewards high-level skills, the advantages of a stable home life and a good education only compound: you're not only more likely to get a better job, but also more likely to gain access to a more successful social circle, marry a higher-status partner, and raise higher-status kids.

Indeed, looking at the current picture, one doesn't need too active an imagination to see how we get to a world very much like the one Cowen describes. What's more, you can see how that bleak world might come about, not as the result of some massive catastrophe— another recession, say, or a trade war with China—but as the gradual, incremental result of countless upgrades by countless businesses reflexively exploiting each new generation of cost-reducing, return-improving efficiency. "We won't really see how we could stop that,"

Cowen says. "One day soon we will look back and see that we produced two nations, a fantastically successful nation, working in the technologically dynamic sectors, and everyone else."[38]

The paradox is that, by many of the classic metrics, this shouldn't be happening. The overall economy continues to grow more efficient and more productive—to generate more dollars of GDP at a lower cost per dollar—every year. Wall Street and other financial markets are booming—in no small part because new technology companies are being launched right and left. The number of private companies doing an initial public offering was up 40 percent in 2013,[39] and is now higher than at any time since the pre-crash peak.[40] And, perhaps inevitably, some of the biggest IPOs are from the tech industry.

Yet tellingly, much of the innovation being pursued seems unlikely to bring the sort of economic revival we truly need. Consider the hullabaloo around Twitter, which went public in late 2013. The social media site bills itself as "the premier platform for public self-expression," in part because tweeting is so easy and efficient that many of us do it almost compulsively. We tweet while toppling Middle Eastern autocrats or witnessing astonishing acts of heroism—but also while sitting in traffic, or going out, or watching television. The result is a near-constant stream of self-expression (currently 347,000 tweets a minute worldwide) that is visible to anyone—notably advertisers, who, by sifting through all our tweets, can be present, so to speak, at the very moment someone's act of self-expression is crystalizing into an act of consumption. The example that Dick Costolo, the CEO of Twitter, offered in his investor presentations was a group of Twitter users tweeting late at night about sleeplessness. Once an advertiser like NyQuil has detected this conversation, Costolo explained, the company can tweet each user with an embedded offer for its ZzzQuil sleeping pills. "These kinds of conversations occur regularly on Twitter," Costolo promised, with the result that advertisers could find nearly endless opportunities "to connect in context to the users." Twitter's IPO was a smashing success. Investors flocked to the stock, and the company's valuation by the end of the day was roughly thirty-one billion dollars, making it one of the most successful IPOs in years —and this before the firm had actually turned a profit.

One can hardly resent Costolo or Twitter for scoring a fat IPO. Yet their success, and the massive excitement around it, only underscores the larger shortcoming in the way innovation and the job market interact in the Impulse Society. The kinds of innovation that brought steady increases in wages in the last century aren't the kinds of innovation that get traction in our efficient market. We're interested either in quick hits like Twitter (which generate speculative waves that investors quickly harvest, but that don't generate many new jobs) or the kind of innovation that actively *reduces* wages and jobs.

So effective are our laborsaving technologies that industry now invests more in technology than in labor: simply put, the return on a robot or server farm or a semantically sensitive algorithm is higher than if you invested the same capital in hiring or training a worker. And as economist Larry Summers has pointed out, the pattern quickly snowballs. As companies invest more capital in laborsaving technologies, not only do they have less capital to pay to labor as wages, but those newly deployed laborsaving technologies create a larger pool of un- or underemployed workers, who then have commensurately less wage-bargaining power. All told, as technology's better returns have drawn more and more capital, while labor has drawn less, the share of the entire economy has moved away from labor. As recently as the 1970s, the share of American economic output that went to employees, in the form of wages, pensions, and benefits, was around 41 percent, with the rest going to investors or to the government in taxes. By 2007, labor's share had shrunk to 31 percent. While some of that fall was due to the declining power of labor unions, one of the main reasons is that massive investments in automation and outsourcing have allowed companies to lower costs and prices, boost sales, and give most of the profits to investors, without lifting wages at all—and, indeed, while lowering wages.[41] And as Summers and others have pointed out, given that new laborsaving technologies raise industrial output while reducing demand for labor, it becomes easier to see how corporate profits and shareholder returns have been able to surge since the recession, while median wages and household income have remained flat. Slowly but surely, the rewards of productivity and efficiency and innovation have tilted away from labor and toward capital.

More and more, America under the Impulse Society comes to resemble, not the most advanced nation on the world, but one of those second-rate economies where the rich and the rest may as well be on other planets. "A generation ago, the United States was a recognizable, if somewhat more unequal, member of the cluster of affluent democracies known as mixed economies, where fast growth was widely shared," write political scientists Jacob Hacker and Paul Pierson. "No more. Since around 1980, we have drifted away from that mixed-economy cluster, and traveled a considerable distance toward another: the capitalist oligarchies, like Brazil, Mexico, and Russia, with their much greater concentration of economic bounty."[42] There is little reason to think the shift won't continue, given how perfectly it fits in with the larger patterns of the Impulse Society. Over the past three decades, employers have gained an increasing measure of power as technology, globalization, the decline of unions, and the cultural acceptance of efficient markets have allowed management steadily more leeway in dealing with their workforces. And like any group that finds itself in possession of greater capability, employers have used it. But this is not simply a question of capability. In earlier times, the managers of the economy intentionally carved off a smaller share of the pie. They did this to keep peace with labor and with its allies in government. But they also took a smaller share because they recognized that a workforce whose wages were rising meant a middle class that could afford more of what business wanted to sell. That big-picture, long-term perspective is almost absent from the business culture of the Impulse Society. Instead, there continues to be an implicit argument that companies have no choice but to drive down labor costs in order to survive one existential crisis after another: globalization, digitalization, recession, Walmart. Yet at a time when corporate profits now make up 11 percent of the nation's total economic output, a share not seen since before the Great Depression,[43] that justification rings more than a little hollow. "Corporate profits as a share of the economy are near their all-time high," argues Princeton economist Alan Krueger, former chair of President Obama's Council of Economic Advisers. "So it is hard to argue that companies do not have the ability to support higher wages."[44]

And yet the culture of the Impulse Society continues to make this argument—sometimes quite publicly. Although many manufac-turers won major wage concessions from employees during the reces-sion, on the theory that reductions were necessary for company survival, many of those same companies have refused to restore wages to their earlier levels, despite the recovery in corporate profits. When workers at the company Caterpillar demanded to know why the manufacturer refused to relax an earlier wage freeze, despite report-ing record profits, CEO Douglas Oberhelman (whose own pay had nearly doubled since 2010) argued that the wage freeze continued to be necessary to keep the company competitive. "I always try to communicate to our people that we can never make enough money," Oberhelman told Bloomberg Businessweek.[45] "We can never make enough profit."

A similar shamelessness applies to cost cutting. As *The Washington Post* reported in late 2013, even as corporate America was reporting near-record profits and shareholder returns, the U.S.

Chamber of Commerce was offering its corporate members advice on how "to chaperone their low-wage employees onto public assistance programs like housing vouchers and food stamps, as a cost-free way of addressing the business problem of high turnover."[46]

The pragmatic response would be to ignore the ethical lapses that are implicit in this corruption of the economy. Those in power will continue to use innovation in ways that let them carve off more of the pie. As long as the pie continues to get larger, perhaps the rest of us should stop fretting over the morality of inequality. The problem is that, in the self-centered economy that is both the hallmark and the engine of the Impulse Society, there is no assurance the pie will continue to grow. Even if we manage to avoid massive social disruption over the increasing divide between haves and have-nots (because the have-nots are all too busy posting pictures of their breakfasts to take to the barricades), the implicit characteristics of the self-centered economy bode poorly for long-term sustainability. In particular, the inclination for ever-faster, ever more narrowly self-serving rewards all but assures that our enormous powers of innovation will be applied toward the wrong goals. So technology companies will continue to pour their cash into "ventures" such as share buybacks. Or they'll spend billions buying up technology patents in order to use those patents to sue competitors with marginally similar technologies. Meanwhile, potential inventors (smart, ambitious kids fresh out of school) will continue to focus on innovations that turn the quickest buck yet may contribute little to moving the economy, or society, forward. As Eliezer Yudkowsky, a research fellow of the Machine Intelligence Research Institute, quips, "If you can build a feature-app and flip it to Google for $20M in an acqui-hire, why bother trying to invent the next Model T?"[47] Given the intense focus on such unproductive work, it's hardly surprising that so much of the "high"-tech industry is struggling to bring out truly innovative or breakthrough products or ideas, and instead subsists on milking existing technologies with ever-weaker derivatives. Such efforts make the likelihood of a real breakthrough (the kind that could keep the pie expanding) less and less likely.

Given the power that our new technologies give us to secure short-term rewards, it's hard to see why we would have any incentive to behave otherwise. In a truly efficient market, such short-termism would be recognized and punished. But in the self-centered economy, the market is in on the scam. Thus, shareholders cheer when Microsoft or Apple or Intel spends tens of billions of dollars on share buybacks. Consider the following: in August 2013, Carl Icahn, the corporate-raider-turned-activist-investor, announced (on Twitter, naturally) that he had acquired a $1 billion stake in Apple, and was demanding that the company spend $150 billion to buy back its own shares. Such a move, Icahn insisted, would lift Apple's share price from $487 to $625 (and, others noted, net the raider a $280 million capital gain[48]). It was a classic Impulse Society move: Icahn has no expertise in computer technology or organizational structure, or any of the things that go into true innovation. He knows only how to use financial technologies to transform his large pile of capital into a larger pile. Some more practical observers argued that Apple's cash might be better spent trying to reinvigorate the company's process of innovation—or, at least, coming up with something a bit more pioneering than the iPhone 5c. But the market was delighted. Share buybacks represented a much more efficient use of capital. Indeed, by the end of the day, Apple's share price was up 3.8 percent. Icahn had increased the company's market value by $20 billion with a single tweet.

CHAPTER 7

In Sickness and in Wealth

At least once a week, physician Anthony Zietman finds himself on the receiving end of an economy fixated on the self. A radiation oncologist at Boston's Massachusetts General Hospital, Zietman routinely meets with men suffering prostate cancer to discuss treatment options. Once upon a time, patients sat docilely as the doctor made his recommendations. Nowadays, says Zietman, "it's not unusual for a patient to come into the office, plunk down a sheaf of Internet pages, and say, '*This* is what I'm having.'" In many cases, "this" is proton beam therapy, a cutting-edge treatment that uses a narrow beam of atomic particles to zap tumors in hard-to-reach places without damaging surrounding tissue. Patients want this precision because other, more traditional treatments can cause impotence and incontinence. But as Zietman carefully explains to each prospective patient, proton therapy's actual advantages are almost nonexistent. The technology's impressive precision is really only advantageous with truly high-risk tumors, such as those on the eye or the spine, where even small errors can be disastrous. For prostate cancer, proton therapy isn't any more effective, or any less likely to cause serious side effects, than standard treatments. It is, however, much more expensive— anywhere from twice to five times the cost of other treatments. That's because making a proton beam requires a particle accelerator, a gymnasium-size machine that can run up to one hundred and fifty million dollars[1]—money, Zietman points out, that is therefore "not being spent on primary care, or a new outpatient clinic, or new surgery center, or something else that is of real value."

Proton prostate therapy is precisely the sort of "product" a truly efficient market would reduce or even eliminate. But thanks to heavy marketing by device makers and hospitals, and a distorted insurance system that is largely oblivious to cost, the practice is growing by leaps and bounds. By 2020 the United States will have thirty-one proton treatment centers—or roughly three times the number it actually needs—and the U.S. health care system will be many billions of dollars closer to a complete meltdown. "We can't afford it," says Zietman. "I mean, if everyone is to have the proton beam, not because it's better, but because they want it, because they'd like the newest, the brightest, the most sensational, it will bankrupt society." Medical treatment, it seems, is the new meeting ground for self and marketplace—a place where our basic fears and insecurities can be harvested for short-term returns.

One can, in fact, make a pretty good case that the entire American health care system is an example of the Impulse Society on accelerants, a microcosm of the self-centered economy powered by its own treadmills and generating its own variant of short-term, narrowly self-interested behavior. This is a "health" culture, after all, that blithely spends hundreds of millions of dollars on unnecessary treatments while leaving fifty million people without even basic health insurance. It is a culture so incapable of reining in immediate gratification that our grandchildren may have to triple their own taxes to pay off our generation's accumulated medical debt. A culture that has encouraged such wildly inflated, even narcissistic, expectations about medical treatment (at least for those of us who can afford health care) that any illness is now regarded as a violation of our individual rights.

Above all, it is a culture that simply seems unable to acknowledge the fact of the self's finitude and impermanence. Each year, we spend billions of dollars denying our passage toward the undeniable (eleven billion a year for cosmetic surgery; two billion for testosterone gels) and even trying to escape it altogether. In late 2013, Google launched a new venture, California Life Company, or Calico, whose mission will be searching for treatments capable of extending human life spans by twenty to one hundred years[2]—treatments that, according to the Pew Research Center, four in ten Americans would now embrace.

Put another way, the American health care system has become an elaborate and depressing case study in the risks of institutionalizing the postmaterialist ideal. In theory, health care is an example of a social system that shields citizens from the risks of a material existence—in this case, the risk of illness and related financial stress. That protection allows those citizens to reach their potential more easily and, ideally, to aspire to a more civic, socially engaged way of life. But if that institutionalization is flawed—as the American health care system clearly is—we get the opposite results. As health care consumers, we citizens have become so self-serving that we're threatening to pull most of society off the rails. In other words, in our imploding health care system, we're able to observe the inherent tensions between the ideals of postmaterialism and the impulses of the self and marketplace—tensions that are now driving the entire Impulse Society in a similarly unattractive direction. More to the point, in the effort to fix our dysfunctional health care system, we're watching the first real attempts to confront these tensions—and to probe the economic, political, and psychological barriers that have made the Impulse Society feel so permanent and impregnable.

This is why the saga of Obamacare[3] is such a central narrative for our times. For all the flaws in the substance and execution of the Affordable Care Act, it marks one of the first comprehensive attempts to rebalance what is, in essence, postmaterialism run completely amuck. The debate over health care is, fundamentally, the debate over whether the Impulse Society can be turned into something sustainable and human. The struggles we've faced in reforming our health care system offer a preview of a much larger struggle up ahead. If our ultimate objective is to encourage a society with broader goals and longer-term horizons, the dysfunctions and potentials in American health culture might have a thing or two to teach us.

This would have been a familiar dilemma for John Knowles. In the late 1960s and 1970s, the Harvard-trained physician waged a highly public campaign against the excesses he saw destroying American medicine. In articles and speeches, in a style more befitting a revivalist preacher than a doctor, Knowles excoriated his fellow physicians for charging exorbitant fees and performing tens of thousands of unnecessary procedures because, as he told *People* magazine, some doctor "is building a home out in the country, or his wife needs a new car."[4] But Knowles was just as critical of the American health consumer, whose personal habits—"overeating, too much drinking, taking pills, staying up at night, engaging in promiscuous sex, driving too fast, and smoking cigarettes"[5]—were also driving up medical costs.

Knowles laid part of the blame for our bad habits on our permissive, "credit-minded culture which does it now and pays for it later, whether in drinking and eating or in buying cars and houses." But the larger factor, in his mind, was the institutional, structural forces that had undermined consumers' sense of individual responsibility for their own health. Even as Americans demanded "unrestricted freedom"[6] in their personal health choices, Knowles argued, we also had come to expect, after decades under the most generous and triumphant health care system in the world, complete protection from the consequences of exercising that health freedom. As Knowles wrote, "The idea of individual responsibility has been submerged to individual rights—rights, or demands, to be guaranteed by government and delivered by public and private institutions."⁷ The idea that flawed social and economic institutions encourage poor individual behavior is hardly new or confined to health care; indeed, it's at the heart of a longstanding debate about the optimal relationship between the state and its citizens. But in the case of health care, we can see just how truly challenging it is to strike the correct balance—and, as important, to fix things when they're so clearly *not* in balance.

A central problem here is that we didn't set out to build our health care institutions with the aim of finding the right state-citizen balance. Quite the contrary: our national health care goals were far more modest and post hoc. Where most European countries sought expressly to provide universal coverage, our governmental efforts— namely, Medicare and Medicaid, both enacted in 1965—were intended mainly to fill in the gaps left by a large private health insurance business. For proponents of universal coverage, this public-private hybrid fell mournfully short. But backers hoped it would offer the best of both public and private worlds—the security of a social safety net coupled with the innovative energy and discipline of private markets. They were half right. The effect of the new federal insurance programs was to push the private health care market into an impressive frenzy of technological innovation. Because Medicare and Medicaid reimbursed hospitals and doctors at market rates (and because most states soon required private insurers to do the same) Congress had not only created a massive new demand for health care, but had removed much of the discipline in the marketplace supplying that health care.

One result was a telescoping of medical innovation. With more generous coverage, demand for health care rose, which spurred rapid advances in treatments and technologies and huge improvements in patient outcomes. In 1960, three of five heart attack victims died. By 2000, thanks to advances such as beta blockers, cardiac care units, blood thinners, angioplasty, and stents, this was down to one in four.⁸ The story was the same across the health care field, which by 2000 had extended the average American life span by another four years.⁹ But our new system encouraged other, less desirable outcomes. Generous coverage weakened any incentives that either patients or providers might have had to conserve medical resources. We used far more health services than we needed, and we also used those services less efficiently. We underspent on proactive measures, such as prevention and screening, and, as a result, racked up larger bills later on, when our health failed and our medical options were fewer and more expensive. Further, as medical consumers, untroubled by cost, demanded steadily more advanced treatments, the market for medical innovation also skewed higher—away from prevention and toward more complex, higher-margin procedures and technologies. And since product development costs were rising, because of regulation, but also because most of the easy treatments had already been developed, each successive generation of medical innovation was more and more costly.

The escalating cost of medical innovation, in turn, unleashed a particularly virulent form of the financialization we saw in earlier chapters. Because medical technology is so expensive today, physicians and hospitals buying new equipment are under tremendous pressure to use those tools more often to make back their investment. Take the case of the two most commonly used medical imaging technologies—computed tomography, or CT scans, and magnetic resonance imaging, or MRI. No one could deny that both technologies have saved hundreds of thousands of lives via early detection of cancers and other ailments. Yet each technology's financial "signature"—a large upfront cost (anywhere from half a million dollars to three million dollars) and relatively low operating costs—naturally inclines the physician-investors to use them as frequently as possible. "Once you've absorbed the fixed costs of installing the technology, you now have the incentive to run it on *every* patient," says Amitabh Chandra, a Harvard economist who studies health care policy and decision making. And because a general-purpose diagnostic tool such as a CT scan or MRI can theoretically be used in any medical situation, there is a natural tendency to overprescribe. "The problem," Chandra says, "is that you can MRI and CT the entire population."[10]

More and more, the underlying economics of medical technology—and thus the behaviors of those developing and using that technology—has come to resemble that of any capitally intensive industry. "It's like a jet airliner," Chandra told me. "If you're United Airlines and you've just bought a new 777, you don't want it sitting on the ground. That 777 should be flying *all* the *time*." And, of course, the more that hospitals and physicians use this costly technology, the more patients come to see such technologies and such routine uses as an essential part of treatment.

The result is the classic Impulse Society paradox: a snowballing pattern of innovation and treatment and expectation that has generated medical miracle after medical miracle—but has also helped push up health care costs about three times faster than the growth of the overall economy. This disparity has metastasized into a widening health care deficit that is consuming an unsustainable share of American economic output. U.S. health care costs, which accounted for just 5 percent of GDP in 1960, now swallow up around 17 percent of a much larger economy (by comparison, no other nation spends more than 12 percent of GDP on health[11]), and is expected to reach 20 percent by 2020. Medical progress is now identical to the upgrade treadmill at Apple or General Motors—except with vastly larger stakes. "It's like the exploration of space," says Daniel Callahan, a medical ethicist and historian at the Hastings Center, which studies health care costs. "No matter how far you go, there is still farther you can go. It's medicine without limits."[12]

All told, this insurance/innovation/expectation-driven health care model has brought our health care culture to the point where even the absurd feels normal. In 2012, New York's Memorial Sloan Kettering Cancer Center, one of the top cancer treatment hospitals in the world, made headlines by refusing to administer Zaltrap, a new drug for late-stage colorectal cancer. Sloan Kettering's decision was laudable: at a cost of eleven thousand dollars a month, Zaltrap was more than twice as expensive as an existing cancer drug, Avistan, yet provided no significant advantages over Avistan. Yet Avistan itself is hardly a bargain: for the typical late-stage colorectal cancer patient, a course of Avistan costs around $80,000; includes some nasty side effects, such as hemorrhaging; and on average, gives a patient just over six weeks of additional life. Stories like these are now routine. Provenge, a new prostate cancer drug that is tailored for each patient's particular body chemistry, costs around $93,000 a treatment (to recover its $1.1 billion development costs[13])—and in return, the average patient gets an extra four months.

We can be grateful that patients today have these sorts of options, but at the same time deeply concerned that, thanks to the financial imperatives of an out-of-balance health sector, patients in such a precarious position must be presented with such an awful dilemma. "The drug companies know that however outrageous the price, there will always be some people willing to buy it," says Callahan. "And with a lot of these expensive drugs, the insurance company may pay for some of it, but not the whole thing. The patients will mortgage their house—or the children mortgage *their* house—and they bankrupt themselves for these drugs." In other countries, such situations are much rarer, in part because most government-run health care systems refuse to pay for such high-cost, low-value treatments and, as a result, patients' expectations are commensurately lower. In Britain, patients diagnosed with certain well-advanced cancers are automatically referred for palliative care and hospice. "You say, 'Well, isn't that incredibly bleak?'" says Zietman, who is from England. "No, it's reality. We can *pretend* we can cure you with additional drugs, but that's just a game of make-believe that really is not rational."

But in the United States, even terminal illness is often seen as a market opportunity, and palliative care is almost an afterthought. The median hospice stay here is under three weeks, and a third of American hospice patients die in the first seven days. Instead, the emphasis is on heroic, late-stage, and usually quite costly treatment—so much so that efforts by government or insurers to dissuade patients from such a costly course are met with protest and litigation. "The conservative view is that these choices should always be left up to the individual," says Callahan. "The problem is that [sick] people usually aren't in a good position to make those choices ... and they often make bad choices. And part of the definition of a good system is one that more or less tries to protect them against bad choices, particularly the kind which involve money." Increasingly, however, our health care system is one that not only doesn't protect people from bad choices, but encourages those bad choices, and indeed, requires them for profit.

The growing disparity between what the health care system can profitably produce and what health care consumers realistically need—the classic symptom of the Impulse Society—would be almost comic were its ramifications not so lethal. The United States not only spends more than any other industrial nation on health care per person, but gets a surprisingly poor health "return" on its investment. In almost every critical category—from life expectancy and infant mortality to patient satisfaction—American health care outcomes lag those of other developed economies.[14]

As symptomatic are the tens of millions of Americans without health care insurance. The statistics are thrown around so often that they barely register anymore, but consider what it means that the richest nation in history tolerates a seventh of its population being without even minimal coverage. No other industrialized nation accepts such disparity. But no other industrialized nation has surrendered so completely to the myopia and narrow self-interest that now define the Impulse Society—and the crisis of the uninsured is very much a symptom of that surrender. It's notable that the ranks of the uninsured began to swell with the economic turbulence of the 1970s and the cost-cutting frenzy that began in the 1980s, when many companies stopped offering health insurance for lower-wage workers. The change was so swift and dramatic that by the end of the 1990s, despite a booming economy, the proportion of low-wage workers without health insurance was higher than it had been in the 1980s. As Judith Feder, a health care expert at Georgetown University, has noted, "The clear lesson of the 1990s was not only that a threatened economy reduces health insurance coverage, but that a prosperous economy cannot guarantee it."

Indeed, if prosperity is defined by a steady treadmill of medical innovation, then "prosperity" may actually make it even harder to render health care more accessible. First, our intensive reliance on expensive new technologies drives much of health cost inflation, thus making health care even less accessible to the poor. Second, our return-obsessed health care business model tilts toward technologies that, in the way they are used, suck up lots of capital but deliver relatively modest social value. Harvard's Chandra notes that for the money we now spend for a man to have a single treatment of proton therapy, we could buy health insurance for three uninsured people. "So that is the choice we are making," Chandra told me. "That's the form of rationing that we have decided to engage in. We're saying we'd rather give proton beam to some people but ration health insurance for these other people. And maybe that's the same choice that a deliberative institution would have made, but I find that very hard to believe. I mean, anyone who has deliberated on this for more than two minutes would say, no, 'this is a crazy choice.'"

But, again, it's a choice entirely in keeping with health care in the Impulse Society, where the goal isn't actually health but health care—that is, treatment for illness. Under a rational model for health care, we'd be interested in doing whatever it took, from diet and exercise to preventative medicine, to keep people healthy or to catch illness before it reached the point of needing massively expensive treatments. But under the current version of consumer capitalism, which prioritizes fast returns and prizes any expenditure as positive economic activity, a costly medical intervention is in some sense the more valuable. In health care, we've reached the point where medical treatment—and by perverse extension, the illnesses that require that treatment—are becoming as essential to economic growth as good health is. As Jonathan Rowe, a journalist and public policy analyst, put it several years ago, "The aim [of the health care system] should be healthy people, not the sale of more medical services and drugs. Now, however, we assess the economic contribution of the medical system on the basis of treatments rather than results ... Next, we will be hearing about 'disease-led recovery.' To stimulate the economy we will have to encourage people to be sick so that the economy can be well."[15]

In this latter context, you can see why health care reform has been so difficult. To begin with, we're trying to rebuild the institutions and norms that influence how we manage our health, and that is no easy task. To be sure, as a purely technical matter, we've no shortage of examples of health care systems that are far more rational than ours—everything from the state-run "single-payer" programs in Canada and Taiwan to market-based models in Switzerland and Singapore. But for many reasons, there has never been a clear consensus about which would work best in the United States—in part because we remain divided as to whether government or the market would be more effective, or less damaging, in managing something as important as health care.

For advocates of a single-payer model, the answer is clear: government is the most rational provider because government can use its massive scale to buy health care at the lowest cost and use its regulatory authority to manage (or, more bluntly, ration) how much health care individuals use. Ideally, that top-down approach helps temper the worst excesses of both marketplace and individual, thereby transforming health care from a volatile and not always accessible consumer commodity into a basic social service. Meanwhile, the savings produced by these efficiencies can go toward financing health care for the uninsured. Advocates of the market-based approach, on the other hand, want government to do little more than ensure that every citizen has the funds necessary to buy a minimum level of coverage on the private market. Because consumers would have limited resources but also greater control over them, they'll be far more careful not only in how much health care they use, but also in how they use it—and this new self-discipline would force hospitals, doctors, and technology providers to become more cost-conscious, too.

But it's not simply a question of choosing the most efficient system. Although the health care debate is often framed as a debate between the market and the state, there has always been a deeper set of questions—questions about the relationship between the consumer and the marketplace, but also between citizen and society (which are not at all the same thing). In particular, as the health care debate has unfolded, we've been pushed to clarify what, if anything, we think society "owes" its citizens and what citizens owe society. "The overarching question is, whether we want to accept a premise that a lot of other countries accept, which is that the health of the people basically is a national responsibility," says Daniel Wikler, a medical ethicist in Harvard's Department of Global Health and Population. "Is it the business of a national government to keep the people healthy and in particular to make sure that people have access to a doctor when they need one?"[16] This is both a political question—can we forge the consensus and find the resources and the program to make it happen?—but also, as Wikler notes, a moral one, "whether your neighbor is going to be in there with you when you get sick and the only thing standing between you and really bad health is the cost of health care, which you can't bear yourself."

This latter question is far from settled. Although a large majority of Americans (56 percent over 33 percent) favored health care reform in the years leading up to Obamacare, more than half felt that the goal of reform should be cutting costs, not extending coverage.[17] Part of that reflects an ideological divide about the role of government and the appropriateness of social safety nets generally. But as Georgetown's Feder points out, it also underscores a very basic dynamic in the health care industry: the desire to maintain the status quo. For the fact is that, despite all the problems in the American health care system, most Americans are reasonably content with what they have. Most Americans have health insurance. Most Americans have tolerable access to health care services. Members of this majority think it regrettable that not everyone has insurance, and aren't against trying to find some sort of solution—as long as it doesn't interfere with their own health care situation. "The barrier to getting everyone covered is that most of us have coverage and we don't want it disrupted, and there is a minority [that is] just left out," says Feder, who worked on the Clinton administration's unsuccessful health care initiative. That reluctance to accept any disruption, Feder says, is why Democratic lawmakers, once the champions of a single-payer model, now rarely even mention the idea. Consumers, Feder told me, "don't want that. People with vested interests want to stay where they are." That's a big reason that most of the health care measures prior to Obamacare centered not on reforming anything, but on adding benefits—as, for example, the quite popular, and quite expensive, Medicare prescription drug benefit enacted in 2003.

This collective reflex of self-preservation helps explain why Barack Obama's Affordable Care Act (ACA) has provoked such a visceral response—a negative reaction that goes well beyond our antipathy at the botched rollout. Although the ACA leaves intact the basic public-private structure of American health care, the law nonetheless goes after some of the key institutional enablers of bad health care practices. Under changes to Medicare's reimbursement structure, for example, providers are no longer paid for the separate services they provide, but for the health outcomes they achieve. It's a shift that is already lowering Medicare's costs, and is probably also playing a part in the recent slowdown in health care cost inflation—the first in decades. Likewise, under a policy known as "comparative effectiveness review,"[18] insurers will be able to reject medical technology or procedures deemed too costly for the benefit they deliver. (This is a standard feature in single-payer systems such as the United Kingdom's.) More controversially, the ACA raises the costs of individual and employer-offered health insurance, exposing consumers to more of the actual costs of health care, and thus to the discipline of the marketplace. The individual mandate, meanwhile, requires those who don't currently want health insurance, often due to their young age and good health, nonetheless to begin paying into the "risk pool" now, in anticipation of the time when they will need it. In theory, the mandate helps correct the individual's natural myopia from imposing a major cost on society.

These changes may not qualify as real reform, since they leave intact the awkward hybrid nature of the American health care system. But they nonetheless represent substantial changes both to the status quo in health care and to the broader debate on the relationship between individual and society—and their full effect will take years to gauge. We will likely see substantial per capita cost reductions in federal insurance spending as reimbursement policies change how doctors and hospitals approach treatment. Also likely is a decline in the obsessive-compulsive technology reflex that is making us a proton beam nation.

But there are certainly other ramifications, potentially less encouraging. For example, will caps on reimbursement for gratuitous technology also have the unintended effect of slowing the rate of medical progress? Countries such as the United Kingdom and France may disallow their own doctors from using costly treatments, but their patients nonetheless benefit from the many medical advances that have been produced by America's hyperactive innovation engine. This is a concern that extends well beyond the medical sphere. More fundamentally, what kind of political pushback will these reforms ultimately engender? When Congress created Medicare and Medicaid in 1965, conservative opposition was overwhelmed not only by a powerful Democratic majority in Washington, but eventually by the fact that a rapidly aging population very much liked the benefit—and society was feeling rich enough to subsidize the elderly. This time around, we're not feeling so rich. As a result, many groups are being asked to pay more or receive less. The early negative reaction to the rollout problems and the policy cancellations may actually pale in comparison to the anger that arises as well-connected constituencies begin to feel the longer-term changes to the status quo.

Significantly, much of the funding to expand insurance to the uninsured will come through reductions in Medicare spending. Thomas Edsall, a longtime observer of government policy, predicts that because those benefiting from insurance extension are predominantly poor and minority, whereas those getting Medicare are predominately middle class and white, the ACA represents a reallocation of public money that will pit one social group against another, very different one. This is a competition, Edsall warns, that could have profound political and electoral implications. "Those who think that a critical mass of white voters has moved past its resistance to programs shifting tax dollars and other resources from the middle class to poorer minorities merely need to look at the election of 2010, which demonstrated how readily this resistance can be used politically," wrote Edsall in a November 2013 *New York Times* op-ed. "The passage of the A.C.A. that year forced such issues to the fore, and Republicans swept the House and state houses across the country. The program's current difficulties have the clear potential to replay events of 2010 in 2014 and possibly 2016."[19] In other words, if we imagine that state power could be used to curb the sort of problematic reflexes (be they in health care or finance or personal behavior) that drive the Impulse Society, we shouldn't be surprised to see some significant pushback. The Impulse Society, in effect, will defend itself.

In some respects, the opposition Obamacare has provoked seems relatively mild, given the degree to which it is attempting to shake up the status quo. Liberals may complain that the ACA falls far short of the long-dreamed-of European-style single-payer model. But as far as many conservatives are concerned, Obamacare represents the first effort in decades to shift the country back toward the New Deal program of economic management that was supposed to have been killed off in the 1980s. More fundamentally, the reaction to Obamacare may force us to reassess the cherished idea that Americans will make personal sacrifices to address a broad social problem. Rather, one could argue that, after decades of an increasingly self-centered ideology and a hyper-responsive consumer economy, when it comes to supporting social justice, personal sacrifice may be a deal breaker.

But in a sense, this is a learned behavior. Without question, past generations have been more willing to make sacrifices for a larger social good. Unfortunately, as with much of the rest of the Impulse Society, our health care culture, with its endlessly snowballing cycles of innovation and expectation, has efficiently cultivated a sense of entitlement and self-service. So, for example, patients not only litigate when insurers refuse to cover a costly experimental treatment; they have also begun using the courts to overturn priority systems for organ transplants—in effect, making end runs around norms and institutions designed to distribute scarce medical resources equitably. Such end runs, increasingly common in the United States, are far rarer in other countries, such as England, where the government has a much stricter medical policy and, importantly, where citizens are far more accepting of rules and regulations. "The British are much better at queuing up—at taking their place in line and *waiting* in line," Kevin Donovan, a physician and expert in bioethics at Georgetown University Medical Center, told me. "The American attitude is that 'There can be good reasons for restrictions and they should be followed—except perhaps in *my* case.'"[20]

In fact, there is an inherent bias toward inegalitarianism in American health culture that government reform alone isn't likely to eliminate—and which points to one of the main challenges in dealing with the broader Impulse Society. This is, again, an artifact of our intensive focus on medical technologies. Many of the most exciting medical innovations are likely to be quite expensive. A good example is the promising field of genetically targeted treatments, where biotech firms tailor drugs to specific diseases in specific and potentially quite small populations. In order for investors to quickly recover the very high development costs, says Harvard's Chandra, biotech firms may have little choice but to focus their research on diseases afflicting the affluent. That means focusing not only on wealthy countries, but on the wealthiest segments within those countries. "Just as you're more likely to target your drugs to the American market as opposed to, say, the market in Afghanistan or Sri Lanka, within the United States you're going to target the diseases that afflict people in Boston and Manhattan much more than the poor and the sick in Arkansas and Kentucky," Chandra told me. And as gene science gains the capacity to identify the genetic components associated with intelligence, ambition, and other precursors to affluence, these gene profiles will also be scanned for potentially treatable diseases. The sorting process will continue at the molecular level.

Given the huge development costs these medical technologies will require, and the industry's ever-more-intense need for prompt returns, it's not so hard to imagine a medical future that looks an awful lot like the medical present—that is, where more and more of the truly life-altering benefits of innovation flow to the part of the market that can most afford them. Even if we managed to enact a single-payer system, we'd still be looking at a health culture very much along the lines of Tyler Cowen's bifurcated, end-of-average society, where the wealthy get not only better health care but also more access to the sorts of innovations that are likely to dramatically extend life spans. What will society look like in thirty years, when Cowen's hyperproductives are not only wealthier than everyone else, but living much longer?

Again and again, our health care culture highlights and accentuates the inequities and imbalances of the Impulse Society—and the reflexes that guide so many of our decisions. We rarely stop to ask whether this innovation or that technique is taking us where we ultimately want to be, or what sorts of trade-offs it implies—our only concern is that it is moving us forward, delivering an immediate return. Few of us are sorry that medical science has eradicated many of the diseases that once cut life short. But as we enter those extra years, we realize that longer lives bring their own substantial costs—few of which are rationally incorporated in our conceptions of health care. Longer lives mean that we're far more likely to suffer chronic, utterly disabling and quite costly diseases such as cancer or stroke or Alzheimer's. Even for those whose final years are relatively disease-free (either through good luck or thanks to some supertreatment), there remains the underlying, inescapable reality of very old age—frailty—which can turn the final years into a physical and emotional ordeal, what Joanne Lynn, a Washington-based gerontologist and health care reform advocate, calls "death by a thousand cuts—the increasing challenges of just day-to-day living."[21] With the aging of the population, frailty and chronic, debilitating diseases will be the dominant reality for postindustrial, postmaterialist society. And yet this is not the medical future we're planning for. Were that the case, we would have long ago begun reallocating more resources to help the elderly cope with frailty—help that often centers less on the latest treatment than on, for instance, ensuring transportation to the doctor's office or adequate nutrition or home visits by a nurse. By contrast, our health care system largely ignores such basic demands as it strives to deliver the latest life-extending innovation—in no small part because those innovations are vastly more profitable.

In the meantime, it is already imposing a penalty on us, in the form of a growing incapacity to accept or even consider our own limits, or the impermanence of our selves. Thanks to the huge success of our medical innovations, we may have made it harder for individuals to face the moment when those successes must ultimately run out. Under the steady pressure of our medical treadmills, our strategies for dealing with aging and, finally, with death itself have become less overt and deliberate. They are guided less and less by explicit personal beliefs or cultural traditions or even by a frank admission of purpose. Instead, when we approach a terminal condition, we defer more and more to the structural "instincts" of the medical marketplace and to the various capital cycles and treadmills that operate there. It's as if aging and death, rather than being seen as an inevitable part of the process of life—and a call for grace and humility and courage—have instead become just another set of unmet consumer demands and unfulfilled consumer desires, another "failure" by the market to confirm the preeminence and permanence of the self.

This, too, is of a piece with the Impulse Society. According to psychologists, the narcissistic personality is particularly unsuited to contemplating death, in part because the self has become so inflated that it cannot even contemplate the idea of nonexistence without profound terror and a desperate campaign of avoidance and denial. As a society, we fear death with the same reflex, and with each increment of life-extending progress, it's possible that our fear will grow deeper and more paralyzing.

In this, the health care debate offers the clearest prognosis for the Impulse Society. Over the next several decades, we must confront crises in everything from health care and finance to structural unemployment, ecological decay, and a fraying social fabric. Yet it is not merely the magnitude or complexity of the crises we face but the fact that, under the Impulse Society, our very capacity to confront crises, of any kind, has diminished. On an individual level, our long years under a personalizing economy have left us unwilling to defer our own gratification or step beyond our comfort zones. Even more seriously, however, many of the public institutions that once helped compensate for these individual shortcomings—notably the media and our political system—have been so weakened under the pressure of the self-centered economy that they, too, are effectively paralyzed.

CHAPTER 8

Forever War

On the evening of January 20, 2009, just hours after Barack Obama was sworn in before the largest inauguration crowd in American history, a dozen Republican leaders gathered at the Caucus Room restaurant in Washington for an emergency strategy session. Over a three-hour dinner and many bottles of wine,* GOP heavyweights such as Congressmen Eric Cantor and Paul Ryan, Senators Jim DeMint and Jon Kyl, and former House Speaker Newt Gingrich dissected the party's election disaster and hammered out plans for a counterattack—or, as one participant later called it, an "insurrection." From day one, Republicans would spare no effort to derail the Obama agenda. At the upcoming Senate confirmation hearings, Republicans would attack Timothy Geithner, Obama's pick for treasury secretary, over his personal finances. In the House, Republicans would obstruct Obama's stimulus plan.[1] The national Republican Party, meanwhile, would run campaign-style attack ads hammering Democratic lawmakers over any possible controversy. The insurrection would violate the tradition of a presidential

* The story of the dinner was broken first by Tom Bevan and Carl M. Cannon in their 2011 book, *Election 2012: The Battle Begins*, and a few months later by Robert Draper in his book *Do Not Ask What Good We Do*.

honeymoon, when the losing party defers, at least temporarily, to the victor's election mandate. But the Caucus Room strategists were not in a deferential mood. "If you act like you're the minority, you're going to stay in the minority," declared Congressman Kevin McCarthy.[2] "We've gotta challenge them on every single bill and challenge them on every single campaign."[3]

The rest, as they say, is history. Over the next year, the spirit of the insurrection went national, emerging in a popular movement, dubbed the Tea Party, whose members were avowedly opposed to activist government generally and the Obama administration in particular. In the 2010 midterm elections, insurrection candidates, backed by energetic activists and a host of wealthy archconservative funders, were swept to power in the House of Representatives and won seats in the Senate. From there, cheered on by conservative talk show hosts, the insurrectionists waged relentless legislative campaigns against most of the president's policies and especially his health care plan. The bitter fight dragged on for four and half years, hobbling American domestic and international policy and, for sixteen surreal days in 2013, shutting down government and threatening an already fragile economic recovery. It was one of the biggest breakdowns in the American political system since the Civil War, and even many conservative Americans were appalled by the insurrectionists' disregard for the wider consequences of their narrow agenda. When Republican leaders finally defied the Tea Party and ended the shutdown, in October 2013, one could almost hear the nation breathe a collective sigh of relief.

Yet there is little reason to imagine that the dynamic at the heart of the insurrection of 2009 won't reappear in some other form in the very near future. None of the political issues that energized the rebellion, such as Obamacare or immigration, has gone away. Wealthy business leaders who backed the Tea Party still hate big government, regulation, and taxes. As important, the economy continues to limp along, leaving an ever-larger part of the population feeling excluded, resentful, and ready to rebel against a government that, in their view, has oppressed and betrayed them. And here is the irony: because many of these once-and-future insurrectionists object, fiercely, to some of the very government initiatives (such as health care reform or financial regulation) that might actually improve the economy, their activism could well prolong the very economic insecurity that fuels insurrections. Put another way, the same vicious cycle of short-termism and narrow self-interest that already dominates other arenas of modern life has now fully emerged in the political system. Welcome to Impulse Politics.

Part of the story here is a long-standing campaign by conservatives to reorganize society according to the discipline of the market-place—and to zealously oppose any government efforts to impede that reorganization. This openly ideological crusade has pitted conservatives and liberals against one another in an increasingly brutal war of attrition that has fractured American political culture at both the national and local levels. But behind this sectarian conflict is another pattern that is far less ideological and far more in keeping with the relentless treadmills of the Impulse Society. Over the last three decades, the entire political system has effectively been taken over by the self-centered economy. Where Republicans were once regarded as the party of business, now even Democrats and the liberal political establishment treats the business class, and especially the financial sector, as an essential partner in a political enterprise that grows costlier, more technologically dependent, and more business-like with each election cycle. Both parties today rely so heavily on infusions of capital (a billion dollars for a presidential campaign) that they have begun to operate almost as adjuncts to the financial market-place and now share many of the same cycles and, increasingly, the same agendas of that marketplace.

Nor is this simply about the corruption of the professional politician. Although many voters are deeply frustrated with the extremism that has hobbled the political system, we, too, have succumbed to a much more personal and extreme form of political engagement. For too many of us, political participation is no longer about the hard work of consensus or compromise or being involved in something larger than ourselves. Rather, it has become another venue for personalized consumption—an opportunity to build our identities using the carefully packaged and quite divisive messages of the political parties.

The result is a political system, and a political culture, as myopic as the financial sector or the consumer economy. Even as we grow more and more efficient in the pursuit of short-term political goals, such as raising campaign funds or delivering the fifteen-second, poll-tested, base-inflaming sound bite, our capacity to use the political process to solve complex, long-range challenges dwindles. The result: a political system so devoted to its own perpetuation that it is capable of little else. So we can mount election campaigns as sophisticated and aggressive as military invasions and as well-financed as an IPO. We can build elaborate and stealthy networks of patronage that gratify the short-term interests of entrenched elites. But confront that same political system with the sort of complicated, enduring problems that now threaten stable, sustainable prosperity—problems such as a hollowed-out job market, or a bankrupt health care system, or crumbling infrastructure, or a suicidal financial market bound for another meltdown—and we've all but lost the ability or the will to act. Here is the ultimate tragedy of the Impulse Society: the very mechanism through which we might begin to redirect our myopic, self-centered institutions is itself so infected by the virus of short-term narrow self-interest that it is hard to know where to start.

To be fair, not all the dysfunction in the American political system is deliberately self-inflicted. The long period of political success that we enjoyed during the first two-thirds of the last century—when we mustered the will to win wars, invest in the future, and curb the more wretched excesses of the industrial model, among other things—was certainly something of a historical aberration. We emerged from the Depression and the Second World War not only rich and powerful, but also relatively unified in purpose and deeply leery of radicalism on either the right or the left. Grave social tensions remained, but in terms of our overt political culture, most Americans were so moderate and centrist that voters often "split the ticket"—that is, voted for one party for president and the other for Congress—and bipartisan legislation was comparatively commonplace. (In 1965, nearly half the GOP voted for Medicare, despite claims that the program was socialistic.[4]) That we would lose some of that cohesiveness and consensus—as was already happening by the late 1960s and early 1970s—was inevitable. The collapse of the postwar economic boom and the string of government failures and scandals, including Vietnam, race riots, out-of-control budget deficits, and Watergate, undercut our postmaterialist idealism and our faith in big government as problem solver. And, ironically, some of our earlier political triumphs, notably on civil rights, provoked conservative backlashes that further dissolved the postwar consensus.

But as we've seen, some of the biggest drivers behind our political unraveling have been intentional. In surrendering to the ideology of the "efficient market" in the mid-1970s, we deliberately restored an older, harsher, more Darwinian economic and social order, with little room for community or collectivity. Companies were turned loose to maximize shareholder value and largely jettison traditional deference to other social values, such as employee welfare or community vitality—and this new corporate personality helped revive economic inequality and erode whatever postwar unity remained. Government, meanwhile, surrendered much of its postwar role as economic referee between business and labor and between market and community, which led to the loss of vital sources of social cohesion. As important, individuals were encouraged to maximize personal pleasure and self-interest. We were empowered to withdraw from society and from traditional norms such as individual discipline and the sacrifice of self for community. And withdraw we have—pulling back from the more public, collective lives that our old, inefficient economic systems obliged us to live and, instead, pursuing lives that are more personalized but also frequently separate and isolating.

We touched on this in chapter 5, in the way many Americans were sorting themselves into communities that matched their cultural and political preferences. By the 1990s, this personalization of the national geography had helped transform the political map: many states and congressional districts that had been relatively evenly divided between Republican voters and Democratic voters were becoming solidly red or blue.[5] But this political sorting wasn't confined to the physical world. With the proliferation of new media formats such as talk radio, cable news, and online sites, we were also dividing into politically distinctive media environments.

Yet, as with so much else in the self-centered economy, our sorting has been driven not only by our own impulses, but also by the market's increasingly efficient capacities to gratify those impulses. Even as voters sought politically compatible environments, those political environments were now seeking us. In the media market, for example, news outlets did everything they could to adapt to and encourage our new, more fragmented political culture, for there is great money in fragments. Advertisers pay top dollar for audiences segregated by political preference—liberals and conservatives shop for different things—and politicized news turned out to be an efficient and profitable way to segregate and harvest like-minded viewing audiences. By the late 1990s, the Fox News Channel, a pioneer in ideologically flavored news, was making a killing cultivating a conservative demographic by means of what Republican media expert David Frum has described as a simple two-part strategy: "provoking the audience into a fever of indignation (to keep them watching) and fomenting mistrust of all other information sources (so that they never change the channel)."[6] Conservatives are still the masters of this model: the main liberal channel MSNBC has less than half of Fox News Channel's audience,[7] and the much larger world of talk radio tilts almost entirely to the right.* But politicized news of any stripe is getting more mainstream as consumers become accustomed to "the fever of indignation"—and as networks get more creative in stoking the fever.† True, that fever might be artificial. The average voter might not be quite as extreme as this new cohort of politicians and experts and media observers claimed. The inflammatory rhetoric and the sound bites might not truly reflect how most of us viewed political issues. But here, too, the efficiencies were overwhelming: for many of us, it simply became easier, and certainly more emotionally gratifying, to embrace the feverish new discourse than to keep doing the sober work of deliberating over each political issue. And as elsewhere in the Impulse Society, the easiest course was the one that we, and our political culture, ultimately took.

In other words, politics are now a brand. In the early days of the consumer economy, marketers discovered that consumers welcomed a strong "name brand" because it spared us the anxiety of choosing among conflicting manufacturing claims every time we shopped. In the same way, under the Impulse Society, formerly complex political concepts such as "conservative" and "liberal" have been distilled into simplistic, but powerful brands. For voters, these brands let us deal with difficult political questions not only faster and more easily, but

* It should be noted that talk radio, by far the largest piece of the politicized news environment, was made possible by Reagan-era deregulation of the airwaves. Until then, the Depression-era Fairness Doctrine had required broadcasters to give equal time to both political parties.

† It's telling that the more ideologically neutral CNN is struggling to hold a prime-time audience, suggesting, as a Pew Research Center analysis put it, that in the new media market, "a channel that chooses not to be overtly liberal or conservative is doomed in the ratings battle."

with far more moral and emotional certainty: our side is good; the other side is evil. For the political establishment and the media business, brands offer a highly efficient means to harvest voter sentiment and convert it into votes or ratings. Politics are now virtually indistinguishable from marketing. Political parties operate like well-funded public relations firms while voters are encouraged to treat politics as another setting for self-expression, identity creation, and emotional fulfillment.

None of which has been especially healthy for democracy. In running our political process as if it were just another wing of the consumer economy, with its emphasis on capital and emotional efficiencies, we have rewired our political culture for disaster. For clearly political decisions shouldn't be treated as just another category of consumer choice. Rather, they require us to be *anti*-consumers—that is, to at least try to look beyond the short-term and the personal and, especially, to resist the "fever of indignation," lest our political passions harden into extremism. But because stoking that fever turns out to be the most efficient means of generating fast political returns—and because modern political parties, like modern business, can never earn "too much" return—fever and extremism have become the chief currencies of our political economy. Slowly but surely, we have created a new sort of treadmill whose primary output is not consensus and progress but discord and paralysis. Thus, it's hardly surprising that the "industrialization" of the political marketplace would only widen the gulf between left and right. Studies of voter attitudes show that the ideological distance between the average Democrat and Republican on a host of core issues, when measured on a standard seven-point ideological scale, nearly doubled between 1972 and 2008.[8] As Emory University political scientist Alan Abramowitz notes, "Over these 36 years, Democratic voters moved from slightly left of center to well to the left of center while Republican voters, who were already well to the right of center, moved even further to the right of center."[9] In short, while Republicans have moved further—the result, perhaps, of their disagreement with the New Deal status quo—both sides have put distance between themselves and what was once the political middle. And that distance is important, because the farther we've drifted from the traditional center, the less willing we've become to compromise on key issues or to tolerate politicians we perceive as compromising.

The consequences of this market-assisted divergence are playing out on multiple levels. On a purely cultural level, we may be as polarized now as at any time since the Civil War. "People are just not interested in interacting with people on the 'other side' anymore," says Abramowitz, one of the top experts in America's shifting political landscape. More and more, "you just avoid those conversations, avoid interaction with people who are different. Why? Because it's uncomfortable, it's *upsetting*."[10] A case in point: in the 1960s, the fraction of Americans who cared whether their children married someone from the "other" political party was less than one in twenty. Today, one in three Democrats and one in two Republicans regard "interparty marriage" as taboo.[11]

The rift in our political culture now runs so deep that we can no longer agree even on such basic notions as the legitimacy of the scientific method or the immorality of false campaign ads. Even the idea that there is one universal truth is now in dispute. "Disagreements in our culture are now not just over values and not just over the facts, they're over how we even conceive of facts, how we come to consider what knowledge *is* a fact," says Michael Lynch, the University of Connecticut professor of philosophy we met in chapter 5. And once we've reached such a state, Lynch argues, democracy is threatened, "because if there is no common standard of knowledge, then there is no common standard of anything. There's not going to be any common vocabulary that we're going to be able to discuss our differences with."

This Montagues-versus-Capulets culture rivalry has translated almost undiminished into the national political culture and, according to Abramowitz and other observers, has produced a generation of congressional lawmakers more ideologically extreme, and less legislatively functional, than any in living memory. All but gone are the moderate Republican lawmakers who were actually to the left of conservative Democrats, or the centrists in both parties capable of bipartisan compromise. Worse, because the country is so evenly divided between red states and blue states, and because every election can potentially shift the congressional balance of power, every legislative vote becomes a strategic winner-take-all opportunity to appease your party's uncompromising constituency while denying your opponents the chance to appease their voters. One example: the escalating use of Senate filibusters to halt opposing legislation or to block judicial nominations. In the 1970s we saw perhaps ten filibusters a year. By the time of the Republican insurrection in 2013, we were seeing seven times that number. "It has gotten to the point where you just filibuster everything—it's obstruction for the sake of obstruction," Abramowitz told me. "It's not even that they necessarily disagree or oppose a nominee or oppose the particular policy. The payoff is just to give the other side a black eye—it's just political gamesmanship." And the cost is a system less and less capable of executing even simple policy—much less the inherently contentious challenges (such as debt reduction, immigration, clean energy, and climate change) that Washington should be grappling with but isn't.

In a functional democracy, political leaders work tirelessly and creatively to heal such breaches and unify the fragmented electorate—or at least to bring enough voters back to the center to create a governable majority. They do this both by compromising their own political aims, but also by inspiring the rest of us to look beyond our private interests and to support the larger, national community—as might occur in a time of war or economic ruin. Yet thanks in large part to the colonization of the political process by the values and strategies of the consumer market, more and more of the modern political class not only is content to leave us in our polarized camps, but also now finds it convenient and profitable to actively encourage further polarization and withdrawal.

Take political campaigns. Divisive, us-versus-them campaign tactics are nothing new—in the 1960s, conservative political strategists began using race as a subtle means to break off conservative southerners from the Democratic Party. But the modern campaign has turned division into a scientific process to be pursued with the same efficiencies of a consumer marketing campaign—and often with the same technologies and experts. By the 1980s, political marketers in both parties were using consumer psychology to target specific demographic groups (the soccer moms, the evangelicals, Medicare seniors) about issues that stirred their passions. The growing complexity of the campaigns made necessary new cadres of political professionals, such as the campaign consultant, whose need to chalk up quick wins—no one hires a losing consultant—introduced yet another element of efficiency into campaigns: increasingly, candidates were advised to move further to the left or the right of their opponents (who were getting the same advice from their consultants) as an expedient way to ensure a win. Political parties, meanwhile, quickly discovered that inflammatory, divisive rhetoric and negative ads, were the most efficient way to motivate "the base" and harvest campaign contributions, which, as political commentator Steven Pearlstein notes, can then be "plowed back into yet more negative advertising along with sophisticated get-out-the-vote efforts on Election Day. This self-reinforcing cycle creates a strong incentive for politicians to abandon the center and move permanently to the ideological extreme. You do not energize the base through moderation and compromise"[12]

And then, in the 2000s, the arrival of Big Data made it possible to divide and conquer at the level of the individual voter. With techniques borrowed from the big consumer products companies, political operatives began parsing voters not only by age, party, and voting history, but also by religious affiliation, credit history, car preference, magazine subscriptions, TV shows, clothing catalogues, news sources, beer affinity, gun ownership, and hundreds of other variables. By mining these rich profiles, campaigns could predict, with depressing accuracy, our reactions to a full range of hot-button political issues—and thus could create personalized messages with the highest probability of motivating voters. This was retail politics taken to an entirely new level—and an entirely new level of intrusion by the political marketplace into the self.

In the 2004 Bush-Kerry election, Bush master strategist Karl Rove used this "microtargeting" technique to secure what turned out to be the decisive demographic, the several million social conservatives and evangelicals who hadn't voted in 2000, and galvanize each of them with personalized messages on topics, such as gay marriage and abortion, that the data predicted would be most motivating.* Democrats, having fallen behind in the Big Data arms race, promptly invested millions of dollars to catch up. By 2008 and 2012, the Obama campaigns, guided by experts hired from Google, Facebook, Twitter, and Craigslist,[13] were sifting through terabytes of personal data from every conceivable source to locate every conceivable Obama voter and calculate the most efficient means of getting that voter to the polls. Measurement was the mantra. Which fund-raising e-mail subject lines generated the most cash? (Thousands of different ones were tested.) Which phone scripts motivated the most voters to register? How likely were voters to vote if asked by a Facebook friend? (One in five, it turned out.[14]) No bit was left unturned. The Obama campaign even aggregated voter lists with cable company billing

---

* As an official with the Bush 2004 reelection victory later boasted, "We were able to develop an exact kind of consumer model that corporate America does every day to predict how people vote—not based on where they live but *how* they live."

records to see which shows Democratic-leaning households were watching—thus allowing the targeting of political ads with unprecedented accuracy and cost-effectiveness.[15]

But as elsewhere in the Impulse Society, it is the very personalizing efficiency of microtargeting that makes the technique so detrimental to the democratic process and the larger community. In many respects, traditional, mass-market political campaigns exert a stabilizing and moderating effect on the political process. Candidates, hoping to reach as large a population as possible, have little choice but to develop broad, inclusive platforms and to moderate their more immoderate positions— an "inefficiency" that nonetheless imposes a tempering, unifying influence on campaigns. Microtargeting, by contrast, minimizes these moderating inefficiencies by allowing candidates to, in effect, create a platform for each like-minded voter, while simply ignoring voters on the "other side." There's less pressure to develop a broad, inclusive platform or come up with a broadly appealing big idea or moderate, centrist message. As election expert Michael Kang puts it, microtargeted campaigns "need not temper their position to attract a majority."

Microtargeting also asks far less of the voter. It is, in fact, the fast food of politics. Where the traditional mass-market campaigns require voters to make an effort—to step out of their individual circumstances and into the rough-and-tumble, competitive political marketplace— with microtargeting, the political marketplace simply comes to the voter, like pizza or Netflix. As with the consumer marketplace, these techniques have closed the gap between politics and the self to an unprecedented degree. Nor are microtargeted voters required to make much in the way of intellectual or civic effort—to consider a big idea or complex concept or, certainly, anything that might require deliberation or compromise. Indeed, the main characteristic of the microtargeted campaign is the *absence* of a big idea. "A lot of us call micro-targeting 'silent' marketing," writes a campaign specialist at a

New York marketing firm. "That's because if you survey voters or consumers during or after an effective micro-targeting campaign they will have a hard time recalling big, dramatic announcements or a catchy ad or the 'big idea.' What they will recall is why the candidate or [product] offer is appealing to them. Micro-targeting done right is stealthy—it flies below the radar."[16] There is now little difference between politics and any other form of marketing; more and more, all are designed to fool the public.

Such stealth is great for the individual campaign; your opponents can't see the entirety of your message. But again, it can hardly be good for a process that is supposed to be collective, deliberative, and public. A campaign that uses continuously upgraded micro-themes to reach sympathetic voters seems unlikely to produce a single, powerful, potentially transcendent idea that might unify the postelection electorate and ease the transition from campaigning to governing. Instead, by Election Day, voters will have been shepherded through such a personal, emotionally charged, one-sided experience that they may struggle to exit the campaign mode and accept the compromises essential to moving ahead. In other words, they may have a hard time believing that even if their candidate lost, the *system* still works. Without that spirit of compromise and confidence, it's hard to see how we move beyond a political culture where our citizens refuse to live next door to someone from the other party and our lawmakers no longer bother with legislation but merely seek to deny the other side any successes in preparation for their own political comeback.

And certainly that is the atmosphere that has followed recent political campaigns, when not only voters but lawmakers seemed unable to switch from campaigning to governing. "Both sides have adopted the attitude that 'we don't need to work with them, and if we just stonewall them we will win in the next election and we will win such an overwhelming victory that we will be able to do everything our way,'" Robert Bixby, executive director of the Concord Coalition, a group that lobbies for deficit reduction, told me. "The goal is always electoral victory, not policy or legislation."[17] As with the self-centered economy, the political marketplace grows more and more enamored of the quick return and is less and less inclined to generate an output of lasting social value. Indeed, in what may be the ultimate symptom of the Impulse Society, the one institution that is supposed to save us from flying apart into a Hobbesian war of all against all has largely been reprogrammed by its business imperatives to make that war perpetual.

But keep in mind that it is not simply a matter of the passions and alienation of the people involved. It is the momentum and efficiencies of the systems that have arisen to harvest those passions and that alienation. It is the political consultants continuing to advise candidates to use extreme tactics because that's the most efficient way for the consultant to score a win and woo new clients. It is the media executives who are unwilling to risk losing audience share or ad revenues by softening their tone. It's the political parties that are all but addicted to negative ads to spur donations to fund more negative ads. The machine is now so thoroughly in control that even the players are getting anxious. In recent years, we've watched Republican leaders squirm because the conservative media echo chamber, which was so useful to the party through 2010, suddenly became a huge liability—a market-led force that now kept the party from turning down the rhetorical volume and adopting a more practical legislative strategy. As Frum, the conservative columnist, argued in 2011, shortly after House Republicans threatened to torpedo debt ceiling talks, "As a commercial proposition, this [conservative news business] model has worked brilliantly in the Obama era. As journalism, not so much. As a tool of political mobilization, it backfires, by inciting followers to the point at which they force leaders into confrontations where everybody loses, like the summertime showdown over the debt ceiling." And yet backing away from that relationship is extremely difficult. As Frum told *Nightline* the year before, "Republicans originally thought that Fox worked for us and now we're discovering we work for Fox. And this balance here has been completely reversed. The thing that sustains a strong Fox network is the thing that undermines a strong Republican party."[18]

Yet there are few signs that members of either party are serious about giving up the marvelous efficiencies of the political machines they have built. Even now, despite recent overtures of bipartisanship, it seems that many of the key players and lever-pullers are merely pausing to reload. Republicans, badly beaten by Obama's Big Data in 2012, have been pouring tens of millions of dollars into their own Big Data effort for 2014 and 2016, under the well-funded auspices of the Koch brothers, Charles and David. Democrats are tapping their own sugar daddies to pay for even more efficiency. At a meeting of liberal donors in Washington in late 2013, retired hedge fund billionaire George Soros announced a $2.5 million cash infusion—a "signal," according to *The New York Times*, that the wealthy "are committing early for the next round."[19]

The names Koch and Soros remind us that the real impulse here isn't the latest technology or our reflexive refusal to compromise. Rather, it's the momentum of a political machine that has become so massive and businesslike, and so dependent on large capital investments, that it operates more like a financial entity than a political one. Campaigns themselves behave like huge high-tech start-ups with massive demand for "investors." Microtargeting and other weapons in the rapidly escalating data arms race are so expensive that campaign costs are rising even faster than health care costs. Between 1988 and 2012, real-dollar spending on presidential campaigns more than quadrupled,[20] to more than $2.0 billion. Congress has also become vastly more expensive. The cost of winning a Senate seat in 2012 was $10.5 million, while the average House seat was $1.7 million[21]—both roughly double the cost in 1986.[22] In total, the tab for the 2012 campaign was $6.3 billion.[23] In such a system, money becomes as central as, and perhaps even more important than, votes.

The rising river of money in turn only accentuates and locks in the patterns of impulse politics. As races become costlier, the market-place of contributors is less and less willing to bet on challengers and more likely to support incumbents, which helps reinforce the existing partisan structure. Between the early 1990s and the early 2000s, campaign spending by (and contributions to) House incumbents rose by 50 percent, while spending by challengers fell by 13 percent,[24] according to an Emory University study.

More fundamentally, the greater demand for capital has led to a political economy that is guided increasingly by the imperatives and reflexes of the financialized economy. Fund-raising is now a continuous, year-round operation—the average House member spends four hours every day calling potential donors. Further, because lawmakers must raise such vast sums, they automatically gravitate to donors and sectors that can write the largest checks, even though that means dealing with the political agendas that come with big checkbooks. That's been particularly awkward for Democratic lawmakers. The party that has traditionally pushed populist causes (such as labor, environmentalism, and minority rights) now must woo a funding base whose agenda is often anything but populist or even progressive. In surveys, wealthy voters are significantly more likely to regard deficit reduction and government spending as having greater priority than unemployment, because the deficit affects interest rates and interest rates have a huge impact on investments. Studies find the wealthy only a third as likely as the general public to believe that the federal government should prioritize full employment and half as likely to support a federal minimum wage high enough to keep a family above the poverty line.[25] As Tom Perriello, a former Democratic congressman, told *The New York Times*, big Democratic donors are "more likely to consider the deficit a bigger crisis than the lack of jobs."[26] This shift in the priorities of funders, says Perriello, who now raises funds for the left-of-center Center for American Progress,[27] is injecting "an enormous anti-populist element" into Democratic politics and policymaking.

That concern is echoed by Dean Baker, an economist and cofounder of the liberal Center for Economic and Policy Research. "The people who pay for campaigns—people who have a lot of money in stock, people who are top executives in corporations—they're doing great right now. They've recovered completely. The stock market is higher than its prerecession levels. Corporate profits are at record highs. They don't see a big unemployment problem." What that means, Baker says, is that if a Democrat lawmaker wants to propose a government program to fight joblessness, he or she isn't likely to get the same sort of support from today's larger donors. "If you go to [a donor] and say, 'Hey, here's this great way we could boost the economy, get [the] unemployment rate down by two to three percentage points,' they're going to say, 'Well, why would we want to do that? You're just going to raise the deficit. So why don't we just bide our time and let the economy sort itself out?' "[28] In today's more capital-intensive politics, populism itself becomes an efficiency to be squeezed from the political machine.

In fact, with the rapid growth of campaign finance, the entire political culture has less room for, and is less responsive to, issues that might matter to the groups Democrats and liberals once championed. One of the biggest contributors today is the financial services industry—the sector with the greatest profit surplus and, in recent years, the greatest incentive to spread some of that surplus around Washington. Between 1992 and 2012, financial sector contributions, in real dollars, have increased almost sevenfold, to $665 million,[29] or more than any other sector,[30] and now account for 11.5 percent of all campaign spending, up from just 4 percent in 1992.[31] In addition, the sector spent nearly half a billion dollars in 2012 lobbying lawmakers and regulators.[32]

The financial sector's influence shows up on many fronts. It is most overt in places like the House Committee on Financial Services, which is responsible for regulating Wall Street and whose members are showered, almost literally, with massive campaign contributions from the financial sector. So lucrative is a seat on the "cash committee" that, since 1981, seventeen new seats have been added, for a total of sixty-one.[33] And once a freshman House member has won a committee seat, he or she is then scrutinized by industry lobbyists much as a professional ball club looks at college athletes. "It is almost like investing in a first-round draft pick for the NBA or NFL," a lobbyist told the *Times'* Eric Lipton in a story about the cash committee.[34] "There is potential there. So we make an investment, and we are hopeful that investment produces a return." Mostly they have been pleased. The House Committee on Financial Services, along with the rest of Congress and even the White House, has managed to blunt or eliminate entirely many of the reforms promised in the wake of the financial meltdown.

Wall Street has always regarded Washington as an asset capable of generating a certain return. But in recent decades, the financialization of national politics has moved to a new level—or, some might say, has returned to its level before the Great Depression. Where postwar administrations kept the finance sector on a short leash, and were often hostile to it, the modern attitude has been far friendlier. And although this new, more finance-friendly stance began under Republicans Nixon and Reagan, the finance sector's biggest political supporters are now often Democrats. In fact, it was Democrats in the 1990s who were largely responsible for the sector's liberation from Depression-era regulation. It was Bill Clinton's treasury secretary, Robert Rubin, a former Goldman Sachs boss, who led the campaign to repeal the 1933 Glass-Steagall Act, which had prevented commercial banks from also playing the financial markets. Rubin also helped defeat efforts to regulate credit swaps and other financial derivatives. Both these deregulatory initiatives would open up huge new streams of revenues and profits for Wall Street—and a huge new source of campaign finance for Democrats. But both actions were also pivotal in the meltdown in 2007, when "too-big-to-fail" banks playing the markets lost hundreds of billions of dollars in unregulated derivatives and nearly destroyed the global financial system.

But, if anything, the alliance between Democrats and Wall Street has remained strong. Although Barack Obama has pursued an unabashedly progressive agenda in many arenas, notably health care, his stance on finance has been largely old-school. After heavily criticizing Wall Street in the 2008 campaign, the new president was quick to establish ties to the financial sector by, among other things, appointing Rubin protégé Timothy Geithner as his own treasury secretary. Geithner, though he should be credited with helping keep the meltdown from becoming worse than it was, never forgot his Wall Street allegiance and was instrumental in, among other things, blocking what many financial experts say would have been a critical financial reform—the breakup of Wall Street banks that have grown so large their gambles put the entire economy at risk. Nor did the Obama administration pursue criminal indictments against the biggest players on Wall Street for their role in the crisis, despite abundant evidence of fraud. Nor, finally, has Obama been willing to go after Wall Street's revived excesses: the massive bonuses and salaries, or the relentless, corrosive influence of investor myopia on corporate strategy. Here is another triumph for the Impulse Society: the financial sector has converted the political culture into a guarantor of excess profits, or "rents," which can then be "reinvested" to generate still new opportunities for rent.

Sadly, the only public institution that stood in the way of a totally financialized political culture, the courts, has recently buckled. In the 2010 ruling *Citizens United v. the Federal Election Commission*, the U.S. Supreme Court removed any limits to campaign contributions made by corporations to political action committees, which may then use that money to run ads to promote or, more frequently, attack candidates. In the first election after the ruling, corporate-funded "superPACs" raised three hundred million dollars.[35] By the 2012 election, that figure had doubled.

Citizens United points out just how far the imperatives of the financial markets, and the ideology of the efficient market, have penetrated and colonized our political culture. In the ruling, Justice Anthony Kennedy argued, as only someone sequestered in Washington could argue, that the effects of the ruling would be largely benign. Even if the ruling created the "appearance of influence [on] or access" to the political process for corporations, Kennedy opined, such an outcome "will not cause the electorate to lose faith in our democracy."[36] Kennedy was about as wrong as one could be. The ruling was made on the grounds that campaign contributions are a form of constitutionally protected expression. That argument is often part of a larger movement, usually offered by corporate lawyers, to grant corporations the same rights and privileges as people—to, in effect, enable the corporation to seek instant gratification simply by buying the desired political outcome, as if it truly were a self. But it is also an idea that deeply offends many Americans who are not corporate lawyers or lobbyists—and especially those whose lives have been upended by so much corporate self-gratification.

Coming on the heels of the financial crisis that was caused in large part by corporate selves chasing short-term returns (and then demanding bailouts with public funds) *Citizens United* may well have been the straw that broke the camel's back. For many ordinary Americans, the entire political system appeared to be little more than an arm of the financial sector—or an extension of the financial market. For, certainly our political system now behaves like the market, with the same myopia and same winner-take-all mentality, the same narrowly self-interested goals—and, above all, the same reverence for assets over individuals.*

For outsiders looking in, national politics seemed to be returning to the wildly corrupt days before Progressive reformers such as Teddy Roosevelt and William Taft—days when congressional members were openly purchased, the public coffers plundered, and the common citizen either ignored or used as fodder. In such a dismal context, it was hardly a surprise to see the reappearance of some seriously angry populism: the Tea Party in 2009, but even more, the Occupy Wall Street movement two years later. When protesters poured into Manhattan's Zuccotti Park in September 2011 to demonstrate against a corrupt financial system and equally corrupt political system, the surprise most of us felt wasn't that a protest was happening, but that it taken so long.

So why *didn't* that anger turn into a full-scale revolution? Given the consequences of our new financialized, efficiency-driven, self-absorbed Impulse Politics—consequences that include the meltdown, but also the gutting of the middle class and the paralysis of our legislative process—one could hardly have imagined better circumstances for a sustained protest movement. And yet the protest movement most focused on those problems, Occupy Wall Street, largely failed to ignite Main Street. Meanwhile, America's other protest movement, the Tea Party, whose platform was largely dedicated to *preventing* any sort of a meaningful reform of those imbalances, was so effective that it took over the Republican Party and shut down the government. Sadly, this is precisely the outcome we would expect in a political

---

* Which should not surprise us. Two of every three U.S. senators and two of every five House members have a net worth of a million dollars or more.

culture that is driven as much by branding and the creation of identity as by a desire for real political change.

Consider the liberal response to the financial crisis. Although the Occupy movement reflected a broad consensus among mainstream liberals that both Wall Street and its government watchdogs were corrupt and in need of serious reform, the movement failed to motivate many mainstream liberals. To be fair, Occupy made little effort to appeal to the mainstream. The group was perversely uninterested in speaking with the media or working with potential allies, such as labor. Nor was it willing, or perhaps able, to offer a coherent agenda. In a real sense, Occupy represented the impulse of political anger without the more deliberative structure or process that might have allowed it to go mainstream. Occupy was more Doer than Planner.

And yet, even if Occupy had been more "professional," it's not at all clear that mainstream liberals were ready for the collective, risky action displayed in Zuccotti Park and, eventually, hundreds of other public spaces around the United States. Since the 1970s, in fact, the American left has had a profoundly awkward relationship with the idea of collectivity or collective action. The counterculture impulse that was so powerful in the 1960s had, by the 1980s, been largely absorbed into a mainstream consumer culture that was happy to translate any political aspiration into a product or service. By the 1990s, many of the radicals of the counterculture had become spokespeople for the consumer culture: Allen Ginsberg sold Gap jeans and William Burroughs hawked Nike Air Max. As for the rest of us, protest and dissent were things we did mainly commercially, and conveniently, via a consumer economy that allowed us to strike out for (personal) freedom every time we went to the shopping mall.

At the same time, much of the New Left—the politically active men and women who marched for civil rights and against the Vietnam War—had been largely assimilated into the American middle class. Political aspiration was giving way to material aspiration. In the late 1960s, liberal student activists answered the conservative policies of Richard Nixon by taking to the streets. Twenty years later, many of those same liberals reacted to the conservatism of Reaganomics not by hitting the streets, but by moving to neighborhoods where people didn't put up Reagan yard signs. Politicians, meanwhile, had all but stopped asking voters to step out of their private interests and embrace some larger national goal. For many boomers, politics have become much more about self-expression and identity, something to be engaged in as it suits our schedules or lifestyles or our need to fill an inner emptiness, but never something that might require discomfort or delayed gratification or hard choices—and certainly not something to get teargassed over.

Not to say that these aging leftists have lost their desire for a less market-oriented society. A quick glance at the popularity of sites such as Daily Kos shows just how large and attentive the American left still is. But Daily Kos is the perfect illustration of how our political aspirations have evolved—or, perhaps, devolved—under the Impulse Society. We have become, in many respects, a nation of armchair liberals—participating in, and raging about, the American political scene from the safety and comfort of our living rooms or office cubicles. Want to encourage Elizabeth Warren to run for president? Click here. Want to tell Harry Reid to end the filibuster? Click here. Want to support Occupy? Click here. But as for getting out into the streets and enduring the level of discomfort or facing the psychological and physical risks that Occupiers faced (and by the way, when is the last time you saw that level of white-on-white police brutality?) well, that isn't something most of us are prepared to risk. Nor is it something our industrialized, financialized, businessified political culture suggests we undertake.

The result is that we no longer have an effective "left" in American politics—or at least, not in the way that we did in the labor heyday of the 1930s or the protest movements of the late postwar period. And that, argues political analyst Peter Beinart, has proven disastrous for the American political process, because it has led Democrats to give up many positions that were once central to the party. Without a credible left wing, without activists willing to hit the streets and disrupt the status quo, Beinart argues, the Democrats cannot negotiate with conservatives. "Unlike Franklin Roosevelt or Lyndon Johnson, Bill Clinton and Barack Obama could never credibly threaten American conservatives that if they didn't pass liberal reforms, left-wing radicals might disrupt the social order," writes Beinart. At the same time, the absence of a left wing has allowed the Democratic Party to become far more comfortable with practices once associated mainly with the right, such as pumping corporate donors for campaign funds and befriending Wall Street. "Democrats have found it easier to forge relationships with the conservative worlds of big business and high finance," Beinart notes, "because they have not faced much countervailing pressure from an independent movement of the left."[37] In a sense, financial deregulation and the mess that followed were a direct result of the left's more self-centered politics. So focused was the left on self-expression and personal fulfillment that it largely neglected its historic function: keeping government from falling totally in the thrall of the marketplace and the blind march for efficiency.

The Tea Party, by contrast, suffered no such absence of support. From the moment of its inception, the revolution on the right found a warm reception from the conservative political machine that was much more geared for action—and vastly better funded—than anything on the left. Where Occupy all but refused to deal with the press, many Tea Party activists were given explicit training in media management. Rallies were carefully organized and coordinated with the media and, importantly, with local lawmakers—many of whom were not only invited to attend, but warned that failure to support the Tea Party agenda would result in an automatic challenge in the next primary election.

This isn't to say that the anger animating the Tea Party was any less genuine than that at Zuccotti Park, or that it was all manufactured by right-wing lobbyists and millionaires. At the heart of the Tea Party movement, and the larger red state "brand," is a deep and genuine anxiety over the loss of important social values, including family, community, and self-reliance. Granted, in the Tea Party universe, these values are often mixed in with far less noble ones, including a fair measure of bigotry. What's more, these conservative values are easily manipulated by political and business elites—and have been since well before Richard Nixon exploited the anxieties of the "silent majority" to win reelection. But Nixon, and the conservatives who followed, such as Ronald Reagan, succeeded because they understood that many Americans, and not just rabid conservatives or libertarians or survivalists, were genuinely troubled by the social costs of the postwar liberal enterprise.

From the conservative standpoint, a big, activist government and a broad social safety net were not only draining the Treasury but also producing a new and unattractive sort of citizen: self-absorbed, besotted with entitlements, out of touch with material realities, and unappreciative of the traditional institutions that had sustained American society. This wasn't merely a complaint about pot-addled hippies and welfare queens. It was a more legitimate fear that a growing part of the population no longer supported or believed in the social institutions and norms essential for a stable, productive, happy culture. These new liberal citizens "reject the American past, deny their relation to the community," lamented conservative historian Daniel Boorstin, warning that this "atavism, this new barbarism, cannot last if the nation is to survive."[38] It was as if conservative Americans had identified the darker side of Inglehart's postmaterialist man, whose selfishness and short-sightedness told us everything we needed to know about why American society was in such a precipitous decline.

And yet the solutions that many conservatives pushed have been startlingly counterproductive. The pious moral crusades of social conservatives such as Jerry Falwell were written off by most mainstream voters as archaic and out of touch. More problematic, however, were the economic prescriptions offered by Reagan and other self-styled fiscal conservatives: massive doses of radical individualism and free-market zeal, untempered by regulation or institutional moderation. Ultimately, these policies would simply accelerate the corrosion of the very social values that conservatives sought to preserve. And yet, even as the consequences of our free-market ideology ripped through society, hammering the job market, exacerbating income inequality, and making life extremely challenging for families, communities, and the would-be self-reliant; conservatives' near-religious faith in efficient markets required them to ignore the contradictions and the collateral damage—or to awkwardly try to justify those costs as the natural order of things. If the left has always been too suspicious of the market, conservatives were now committing the opposite error. Modern conservative ideology "typically exhibits the weakness of the left in reverse: it is highly sensitive to the alienations of big government, but blind to the analogous effects of big business," noted conservative social critics Richard John Neuhaus and Peter Berger at the height of the Reagan revolution. That blindness, added Edward Luttwak, at the conservative Center for Strategic and International Studies, was "the blatant contradiction at the very core of what has become mainstream Republican ideology."[39]

Why have conservatives been so reluctant to consider the market's divisive, corrosive effects? Part of it is a fear, not entirely unjustified, that government efforts to control the economy almost always create a new set of problems; witness how the heavy government presence in the housing market contributed the housing bubble. But to truly understand the right's blindness to the paradoxes of the free market, we need to go back to the rise of political branding. Over the last two decades, political parties, consultants, and media outlets have successfully converted individual political participation into something almost indistinguishable from a consumer product—a means by which a voter can fulfill aspirations and maintain identity without the effort or awkwardness of deliberation and compromise.

Yet if branding has brought short-term returns for political parties—especially, in recent years, for conservatives—it has also left us with a political culture largely incapable of advancing policy or making critical choices. Under the current conservative brand, for example, there is little room for compromise—in no small part because compromise has been deemed morally incompatible with the "authentic" conservative identity. As a result, conservative voters and political leaders have little ideological room to maneuver—and no place to go except to move further from the center and deeper into extremism.

But the contradictions of the conservative brand are now coming to the surface. As free-market policy decimates the job market, for example, it becomes more difficult for conservatives to both embrace free-market ideology and insist that individuals are entirely responsible for their own economic outcomes: in today's economy, a man or woman can strive wholeheartedly for self-sufficiency and still end up going backward. Over the last decade, in fact, the right-wing brand has steadily lost much of its real-world basis. Where Reagan era conservatism was inspired by demonstrable flaws in the liberal New Deal agenda—such as the collapse of Great Society programs and the corruption and complacency in many unions—today's conservative brand has a much softer foundation in reality. Certainly, after the economic and social devastation of the financial crisis, a reality-based conservative movement would have been forced to reconsider the wisdom of an unfettered financial marketplace.

And yet, thanks to the penetration of right-wing branding, many conservatives simply refuse to acknowledge even the possibility of a failure of the efficient marketplace. According to surveys, many self-identifying conservatives blame the meltdown on government-backed home loans while the slow, jobless recovery is seen as the result of excessive government regulation. That the efficient market itself might be corrupt and hugely biased toward inequality and against the middle class never enters the picture. But here, too, brand conservatism wears thin.

Surveys also find that younger conservatives, particularly those whose economic fortunes have recently faltered, aren't nearly so enamored of the market—or so reflexively opposed to a government role in that market. And yet, brand conservatism has so dominated the Republican party apparatus—not least in the selection of candidates during the primary elections—that the brand remains just as extreme as ever.

This dynamic has left the Republican Party almost incapable of offering real policy proposals for any economic problems. Case in point: many Republican lawmakers recognize that the current capital gains tax is unsustainable. It not only taxes millionaires at a lower rate than it does middle-class wage earners; it also encourages some of the worst kinds of short-termism in the market because it allows shareholders to churn shares with a minimum tax penalty. In a functional political culture, capital gains would be taxed in a way that encouraged investors to hold on to their stock for five years or more. "I know some pretty centrist lawmakers who would be very open to the idea of having the capital gains rate go up on short-term sales," says the AFL-CIO's Damon Silvers, who is an expert on corporate short-termism. "I think that kind of deal could be done. The problem with that isn't so much the corporate community—it's the Tea Party, because you're talking about raising taxes and the Tea Party is not for that. In fact, the Tea Party's primary reason for existence is to *not* be for that."

Political culture is a complex beast to be sure, and there are many drivers behind the widening gap between left and right. For instance, there is mounting behavioral research evidence suggesting that liberals and conservatives simply respond differently to uncertainty and turmoil—and that conservatives are far more psychologically inclined to leave individuals to shoulder economic misfortune on their own. There is also research indicating that conservatives are far less comfortable with challenges to authority—and thus, more resistant to any reforms serious enough to confront a deeply entrenched status quo. But as our exploration of the Impulse Society has made clear, a more fundamental factor in conservatives' strange loyalty to a clearly corrupted market is that conservatives, through the treadmill of an industrialized, individualized, hyper-efficient, ego-fueled impulse politics, have backed themselves into an identity that no longer acknowledges the necessity of compromise—or even includes the concept in its lexicon. This isn't to say that the liberal machine hasn't exploited identity politics or that contemporary political culture isn't also suffering to some degree from an ideology of victimhood.* Yet in this, the left hasn't strayed as far as the right. In study after study, it is conservatives who have migrated further from the center and it is conservatives whose positions have most hardened. It may simply be that the modern world, with its relentless emphasis on individual empowerment and self-fulfillment—and the de-emphasis on community and stability—is more unnerving to conservatives. Whatever the causes, the result is that today, conservatives have much further to travel before they're ready to confront the contradictions of a discredited free-market ideology. And until conservatives take up that challenge, our entire political system can't truly overcome the paradoxes of a self-centered economy that, increasingly, prioritizes immediate gratification and narrow self-interest over deliberation and the interests of the larger community.

Yet even in the cynical arena of American politics, hope has proven to be a patient species. For example, younger Americans, for all their reputed disengagement from formal politics, are showing signs of coming alive as a political force. Surveys find that while Millennials don't vote nearly as regularly as their older peers, they are more likely to be actively involved in other ways. They are more likely to volunteer and, importantly, more likely to incorporate their political values in all aspects of their lives, and not regard political engagement as something that happens only at election time. What's more, they are far less likely

---

* Although nowhere nearly to the degree that right-wing ideologues would like us all to believe.

to embrace the sorts of branded politics that older citizens do. Conservative Millennials, for instance, are far more tolerant of ethnic diversity than are older conservatives and are likewise far less troubled by gay marriage. And, significantly, conservative Millennials are more likely to be suspicious of big business, and to view government as a potentially useful force in correcting economic imbalances—an attitude that may result from the fact that many Millennials have come of age in an era notable for its business corruption. Political observers like Peter Beinart have argued that the political party or leader who finds the right political and economic message to reach the Millennials—for a while, Elizabeth Warren was being touted as the ideal Millennial candidate—will have a powerful new voting block, and some serious leverage for political and financial reform.[40]

Yet, significantly, this new block may not fall into traditional right-left, conservative-liberal categories. Rather, after years of partisan gridlock and brand politics, we may be witnessing the slow emergence of a new political middle. Recent surveys have found a large number of voters, Republican, Democrat, and Independent, who actually agree on a wide range of issues—from abortion rights and background checks to the minimum wage and the separation of church and state. And while these new centrists hardly vote as one, notes Kathleen Parker, a right-of-center columnist at *The Washington Post*, "what they share is greater than the sum of the extreme parts. Mostly they share a disdain for ideological purity."[41] Certainly, that block made its presence known in the 2012 election, when a backlash to Tea Party extremism contributed to decisive Republican defeats. But Middle America wasn't simply rejecting the imbalanced politics of the extreme right. It was affirming an older, more balanced idea of America. As E. J. Dionne Jr., the *Post*'s liberal columnist and author of *Our Divided Political Heart*, puts it, the 2012 election was essentially an endorsement of the postwar consensus about the proper balance between "individualism and community, private and public endeavor, the market's achievements and government's essential role in cleaning up the problems the market leaves behind."[42]

Conservative politicians might not have used precisely those terms. But certainly, in the aftermath of the 2012 election, it was clear that mainstream Republicans were, at the very least, ready to take back the party from extremists and move the "brand" back toward the center. The rebuke of the Tea Party in late 2013 was a clear sign that even in the cloistered realm of Washington politics—the ultimate in "sorted" communities—there is recognition that the status quo is no longer sufficient.

Cynics might argue that the Tea Party's defeat came at the behest of the business community and the finance sector especially—players who feared that Tea Party extremism was undermining the Republican Party's ability to forestall regulatory reform. But the rebuke also reflected the fact that our political culture has finally reached a tipping point. Voters are clearly fed up after what has now been decades of political trench warfare. And, frankly, even some of the more ideologically minded lawmakers seemed relieved that the Tea Party rebellion stumbled. At a very basic, human level, the aftermath of the government shutdown provided all sides with a much-needed break. After months of relentlessly escalating partisanship, lawmakers were able to step back, however briefly, and get some distance from the treadmill that is driving our political culture toward the precipice. It was in that newly opened space that lawmakers managed to craft some small but crucial compromise bills. No one expected the peace to last. The discord machine was clearly just pausing in preparation for the midterm elections in 2014. But even the temporary respite was enough to let us see that what political players need, first and foremost, is a way to step back from the political machine and create some space—space to reflect, to deliberate, to *choose* a course of action rather than simply allowing the machine's momentum to drive our decisions and strategies and destiny. Ironically, in that brief moment, it was as if Washington, capital city for the Impulse Society, was showing the rest of us how that society might be disarmed.

Part Three

We Society

CHAPTER 9

Making Space

On some levels, the revolt against the Impulse Society has been under way for decades. In any community, on any day of the week, you can find people working diligently and often desperately to put a little space between themselves and a socioeconomic system that prioritizes efficiency and quick returns over any other values. It might be the family down the street that decides one day to unplug from smartphones and social networks in the hope of reclaiming some familial intimacy. Or it might be the overworked software engineer who talks his boss into a leave of absence so he can get to know his own preschool kids. It's the lady who no longer shops online or uses credit cards because she is tired of being stalked by third-party marketers and Russian cyber thieves. It's the political junkie who swears off Fox and Daily Kos because he sees the media echo chamber destroying his belief in democracy. And certainly it's someone such as Brett Walker, setting himself free from the digital underworld. This uprising against the Impulse Society may be undeclared. But it's happening anywhere people have recognized that they're going to lose something essential and irreplaceable unless they get some distance from the inertia, expectations, and values of a socioeconomic treadmill running largely on autopilot.

Our acts of insubordination are driven by desperation and anger—but also by a loss of faith. In the aftermath of our financial and political meltdowns, many of us no longer trust the basic structures and assumptions underlying society. It's not only that our confidence in the political system is at a historic low. We've also concluded, many of us, that our economic system is effectively working against us—that it has been so thoroughly corrupted by a quick-returns, winner-take-all mentality that income inequality, corporate brutality, and periodic market meltdowns are the new reality. We've seen the other kinds of market failure as well. We've seen the religion of cost cutting taken to absurd, even destructive extremes—as when Bangladesh sweatshops collapse because contractors skimp on concrete; or when a corner-cutting oil company spews a hundred million gallons of crude into the Gulf. We've seen the way Big Data and other digital technologies have mainly provided big business with new tools to track and manipulate us with the stealth of our national security apparatus. More fundamentally, we've seen the breakdown not only of the efficient market, but also of the "market society"—one that promised to lift the commonwealth via the unfettered pursuit of self-interest, but that instead brought us a mainstream culture so fragmented by the quest for immediate gratification, and so emptied of tradition and meaning, that even many middle-of-the-road, decidedly unradical individuals have woken up to the profound difference between getting what you want and getting what you need.

Yet our efforts at pushing back against this wayward system have been halting. We may recognize the need to reassert more humane priorities, but the structural drivers that gave rise to the Impulse Society are still very much in place and entirely unmoved by our dissatisfaction. The economic realities of globalization and the technology treadmill continue to grind down any form of inefficiency. Investors remain just as intent in the hunt for yield; executive compensation and corporate strategy are still in the thrall of quarterly earnings and share price. Politicians and political machines are still rewarded for extremism and quick wins. Consumer culture, meanwhile, continues to insist that a life defined increasingly by "me" and "now" is not only appropriate but necessary—and that any real effort to step back or unplug is to risk falling behind and failing.

And in some ways, consumer culture is right. Psychologically, many of us are so beholden to the relentless propositions of the Impulse Society that to create even a small measure of space around us would feel like real exile. And economically, one needn't be paranoid to fear that unplugging will be harshly penalized. This isn't your grandfather's booming, forgiving, encouraging economy, where the prosperity of previous generations allowed us to take chances, as individuals and as a society. The mood today is far more cautious and restrained—even fearful. In the current job market, to unplug even momentarily—say, by refusing to be on call 24/7 or to become known as the "outspoken" employee—is to run the very real risk of permanent banishment from the job market. As a result, our acts of space creation tend to be more modest and less openly defiant—more focused on day-to-day self-preservation than on anything remotely approaching social transformation. This wariness afflicts our entire culture, from the lone worker afraid to leave a soul-killing job to CEOs and politicians unwilling to take on their respective establishments. Some of this is simple pragmatism, but there is a large element here of capitulation: it's as if we believe that everything happening today—the short-termism and the economic inequality, the personal excess and extreme self-absorption, the "I-trumps-we" culture—is inevitable, the logical outcome of an efficient socioeconomic evolution that, by definition, is producing the maximum possible good. Simply put, the Impulse Society is what social progress looks like now.

But this is manifestly and demonstrably false. There are other possible economic outcomes, with different social and cultural consequences. We could point to alternative models in western Europe and parts of Asia—Germany, say, or Singapore—where societies have significantly different expectations for their economic systems—and significantly less tolerance for the excesses and indignities we regard as unavoidable. For that matter, Americans need look no further than our own history to see how a people can choose to make the economy produce more of what is necessary for individuals and for society as a whole. Conservatives often dismiss such alternative scenarios, whether from abroad or from our own past, as case studies in liberal overreach and unwarranted government intrusion into the marketplace—and these complaints are not entirely undeserved. But the basic argument—that it is possible and thus necessary to take steps to produce more sustainable, equitable, humane economic outcomes—is neither flawed nor particularly "liberal."

From the very beginnings of the Industrial Revolution, it was understood that "commercial society," as Adam Smith called capitalism, would need constant poking and prodding and nudging to ensure that its massive efficiencies benefited as wide a public as possible. As Smith wrote in *The Wealth of Nations*,[1] "No society can surely be flourishing and happy, of which the far greater part of the members are poor and miserable." Today, conservatives routinely invoke Smith and his invisible hand to argue for unfettered markets. But in fact, Smith recognized that markets needed occasional fettering—he favored, among other things, a progressive tax on the wealthy and, especially, hefty regulation of finance to prevent the consolidation of economic power in the hands of the few. Such regulatory intrusions, Smith readily acknowledged, were "in some respect a violation of natural liberty" of bankers and others with economic power. But this measured reduction in the individual liberty of the few was essential if a nation were serious in its efforts to protect "the security of the whole society."[2] As Dutch economic essayist Thomas Wells puts it, "Commercial society was for Smith an ethical project whose greatest potential benefits had to be struggled for." The success of that project,

Wells notes, "was not predetermined, but had to be worked for."[3] The question for us is, toward what end? What is the "output" we hope to achieve from a post-Impulse economy and how might we begin to get there?

MORE IS STILL BETTER . . . RIGHT?

Fittingly, Smith offers us a good place to start, with his notion of "the security of the whole society." One of the ironies of the Impulse Society is that, having internalized and institutionalized the values of the efficient market, our culture has atomized into a cloud of separate individuals (consumers but also corporations and even political parties) all seeking their own self-interest. This fragmentation has been hugely successful for individuals—or at least, some individuals—because it has allowed and encouraged greater individual advancement: more wealth, more consumption, more gratification and self-expression generally. But fragmentation has also steadily undermined the "the security of the whole society," in part because it has recast the meaning of individual existence. We've gone from being members of a "whole society" to being competitors in a race for individual gratification. What has emerged is a Darwinian, winner-take-all struggle that leaves little obvious space for social goals or even for the idea of a "commonwealth," because it is no longer a wealth that is shared.

Nothing captures this unsustainable state of affairs more acutely than our insistence that the health of the society can be measured simply by looking at the rate of economic growth. As long as the economy is cranking out more—more factories, more units, more returns—at a lower cost, we tell ourselves that everything is proceeding as it should be. Such a fiction has a basis in fact, of course. Historically, a larger pie has meant bigger slices for everyone. During the postwar period especially, rapid, efficient growth brought not only more wealth, but better jobs and wages; more innovative, helpful products; and higher aspirations, which lifted society as a whole. Since the rise of the Impulse Society, however, that connection has faltered. In recent decades, we've demonstrated that it's possible to have a roaring GDP and a failing society. It's not simply that more and more of the growth is being rerouted to a smaller population of beneficiaries, via the efficiencies of financialization and crony capitalism. It's also that, in a socioeconomic system whose values are set by the marketplace, economic "success" no longer necessarily coincides with social success. Indeed, it is part of the perverse nature of the self-centered economy that our social failures are often the source of our roaring GDP. In a corporate environment increasingly skewed toward quick wins, quarterly earnings, and share price, companies (and their managers) can succeed, and GDP can soar through strategies that are profoundly destabilizing for employees and society as a whole. This disconnect is one of the reasons U.S. companies can be rewarded for spending roughly half a trillion dollars a year on share buybacks even as wages stagnate, investment in worker training declines, and corporate spending on long-term basic research is in free fall. Under an economic model that makes no distinction between activity that is genuinely productive and activity that is merely "capitally efficient," there is no formal tension between artificially engineered shareholder profits and a workforce that slips further down Maslow's hierarchy of needs every year.

But this paradoxical relationship between economic growth and social decline isn't confined to the corporate landscape; it's a signature pattern across the Impulse Society. A sick patient is worth more than a healthy one, because the former generates far more in the way of revenues. A shuttered small-town downtown is worth more than a vibrant one because the former implies that the global retail supply chain has successfully eliminated another inefficiency. Deforestation, maxed-out credit cards, rising atmospheric carbon dioxide, increasing rates of prescription drug abuse—all count as net growth because they reflect the movement of more units through a system that registers only short-term gain and ignores long-term costs. Just as perversely, even as our growth- and efficiency-obsessed economy fails to properly account for social costs, it also largely ignores much of the real wealth we create outside normal economic channels. Activities that don't involve a commercial transaction: volunteering at the senior center, for example, or teaching your children to cook at home instead of eating out, or playing with them after dinner instead of turning them loose with their gadgets—none of these is credited with adding to GDP, even though all are arguably as vital to our economic health as anything we might buy. As journalist and policy wonk Jonathan Rowe once quipped, under our current standards of economic success, "the worst families in America are those that actually function as families—that cook their own meals, take walks after dinner, and talk together instead of just farming the kids out to the commercial culture. Cooking at home, talking with kids, walking instead of driving, involve less expenditure of money than do their commercial counterparts. Solid marriages involve less expenditure for counseling and divorce. Thus they are threats to the economy as portrayed in the GDP."

For decades, activists of various stripes have argued that our disastrously singular focus on growth should be replaced by a new economic measure that accounts for the costs and benefits that efficient markets get so wrong. In the 1980s and 1990s, some economists proposed replacing the concept of GDP with a more complex metric that considered nonfinancial social costs and benefits—in the hope that such a new metric would gradually encourage countries and companies to take a broader approach to economic success. As Joseph Stiglitz, a former World Bank economist involved in some of these efforts, later explained, "What you measure affects what you do. If you don't measure the right thing, you don't do the right thing."[4]

Those early efforts didn't garner a lot of political support. In fact, in the 1990s, Congress threatened to defund federal agencies studying what a new GDP might look like. But since the financial crisis, the idea of a new economic metric has gained some momentum and has fostered a broad and very necessary debate about what, exactly, our economy is supposed to be producing—and what a new, more genuinely productive economy might look like. It's still merely talk at this point. But even to have that discussion is a critical first step among many toward taking back control of our destiny.

Some of the proposals to emerge from this debate are not for the faint of heart. Herman Daly, another former World Bank economist and the current godfather of environmental economics, has proposed what he calls a "steady state economy," in which society works aggressively and deliberately with regulations, taxes, and other policy levers to confine all economic activity "within the regenerative and assimilative capacities of the ecosystem."[5]* The concept of economic growth within natural limits has been developed further by environmentalists, among them Bill McKibben, whose "deep economy" would shape economic activity to maximize three outputs currently excluded by GDP: long-term, ecological sustainability; income equality; and human happiness. Such an economy, as McKibben told *Salon* a few years ago, is one that "cares less about quantity than about quality; that takes as its goal the production of human satisfaction as much as surplus material; and that is focused on the idea that it might endure and considers durability at least as important as increases in size."[6]

Proposals like these, which call for a more or less complete overhaul of the capitalist system, or a rejection of capitalism entirely,

---

* Daly would curb our appetite for unsustainable growth by, among other things, requiring a heavy tax on raw materials (to limit endlessly rising throughput) and taxes and subsidies aimed at reducing massive income inequality. In Daly's view, the ratio between the richest and the median worker should be no greater than one hundred to one. The idea, Daly argues, is to create an economic model "that rewards real differences and contributions rather than just multiplying privilege."

will not sit well with mainstream culture. This is especially true in a culture, like ours, that has never really flirted with alternatives to a market economy and which, for all the growing pessimism, still regards the status quo as fixable. Far more palatable to us are ideas that fall under the label "liberal" or "progressive," and that aim to push the existing socioeconomic system toward a more sustainable, humane trajectory through smaller, more politically plausible adjustments in our economic assumptions and goals. For example, some environmentally inclined economists (and economically minded environmentalists) want to bolster GDP by adding a metric for carbon—that is, a measurement of how much carbon dioxide the U.S. economy generates for every dollar of economic output—and tie that metric to a tax on carbon. In theory, by making carbon more expensive, the market then automatically begins to search out low- and no-carbon technologies. Granted, such a tax is still a stretch in the current political climate. But many economic policy experts, including such prominent conservative economists as former Reagan adviser Arthur Laffer and Romney adviser Gregory Mankiw,[7] expect that a carbon tax will eventually emerge as the most practical way to curb CO_2 emissions while encouraging a boom in next-generation energy technologies.

Other progressive notions include metrics that look beyond economic growth to the human benefits that economic growth is supposed to provide. Stiglitz and fellow economist Amartya Sen, for example, proposed targeting such real-life measures as individual incomes, the availability of health care, and the quality and accessibility of education.[8] Others want existing government metrics (such as the Federal Reserve's inflation target) adjusted to match new, more socially progressive goals. Liberal economists such as Dean Baker and Paul Krugman, for instance, have argued that the current emphasis on keeping inflation low, through "austerity" cuts to government spending, is one of the reasons that unemployment has remained so high. "It's not that we just get a natural [high] rate of unemployment," Baker says. "We got there because of fiscal policy."

The point here is that we have much more influence over economic outcomes, such as unemployment or access to health care, than is often portrayed in the media or by free-market advocates. Governments have levers they can pull (taxes, subsidies, regulations, and the like) to shift the social "outputs" of the economy based on social and political priorities. For much of the last four decades, we have used those levers selectively, erring in favor of letting markets determine the optimal mix of social outputs, and the optimal balance among competing social goals. But that abdication to the market is no longer feasible: left to itself, the market grows corrupt and increasingly favors outcomes that are short-term, unfair, and simply unsustainable. If we want different results, we're going to have to take the system off autopilot and start steering again.

More fundamentally, we're going to need to have a real debate about where we want our economy to go and what our economic priorities and values are. Are we satisfied with the current shift in returns toward capital, or do we think the balance should be tipped back toward workers? Are we comfortable with a technology treadmill dedicated to incremental innovation and quick wins, or do we want to make the sort of high-stakes technology bets that could jump-start new industries while addressing some serious resource issues? Should we tolerate an economic order that leaves a growing number of us unable to protect the things we truly value, or one that aims to give working families the same opportunities, security, and confidence their parents and grandparents enjoyed? These are hardly simple questions. They are complex and necessitate real trade-offs. Managing those trade-offs will require patience and a willingness to deliberate and to compromise—criteria that our political culture (and the Impulse Society generally) does not prioritize and, indeed, regards as inefficiencies to be bypassed or eliminated altogether.

Nonetheless, to come up with a new set of metrics, one that looks past GDP and bottom-line profit-and-loss calculations and seeks instead to gauge the health of our whole society, would be an important step in moving away from the imperatives of the Impulse Society. It would force us into a broad, society-wide discussion about what we value and the sorts of trade-offs necessary to support those values. More fundamentally, it would pave the way for action to begin bringing those values back to the fore. And action is critical. One could argue that because any such efforts will ultimately depend on our political system and the give-and-take of our democratic process, our first steps must be in the political sphere. And yet, because the main drivers of the Impulse Society are economic and, more specifically, corporate, it's logical to turn first to a handful of practical steps that could be taken in the business world (and which, in fact, are already under discussion) to begin to change the course of business in society at large.

TELLING THE MARKET TO BACK OFF

For decades, conservatives complained that government was so deeply embedded in the economy, and had so much influence on the decisions of producers and consumers alike, that prosperity was no longer possible. Today, we can make a similar complaint about the financial markets, whose penetration into every part of our economic lives lies at the heart of the Impulse Society. In everything from the expansion of consumer credit to the rise of "activist" shareholders, the financial sector has gradually injected its requirements for high yields, quick returns, and capital efficiency into all walks of commercial life—and much of the rest of society as well. Financialization's most infamous symptom is the overuse of consumer credit, and, clearly, we could strike a serious blow against the Impulse Society by helping consumers to rethink the practice of gratifying the present by borrowing from the future. More important, however, has been financialization's influence on the behavior of businesses and especially large businesses, which play such an oversize role in everything from employment and innovation to public policy. Reducing finance's influence in the business world is thus a key step in breaking the economic foundations of the Impulse Society and allowing the reemergence of a more sustainable, socially productive economic system.

At the corporate level, financialization's most pernicious effects show up in myopic strategies that sacrifice long-term stability for short-term gain. As we've seen, industries that once made substantial long-term investments in innovation and in their workforces do less of both in order to satisfy the equally shortsighted agendas of large investors. To curb this tendency, we need to eliminate the incentives that now make short-termism so attractive to investors and corporations, and there is no shortage of proposals to do just that. Many experts have called for a transaction tax on investors each time they buy or sell a security, derivative, or other financial asset. By making it more expensive to chase incremental changes in stock price, the tax might encourage investors to hold company shares for longer periods. That, in turn, could take some of the quarterly earnings pressure off company executives and let them embrace a longer-term approach to cost cutting, employees, and investment in innovation.

Other proposals target the perverse incentives of executive compensation—for example, by paying senior executives with "restricted" stock that can't be sold for five years or for several years after an executive leaves a company, thus removing the enticement to go for quick earnings boosts.[9] (Under one proposal, companies would even be able to "claw back" stock compensation if, as *The Wall Street Journal* put it, "a business built on short-term risk-taking blows up."[10]) Another particularly intriguing idea calls for linking compensation to innovation: pay depends on how much of a company's current profits are being generated from products based on newly developed technologies.[11]

Executives themselves have shown little warmth for such ideas. But experts who study compensation and corporate governance say many companies would welcome the chance to bring compensation under control for very self-serving reasons. Sky-high executive compensation not only hurts employee morale and invites constant criticism from the media and politicians, but also rarely correlates with corporate performance.[12] To the contrary, one study found that two out of five of the highest-paid American CEOs had been at companies that were either bailed out or busted for fraud, or had themselves been terminated.

In the same vein, advocates for a definancialized business sector would severely restrict the practice of share buybacks, which currently presents executives with far too great a temptation to stoke their own compensation by financially engineering a higher share price. Anti-buyback advocates note that the federal government could fairly easily prohibit buybacks simply by rescinding a rule change made under Reagan by the U.S. Securities and Exchange Commission in 1982. Prior to that rule change, buybacks were formally recognized for what they are: an illegal manipulation of the market. It's time to call a spade a spade.

What all these initiatives have in common is a serious interest in pushing companies back onto a longer strategic horizon. That's critical for such issues as long-term investment in innovation. But it's even more important for the future of labor. We're not going to turn off the automation trend, any more than we're going to halt global trade. But companies could significantly change the way these trends impact labor by restoring the idea that the workforce isn't merely a cost to be reduced, but rather, a prized asset to be assiduously maintained and upgraded. This idea was largely discarded during the shareholder revolution, when management, newly fixated on any cost reductions that might boost quarterly earnings and share price, ratcheted back investments in worker training—and then cut workers when they couldn't compete with machines or cheap foreign labor. Compounding the crisis, even as companies cut staff, there was little effort to preserve the skills in that rapidly growing army of unemployed. Contrast this with what occurred in many European countries, where firms are required to play a major role in assisting laid-off workers with retraining, to ensure that expertise—(human capital)—isn't simply lost. It's an effort that has paid off in the past: as recessions end, European companies can much more quickly put laid-off workers back to work. In the United States, retraining efforts have historically been far less comprehensive—thanks in no small part to the conservative, antitax, antigovernment politics that flowered in the 1980s. As a result, American policy for coping with long-term job loss is patchwork and decidedly myopic. We praise ourselves for extending unemployment benefits, but there is little effort to address the deeper problem systematically; for example, by keeping tabs on the unemployed as they try to find work or retrain themselves. "No one even knows who these people are," says economist William Lazonick. "There is a huge waste of human capital going on in the United States—people who have had lots of education and lots of experience—the things we need or that we claim we need [for a manufacturing renaissance]—but they're just being thrown out of work and there is no institutional mechanism for preserving that human capital."

For many liberals today, the go-to solution has been to increase the corporate tax rate and reallocate growing corporate profits to fund long-neglected areas such as worker retraining. And liberals have a strong case: since 2000, conservatives have cut taxes far too steeply to cover mounting government expenditures for, among other things, two wars and an ongoing recession-recovery effort. And lest conservatives forget, this isn't the first time they've cut too deeply: in 1981, newly elected president Reagan slashed taxes so sharply that the national debt more than quadrupled, to three trillion dollars.[13] The difference then was that Reagan recognized the mistake and subsequently raised taxes four times over the next seven years[14]—including the steepest increase in corporate income tax in history and a hike in payroll taxes that was used to fund Medicare.* Today, by contrast, the conservative brand has grown so reflexively antitax and antigovernment that a tax increase can't be discussed, even while much of the nation's workforce falls behind other countries' and public infrastructure decays.

Before liberals put on the tax-and-spend hats, however, we should acknowledge the absurdity of taxing corporations to fund the retraining of workers that corporations themselves have jettisoned. A far better approach would be to induce those same reprobate firms, perhaps through tax credits, to use some of that pretax wealth to better their treatment of their labor "asset." Lazonick, for example, argues that if big firms took even a small fraction of the cash currently spent on share buybacks and reallocated it to ongoing employee training, they would boost their productivity and innovation. That could reduce the need for layoffs in the first place—and, at the very least, would make it easier for laid-off workers to find work elsewhere. Take the case of Apple: with 5 percent of the one hundred billion dollars Apple has committed to share buybacks, the company could create an internal "university" for its employees, with top-notch instructors and accredited programs in skills that are in demand both inside Apple and in the tech sector generally. Such a program, Lazonick says, would be free to all employees— not least the roughly forty thousand currently working in Apple's retail stores—and would let them train for promotions within the company or reenter the job market with a substantially improved résumé and job skills. Lazonick says such in-house universities are common in

---

* As *The Daily Beast*'s Peter Beinart quipped a few years ago, "Let's put this in language today's tea-baggers can understand: Reagan raised taxes to pay for government-run health care."

developing countries such as India, where corporations recognize the long-term self-interest of expanding the overall pool of trained personnel in the industry. Contrast this to the United States, where many firms, in classic Impulse style, cope with skill shortages as cheaply as possible: by lobbying Washington to let in more skilled immigrants from places such as India.

Granted, a few wealthy companies launching in-house universities will hardly bring back the paternalistic corporate welfare state of the postwar period. But such initiatives would send a powerful message through the business community, which already seeks to emulate the strategies of megasuccessful companies such as Apple. More fundamentally, such initiatives would serve as a powerful acknowledgment that the dominant values of the current socioeconomic model simply aren't sustainable. Relegating labor to a mere "cost" may have seemed eminently logical thirty years ago, but it has fostered an animosity in the workforce that is becoming harder for corporations to manage. By stepping back from that unsustainable strategy, and putting some distance between workers and the ruthless imperatives and bottom-line values of the efficient market, companies might begin to restore the collective aspirations that once made the American workforce the most productive in the world—before such aspirations were eliminated by the efficient market as merely another inefficiency.

At the end of the day, however, the economic imbalances of the Impulse Society won't be corrected by voluntary corporate initiatives to retrain workers or tackle short-termism.* Financialization is so entrenched in the economy that it will eventually require outside intervention not simply to restore an equitable balance between labor and capital, but also to shield us all from the devastating corrections that are inevitable under a quick-returns, winner-take-all business model term yield. Fittingly, the most compelling argument for such

---

* See the less-than-total triumph of the "corporate sustainability" movement.

draconian, top-down action is found in the financial sector itself, which shows little inclination to fix its own worst practices voluntarily. To the contrary, the big investment banks not only are engaging in many of the same high-risk behaviors that took down the economy in 2008, but are now so large as to be effectively beyond the sort of conventional regulatory fixes that might prevent another meltdown. Consider: just twelve banks, including JPMorgan, Citicorp, and Goldman Sachs, control 69 percent of the entire U.S. banking industry[15]—a share so large that, no matter how egregious or reckless the banks' behavior, the government can't let them fail lest they take the rest of the economy down with them. Indeed, megabanks are not only too big to fail or regulate, but also too big for government even to prosecute for blatantly criminal activities. As U.S. attorney general Eric Holder admitted in congressional testimony in 2013, U.S. megabanks are so large that "if you do bring a criminal charge, it will have a negative impact on the national economy, perhaps even the world economy."[16] As the saying goes, megabanks are not only "too big to fail," but "too big to jail."

For this reason, financial policy experts have long argued that the risks of a financialized economy won't truly be curbed until so-called TBTF ("too big to fail") banks have been broken up into smaller, more regulatable entities. And while such an extreme measure may seem wildly improbable in the current partisan climate, the case can be made that this would be not only a politically feasible initiative, but precisely the sort of initiative that could clear a path through the political paralysis of Impulse politics.

THE END OF BRAND POLITICS

The Impulse Society's biggest ally isn't the technology treadmill or the relentless drive for efficiency; rather, it's the current impasse in our political culture, and our culture generally, over the proper role of government as the fixer of social ills. This is hardly a novel debate. Over the last century, the consensus has swung from the liberal-progressive conceit that government can and should fix every social problem to the more recent conservative conceit (equally absurd) that government can fix none of them and shouldn't try. Granted, conservatives can point to supporting evidence. Government is not particularly efficient at allocating resources or predicting outcomes or harnessing personal ambition—those are things markets have always done better. Nor can government ever be a substitute for community, or family, or an attitude of individual self-reliance—though governments have certainly tried often enough. But government has always had a critical relationship to these economic and social functions; it can make space for them. Government can encourage the market's allocative and motivational efficacies by attacking the corrupting influence of the rentiers and gamers. And, just as important, government can make it easier for Americans to flourish as communities, families, and self-reliant individuals by providing them with some measure of protection from material risks. Government can offer some security from accidents and natural disasters, for example, or from tyrannical and repressive local majorities—or, as we've focused on here, from the predations of the marketplace that would otherwise steamroller family, community, tradition, and culture. In some cases, *only* federal government has the power to stop that steamroller. It's hardly coincidental that the withdrawal of the government from the marketplace, beginning in the 1980s, has paralleled the emergence of many of the socially fragmenting economic patterns that constitute the Impulse Society.

Again, the necessity of this governmental role is hardly a liberal idea. It was a central insight of an earlier generation of Republicans—not least the reform-minded Republicans of the Progressive Era, who recognized that only the federal government had the capacity to take on corporations grown so large from their efficiencies, technologies, and monopolistic strategies that they were otherwise unstoppable. If there were ever a time for another intervention, this would be it—except that our political culture is hobbled. It has been corrupted by the forces of financialization, which have converted the political process into a "sector," almost indistinguishable from the finance sector, where dollars are now as important as votes. As serious, however, the political process has been all but paralyzed by a "brand" conservatism. That brand reflexively dismisses government's proper role as a backstop for essential social and economic functions—and then refuses to acknowledge that it was the withdrawal of that backstop role that enabled much of the financial corruption that has hurt communities, families, and individuals. Again and again, our contemporary brand of conservatism finds itself in opposition to the very values that conservatives have traditionally fought to defend.

Yet in this contradiction is a way forward. It's worth noting that some of the loudest voices calling for financial reform are conservative. Likewise, when the Obama administration failed to break up the TBTF banks or to restrict their capacity to make high-risk gambles, the failure outraged not only liberals but many on the right as well. To genuine conservatives, the implicit guarantee of a government bailout is nothing but a market-distorting government subsidy that allows TBTF banks to take risks that smaller banks must avoid. Says Richard Fisher, a conservative economist and president of the Federal Reserve Bank of Dallas, "Such firms capture the financial upside of their actions but largely avoid payment—bankruptcy and closure—for actions gone wrong, in violation of one of the basic tenets of market capitalism (at least as it is supposed to be practiced in the United States)."[17] Conservative antipathy for TBTF banks is so strong that in 2013, David Vitter, a staunchly conservative Republican senator from Louisiana, joined the very liberal Democrat Sherrod Brown of Ohio on a bill to force megabanks to dramatically cut the amount of debt they take on. Although the bill was stalled by the banking lobby, it garnered broad bipartisan support, not least among conservative commentators such as Peggy Noonan at *The Wall Street Journal* and *The Washington Post*'s George Will (for whom TBTF exemplifies "the pernicious practice of socializing losses while keeping profits private"[18]). Put another way, in the fight to reregulate TBTF banks, we have an opportunity not only to take on financialization, but also to open much-needed political space where the right and the left might begin to shift back to the bipartisanship that was routine before politics became a form of winner-take-all brand warfare.

One could imagine how such a bipartisan moment might unfold. It begins with an appearance by the Fed's Fisher on Fox News, laying out a plan he and colleagues introduced in early 2013 that would force TBTF banks to separate into smaller, more manageable entities. (The key would be to withdraw the federal safety net from all but traditional lending activities and to empower regulators to disassemble banks that declined to reorganize voluntarily.[19]) Fisher's plan would reverberate through the conservative blogosphere, but it would also resonate in the left-leaning media. As public support swelled, Senators Vitter and Brown would fold the Fisher plan into new legislation that would enjoy broad bipartisan backing. The dozen or so TBTF banks would lobby heavily to kill the measure, but with popular opinion firmly against them, their bargaining position would be weak. Even if the megabanks avoided outright breakups, they likely would be forced to accept a reimposition of a Glass-Steagall-like Depression-era firewall between their commercial lending and their investment activities. The financial sector would now be free of a major source of systemic risk. As important, partisans inside and outside Washington would have demonstrated the capacity for consensus on an issue of national importance. That kind of political success could strike a serious blow against impulse politics, which currently feed on discord and dysfunction. By providing a clear example of the political process in

action, the divisive political brands that both liberals and conservatives have created in recent decades would be weakened.

This has happened before. Keith Poole, a political scientist at the
University of Georgia and an expert in political polarization, notes
that the United States did "depolarize" just over a century ago, as
moderates from both parties united under efforts to reform business.
For history to repeat itself, Poole says, we'd need to see the election
of dozens of moderate candidates from both parties. And while that
hasn't been possible in an era of deep polarization (which tends to put
off moderate candidates), that could change, Poole says, "if there are
more deals between the two parties in Congress, thereby making
moderate positions more attractive for candidates."[20] A campaign to
disassemble the big banks might be just the sort of deal.

And even a temporary weakening of brand politics could provide
a crucial beachhead for the real assault on impulse politics. With a few
more moderates in its ranks, Congress might finally have the capacity
to take on the final and deepest form of financialization, and the ultimate expression of the Impulse Society: campaign finance. Since the
Citizens United ruling in 2010, hundreds of millions of dollars in
contributions from so-called super-PACs have all but completed the
financialization of politics: no longer does our political system merely
mirror the market; now it has merged with the market. Traditionally,
this is an issue that liberals have owned. And, indeed, liberal
Democrats such as Elizabeth Warren and New York governor Andrew
Cuomo clearly see the issue's potential to become, as *Capital New
York* magazine put it, "a big-ticket item with national implications—as
big, if not bigger, than [*sic*] gay marriage and gun control."[21] And yet,
there is no reason that campaign finance reform couldn't become a
rallying issue for conservatives as well. The separation of economics
and politics is actually a conservative principle—or was, before the
sluicing of campaign contributions corrupted those on both the right
and the left. As Barry Goldwater, the godfather of the modern

conservative movement, noted back in 1960, "In order to achieve the widest possible distribution of political power, financial contributions to political campaigns should be made by individuals alone. I see no reason for labor unions—or corporations—to participate in politics. Both were created for economic purposes and their activities should be restricted accordingly." And, in fact, although congressional Republicans have been largely uninterested in taking up campaign finance reform, there are signs that the issue is catching fire among conservatives outside Washington. Polls show considerable support among conservative voters and state lawmakers for a constitutional amendment that would exclude corporations, unions, and other organizations from free speech protections for megasize campaign donations. According to one poll, seven of ten Republicans support such an amendment.[22] "The fact is, a great many people feel that they're not being heard, that their interests are being passed over to promote the interests of Big Business and Big Labor," notes Chris Myers, a conservative blogger on *Red State*. "But here's a chance for conservatives to demonstrate clearly that we stand for what people really care about. Isn't that what we always say we're trying to do, anyway?"[23]

What is interesting is that, in the wake of the Tea Party melt-down, we're already seeing conservative thought leaders shifting toward the center—and away from the brand conservatism of Impulse politics. As Ross Douthat, one of *The New York Times*' conservative columnists, has pointed out, a pragmatic, solutions-oriented "reform conservatism" has recently been emerging from center-right think tanks and from pragmatic conservative politicians concerned with the movement's currently suicidal trajectory. Reform conservatism's ideas—promoting early childhood education, for example, allowing states to manage their own transportation projects with their own fuel taxes—emphasize the brass tacks realism of traditional conservatism that has always appealed to Middle America. As important, that realism once formed the basis for a lot of bipartisan compromise and effective legislation. It was always the pragmatists on the left and on the right who found ways to work together on big issues, such as tax reform. And while pragmatism has been the first thing to suffer under brand politics in the Impulse Society, there are models for bringing it back. As David Brooks, another conservative voice at *The New York Times*, points out, conservative politicians of the nineteenth century— Abraham Lincoln, Henry Clay, Daniel Webster, and other Whigs— built powerful majorities by focusing on basic, nonpartisan issues such as social mobility and economic opportunity and, importantly, by "using the power of government to give marginalized Americans the tools to compete in a capitalist economy." This was an early, effective example of the politics of the middle. And, importantly, Brooks notes, Whigs advanced this pragmatic centrism as an alternative to the rancorous partisanship of the "divisive populist Jacksonians." For the practical Whigs, it was "better to help people move between classes than to pit classes against each other."[24] Brooks argues that an "opportunity coalition" today could enjoy similarly broad support by "scrambling the current political categories" and focusing on ways to improve social mobility—for example, by rebuilding early childhood education or helping disadvantaged families create better parenting patterns. Liberals might be tempted to dismiss this all as a desperate effort at self-preservation for a Republican Party on the brink of a internecine meltdown. But reform conservatism may also be the first step toward a new politics of the middle—an acknowledgment that, for most of us, the brand politics of either side never truly fit our concerns and aspirations. That realization may be an opening for political pragmatists of all stripes to refocus the debate on common interests and potential solutions. And such pragmatism, however tentative, could initiate a shift away from the cynical politics of brand and back toward a politics of reality and of possibility.

❖   ❖   ❖

Assuming such a politics of possibility itself becomes plausible once again, it's clear that we're going to need more than the reregulation of finance to steer the Impulse Society back on a more sustainable trajectory. One of the main benefits of getting finance out of the political system is that it would allow us to put politics back into finance—that is, to restore America's long-term obligation to essential public investments. In short, government would again be freer to do what government is best positioned to do: make the long-term commitments in the collective, public interest that are beyond the capacity or inclination of individuals, communities, or business. This was the logic behind the Progressive agenda a century ago: as the maturing consumer marketplace stepped up overall investment in private goods, government stepped in to ensure adequate investment in public goods.

Here, too, we find room for left-right compromise. Without question, liberals must concede to some degree of real entitlement reform (means testing for Medicare, for example) and regulatory reform, especially for small businesses. But conservatives, too, must move beyond their obsolete brand and acknowledge that after decades of reflexive tax cuts and partisan budget battles, the United States now suffers the largest deficit in public investment of any industrial economy. To cite a few examples: spending on roads, bridges, and other infrastructure falls short of need by around a quarter of a trillion dollars every year.[25] (Across the United States, reports *The Wall Street Journal*, state governments are allowing thousands of miles of road to "erode to gravel."[26]) In spending on early child care and education as a percentage of GDP, the United States ranks twenty-eighth out of thirty-seven developed countries. Twenty-three nations have faster broadband networks. The list is embarrassingly long. Nearly 90 percent of our energy still comes from fossil fuel—the Chinese government now spends nearly twice as much on clean energy research.

Reversing this deficit in public investment would require a substantial shift in the current political mind-set, which is now dominated by the branded conservative aversion to deficit spending or even a modest increase in taxes. But armed with an emerging bipartisan backing, political leaders could begin to make the case for increased investment in specific initiatives (for example, infrastructure and energy). Such a rhetorical campaign would emphasize the critical role that public investment played in previous booms—the postwar boom, but also the digital boom, which couldn't have happened without decades of heavy public spending. More fundamentally, it would make the case that a similar commitment today (for example, to fund research into next-generation energy technology) could jump-start an economic resurgence. Case in point: a significant commitment to research into nuclear fusion (where atoms are combined, rather than split, to produce vast amounts of energy) could yield the sort of game-changing technology needed for a third industrial revolution. Fusion is clean—there is little radiation produced—and the fuel (notably, a hydrogen isotope known as deuterium) is almost infinitely abundant in seawater. The potential here is for a low-carbon energy that is dramatically cheaper than anything on the market today. Given energy's central role in a globalized economy, this could fundamentally remake the economy and launch dozens of new or expanded sectors—all while allowing the phasing out of carbon-heavy fuels. Currently, federal support for fusion research is declining. But even a modest push for fusion—by some estimates, it would cost thirty billion dollars to develop a working fusion reactor by 2034—could pay extraordinary social returns. And while no company is willing to invest that much and wait so long for a return, this is precisely the sort of investment that government can, and should, make. As columnist George Will puts it, fusion "is a perfect example of a public good the private sector cannot pursue and the public sector should not slight."

*   *   *

Admittedly, pushing for greater public investment today would require the sort of sustained, vocal political commitment that mainstream politicians are increasingly wary of making: in the world of financialized, poll-tested, impulse politics, it's far more efficient to follow, or manipulate, voter sentiment than to lead it. Also, voters have been taught to fear public investment, or government generally, as invariably inefficient, unwarranted, and corrupt. But for those political leaders willing to move past "brand" politics, there is no shortage of historical precedent from which to take heart. In the early 1960s, John Kennedy grabbed voters with his vow to put a man on the moon by the end of the decade. In the 1950s, Eisenhower built public support for the national highway system, then the most costly public works project in history. During the Depression, Franklin Roosevelt repeatedly made the case for massive public works projects. And before that, Teddy Roosevelt crusaded for public spending on education, parks, and public health. These were hardly simple sales jobs. In pushing for public works spending, for example, Franklin Roosevelt carefully laid out the then-novel concept known as Keynesian economics: that government could restart a stalled economy by priming demand.

Today, our political leaders are less persuasive. Liberal economists have criticized Obama not only for failing to push through real financial reform; they have also complained that he has been unwilling to attack the efficient-markets ideology that helped bring on the financial crisis or to argue for the need for a fundamentally new direction in economic policy. The more cynical insist that Obama has been hobbled by his close ties to Wall Street. But one could equally argue that most of the American public, for all our professed hunger for "change we can believe in," was not truly prepared, philosophically, for the kind of change we truly needed. Rather, many of us are so anxious about economic conditions, and so distrustful of government and business, that we are losing the confidence to step beyond our personal interests and push for something larger. Put another way, we did not lend the president much in the way of assistance. And as *The Times'* Brooks points out, Obama has "been made aware of how little a president can accomplish unless there is organized support from the outside."[27]

Ideally, we can reverse this attitude of disengagement by altering the social and economic conditions feeding it. We can clean up politics and thus make citizens *want* to engage politically. We can use economic reform and public investment to revive the kind of economic opportunities that inspired earlier generations to "go large" and step outside of their narrow self-interest. By restoring the balance between citizen and marketplace, and between the marketplace and our political institutions, we enable individuals to shift back toward a more generous, broad-minded and long-term outlook.

To be sure, none of those high-level, systemic changes can happen unless citizens begin *demanding* that they happen—something that, admittedly, has become hard to imagine in recent decades. Thanks to political and economic corruption that has made us cynical and apathetic—and a consumer market that insists we can get what we want on our own—mainstream culture has gradually come to embrace the status quo and the idea of a market-led society, with all its widening imperfections and inequalities. But on an individual level, that acquiescence seems to be changing—out of necessity. For more and more of us, the status quo simply doesn't work anymore. We can no longer wish away the hollowing out of the middle class, the myopia of our business class, or our looming infrastructure failures. We can no longer ignore the absurdity that, in the richest nation in history, the average citizen is increasingly insecure and fearful of being left behind. Nor can we any longer persuade ourselves that our market and political systems will somehow reform themselves: the system is so broken that we no longer have the luxury of denial and apathy. More and more of us recognize that the pessimistic story lines that make the Impulse Society seem so intractable—the entrenched political dysfunction, the permanently myopic winner-take-all market, the chronic self-absorption of individuals—are themselves part of the Impulse Society, a meta brand that has made real reform seem impossible. But more of us see through this brand and know that reform *is* possible. Now, even as technocrats and academics and a few reform-minded politicians and businesspeople grapple with the myopia of the political system and the business world, the rest of us need to put that knowledge into action and step into the fray. Capitalizing on the urgency and unease that is now all but universal, we need to demonstrate, to ourselves and to the broader community, that change is possible and that the institutions now driving the Impulse Society can become bulwarks against it.

MIND THE GAP

A few years ago, a friend of mine took that sense of disquiet and acted on it. Marcie had been a rising star in a national architecture firm when she began to seriously question whether she was actually adding much in the way of value to society. She loved designing buildings, but the architecture profession has become so dominated by a cost-cutting, high-volume mentality that creativity is an ever-smaller part of the job. "Most of the time, you're just figuring out how to take money out of the project," Marcie told me. "You'd design something and everyone would love it and then they'd say, 'ok, let's "value-engineer" the hell out of it.' And I started thinking, 'this building was going to be standing for fifty years, with my name is on it, and I don't really agree with how we're doing it.'" As it happened, Marcie had been volunteering with the local school district and leading students tours of the architecture downtown. She loved the kids' enthusiasm and curiosity and the way that she could, in the space of a few hours, change how they saw the world—and somehow, those small transformations felt as creative and as important as anything she was doing at work.

Driving home from the office one evening, Marcie was listening to a radio interview with a politician. He was talking about why he had quit a lucrative job to run for public office, and he quoted the ancient line from Hillel the Elder— "And if I am only for myself, then what am I? And if not now, when?" The sentiment struck a chord with Marcie. "I thought, 'that's exactly how I feel. *I* want to do something that is more important, more valuable.'" So she quit. She left the architecture firm, went back to school for her master's in education, and now spends her days "designing" effective classroom experiences. "Just the impact you can have," she told me. "I mean, I can have a single conversation with a kid that will totally change his life." Marcie admits that stepping away from architecture wasn't easy. She was giving up not only a higher income, but also the ego strokes of a high-visibility job—"When you tell someone you're a teacher, they change the subject," Marcie says. But the further she moved from the professional treadmill she had been on, the more clearly she could see the disconnect between the market's definition of a "successful" job and the kind of success that reflected her own personal values—values tightly bound up with the need to be involved with, and to affect, the lives of others. "It was very much a kind of growing up and realizing, 'Ok, maybe teaching kids really is more important than imagining myself designing buildings.' And that's been true. I love it, and I've never looked back."

To me, Marcie's story is a poignant illustration of this idea of making space—of pushing back from the patterns and values of the Impulse Society so we can glimpse how out of balance things have become—but also so we can see how we might constructively respond to that imbalance. Earlier, we explored the need to create distance between the financial market and the economy and between the market and the political sphere. But to truly move beyond the

Impulse Society, we need to widen the gap between the individual and the market and begin reversing the century-long merger of market and self. Only then can the self gain some relief from the short-term values of the marketplace and reconnect to values that are more essential, more permanent, and more human. As important, it is only as we step back that we realize that much of what we're so frantically seeking in the consumer marketplace actually lies elsewhere. So much of what many of us hunger for today is *connection*—making deep, authentic, meaningful relationships with others; we're still driven, as sociologist Robert Nisbet put it half a century ago, by "the quest for community." We can't fulfill that quest, by definition, in a consumer culture that prioritizes immediate, self-centered satisfaction. Indeed, the connection we really long for here is the very opposite—a connection to something permanent and larger than ourselves. By seeking that connection in the marketplace, we have not only left this basic need unfulfilled, but have also undercut and weakened the very thing that could fulfill us.

So we push back—are already pushing back. Across the nation, we undertake a hundred million minor acts of defiance that reflect our different priorities and fears and choices. But ultimately, we must somehow acknowledge a larger unifying purpose. We need to leverage these individual quests for connection and community into the broad social and political actions that can protect and restore the values of community and the emphasis on larger, long-term goals. And this will only happen by acting collectively. If self and community have collapsed together under the Impulse Society, they must also rise together.

In a broad sense, we already know what to do. We understand, most of us, that the key to both the birth of the Impulse Society and to our hope of taming it lies in the relationship between the self and community. When this reciprocal relationship is healthy, it becomes mutually empowering. Community is healthy and the individual, shored up by the basic values of community—shared purpose, cooperation, self-sacrifice, patience, and long-term commitment—has the power to give back to community. The relationship becomes a virtuous circle, where each side is supported and enlarged by the other. Yes, we allowed that virtuous circle to break down. We persuaded ourselves that an individual could gain all necessary strength and resilience in the marketplace—and community would take care of itself. But as we personalized our gratification, the virtuous circle turned vicious, and the reciprocal relationship between self and community became mutually disempowering, weakening both self and community. This is the toxic reality at the heart of the Impulse Society. The more the market has freed us from the obligations and influences of community, the more our actual power and freedom as individuals has diminished—and the less we can resist the market's divide-and-conquer pattern, or even challenge the outcomes. Look at how we failed to halt the market's undermining of community. Or how willing so many of us have been to accept widening inequality as a fait accompli. In so many ways and on so many levels, the Impulse Society had us right where it wanted us.

But our acquiescence has reached a limit. The very act of pushing back from the market is itself a political act, an acknowledgment that we're not getting what we really need—but also that what we do need is close at hand. Moving clear of the values of the market, the values of community flow back into our lives. Even in modest measure, the pleasure and the sense of authenticity we gain from reconnecting can spur us to create more space so we can make that connection deeper and more lasting. Slowly but surely, the virtuous cycle begins to turn. It's hardly easy or assured. After decades of neglect, many of the social structures necessary for healthy communities have degraded and atrophied. And because many of us have slipped a rung or two down Maslow's ladder, we may lack the time or wherewithal to carve out the necessary space. Yet even in these circumstances, our search for social connection and a larger purpose persists. Give us even the smallest opportunity and encouragement—the creation of even the smallest space—and our desire to rejoin self and community breaks out and blooms like weeds in cracked city pavement, simultaneously reaching toward the sun while driving its roots deep into the foundations of the Impulse Society.

You can see this desire bloom every week at every church and synagogue and mosque as we turn to the collective and the communal to restore us. You can see it in the tribal energy of the Friday night high school football games and the gathered optimism of a high school graduation. You can see it in the certainty of purpose at a Rotary fundraiser, the intensity of a public land use hearing, the pleasures of a farmers' market. Perhaps most of all, you can see it in our near universal reverence for that most basic unit of community, the family, whose values—cooperation, nurturing, and long-term commitment—most of which were the values of the marketplace and the political arena. Our hunger for community and connection is there: what's missing is a concerted effort, at all levels of society, to clear away the political and economic debris—the structural biases, the corruption, and the brand cynicism—and let this quest for community drive us back into a more balanced, more sane position.

Even without wholesale reform, this move back toward community is already happening at the margins. Our growing obsession with "local" bespeaks a renewed appreciation for what Nisbet called "intermediate institutions," the family, church, neighborhood, school, and other small, local social structures that could support individuals and protect them from larger forces, whether natural or human-made. And such enthusiasm is well placed. It's at the local scale where social relationships have the intensity and frequency and sheer familiarity to most clearly show individuals the benefit of reciprocal connection between self and community. "Our ability to comprehend a common good, and our willingness to act on its behalf—to feel a sense of obligation and indebtedness to our inheritance from the past and a sense of duty born of gratitude toward the future—requires a fairly intimate scale," writes Patrick Deneen, an associate professor of constituitional studies at Notre Dame and an expert in classical thought. It's at the local scale that we can have "some sensory connection of our actions upon others and theirs upon us." Similarly, it's also at the local scale that we can most easily draw the distinction between the market and the nonmarket, and to underline the latter's values, such as authenticity, morality, quality, and community itself.

And yet, for all its importance, we should also acknowledge that this Jeffersonian ideal of small, tight, familiar communities is only part of the story of renewal. Local no longer describes the world we live in and our conception of "community" must be large enough to take in national and even global questions and diverse enough for the full spectrum of human experience and ingenuity. So, for instance, we clearly need to revive the idea of work as a real social connection and a legitimate, important locus of community. The era of commanding labor unions and workplace solidarity may or may not be recoverable. Regardless, if we're to have any chance of salvaging the middle class, "the worker" needs to reemerge as a member of collective, connected, self-aware, assertive community.

We also need to embrace the potential of new categories of community—even those that have come under fire in this account, notably the digital community. We need to be frank in our recognition that the online environment has serious limits as a venue for the kind of restorative community that is missing today; Facebook and Twitter are simply no substitute for the intimacy of a neighborhood meeting, a PTA fund-raiser, the family dinner—nor does "following" a political leader or cause excuse us from the civic obligations of state and national political engagement. More fundamentally, we need to acknowledge that digital social networks today fully embody the efficient market, with all of that market's treadmill patterns and emphasis on quick rewards, self-promotion, and incomplete, disposable interactions—the very things we're hoping to move away from. Yet if we could somehow contain the market aspect of the digital world—compartmentalize it or, more plausibly, make users more conscious of the market's ubiquitous presence in the digital realm (one imagines a mandatory "tech ed" for all sixth graders), the potential for this technology as a cornerstone for kinds of social connection we can't even imagine is probably unlimited. Think back to how the Internet began—a community brought together by a desire to share information out of the glare of mainstream culture. Why shouldn't that spirit animate a new arena for civic discourse—a larger and more routine version of the online town hall that is already emerging?

And yet, for all of digital's mixed blessings, we need to acknowledge the untapped community potential in the non-digital world. During the postwar period, decades before digital had even been imagined, we managed an incredible degree of community building and civic engagement and social capital. We mustn't let the dazzle of the digital world—and the relentless community-speak of its producers—distract us from the untapped potential to restore community "offline." There are literally thousands of venues for meaningful, important social connection—everything from volunteering to rec league sports to unplugged family nights—that offer ways to engage and restart the virtuous cycle between the individual and the larger community.

In fact, it is to the largest community that we must ultimately bring our rebuilding efforts. As important as small-scale efforts are, there is an urgent need to restore the idea of broad *national* community—one that reflects our obligations as citizens in a large, sprawling, troubled democracy. This national community may be entirely lacking in the intimacy and familiarity and genuineness of the more local variants. But given that many of the challenges we face require national scale and leverage, restoring a national community isn't something we have a choice about. Only a national community has the resources to tackle problems such as climate change or creating a new energy system. More fundamentally, only a functional, moderately cohesive national community can set the larger goals for our entire society— priorities that will in turn affect our community-building efforts at the local, personal level. Only a national community can provide political and economic "cover" for local and state efforts. Only a national community can make the long-term investments in physical and human capital and ensure that those investments are steering toward sensible long-term objectives and creating a durable, mutually empowering relationship between national and local, state and individual.

The idea of revitalized national community would pose a challenge to many on today's right, still addled with brand conservatism's knee-jerk distrust of government. But even a modest shift in our political culture—a tamping down, for example, of the politically divisive media echo chamber—could enable conservatives to see the strategic benefits in a nonbrand politics that allows constructive engagement and the possibility of change. This, too, could become a self-perpetuating pattern. As pragmatic conservatives will already acknowledge, the postwar economic miracle was as much as anything the result of a virtuous circle between national and local. Massive top-down programs—in everything from social insurance and workplace regulation to huge investments in public infrastructure—helped foster a sense of individual security and optimism in the future and allowed communities to flourish at every level.

The "return" on these social investments was astonishing. As Robert Putnam and others have documented, those flourishing post-war communities responded with unprecedented levels of social and political engagement—volunteerism, patriotism, an esprit de corps and, yes, self-sacrifice, that enabled the entire country to overcome epic challenges. True, we now see that reciprocating relationship at election time, when the top and the bottom of both parties are fully engaged—and, often, enraged. But what we need to move to is a more maintainable engagement, where leaders and the electorate remain engaged in policy and debate at a more low-key, constructive, and sustainable level—and where the voices of echo-chamber extremism are no longer allowed to frame the debate, but instead are pushed back to the fringes where they belong.

Perhaps the most hopeful sign is the rising level of anger and debate over inequality. In the yawning gap between rich and poor, we're seeing the gravest threat to the ideal of community and democracy. Absent economic security and certainty, individuals slowly lose the high-minded aspirations of the postmaterialist and can no longer easily step away from their own interests to invest in their communities. Community declines at the very moment that citizens most need it—an especially brutal example of the virtuous circle turning vicious. Yet it is on the challenge of income inequality that a national community can be most effective. By embarking on a sustained effort to restore some balance and fairness to the marketplace, through reforms such as the ones we've talked about, we could begin pushing that circle back into positive territory. By making people more secure, by encouraging the idea that the larger society has our interests and well-being at heart, we will be more willing to step out of ourselves and to devote more time to our families, our neighbors, our schools. As important, by making progress on inequality, by demonstrating that the economy is not solely for the wealthy and the politically connected, we begin to restore the faith that the rest of us once had in the broader American experiment, and in democracy as a whole. Even simply *talking* about inequality, as politicians from both parties are finally starting to do, is a way to signal to a cynical, ignored population that it's finally safe to start acting like a nation.

True, for decades, a national community has been hard to

imagine—thanks in part to economic failure, to political partisanship and financialization, and to voters who treat politics as another venue for consumption and identity creation. Yet recently, we've seen the possibility of a thaw—brief glimpses of compromise that might point to a larger rapprochement. Admittedly, it is a slim reed; but it is also a window of opportunity for an electorate that recognizes the unsustainability of Impulse politics and the absurdity of a political system that simply can't get anything done. To create the space that allows us to see how badly our political institutions are performing is to begin to demand that those institutions be restored, however imperfectly, to their intended function—channeling our individual self-interest into an instrument for long-term, collective good.

Here is another example of the virtuous circle. A national political culture that begins to talk about the real problems—not death panels or the legality of pot or the president's birth certificate—but issues that are driving our economic and social destinies. The challenges facing the modern family; the decline of business and work ethics; the mismanagement of innovation; the ticking time bombs of unregulated financial markets and unchecked campaign finance: a political culture that could address issues like these is one that people could buy into, could care about. For these are issues that cut across party lines. We may bemoan the fact that we're fragmenting into a national patchwork of red and blue. That mustn't preclude us from finding or creating common ground and crosscurrents that transcend our legitimate differences and reaffirm our joint commitment to basic principles of a just, free society. And in so doing, in shutting off the echo chambers and the toxic assumptions of incompatibility and rediscovering the areas of common interest and the politics of the middle, perhaps we will begin to realize, most of us, that we're not quite so red or so blue after all.

You can see how this virtuous pattern could play out in other arenas and how other national issues could resolve in a similar top-down, bottom-up way. On climate change, for example, we've stalled out on a national level. Efforts to enact a carbon tax have been thwarted by a financialized political system that enables the energy industry to avoid the risk of change—a classic Impulse Society pattern. At the same time, however, there is movement at the state and local level that, properly marshaled, could translate into a national movement. In California, for instance, residents' much closer proximity to the ravages of a changing climate—drought, fires, dust storms—has helped translate local concerns into constructive state policies—policies that could become a model for other states and, eventually, for the federal government, much as a Massachusetts' health care system evolved into a national program. And to speed that evolution, a burgeoning national community of local activists, heavily made up by Millennials, is using new "occupation" tactics to ramp up the political pressure nationally in ways that more established green groups no longer do. Case in point: more than 75,000 activists stand ready to block the development of Keystone XL, a pipeline project that would carry carbon-heavy oil from the Canadian tar sands—a threat that may help explain why the Obama administration has stalled the project's approval.

Perhaps the greatest opportunity for this top-down, bottom-up dynamic is in education. The sector has suffered under the Impulse Society. Our dismal academic performance, compared to "lesser" industrial nations, is already undercutting our capacity to revive our economy or even think about long-term prosperity. But the opportunities for engagement and improvement and community building are rich and waiting to be explored. At the national level, the modest success of "Common Core," the federal attempt to bring uniform national standards to schools in every state, has already gained momentum, despite local umbrage at the idea of national standards. And at the local level, reformers are experimenting with everything from charter schools to a new "flipped" model, where students watch online lectures at home and do their "homework" in the classroom. Many of these experiments are controversial. But their mere existence reflects the sort of involved, do-it-yourself energy that used to characterize our entire culture—and which, with the right encouragement, could once again.

Indeed, of all the sectors of modern society, education may be the one most likely to motivate individuals to become engaged and take action. Education is often our first opportunity as adults to formally participate in a community beyond our family or neighborhood. It's also frequently our first chance to engage with government: when we're unhappy with our children's schooling, we're highly motivated to do something about it—whether that means fund-raising for classroom equipment, campaigning for the local levy, or running for a seat on the school board. And as my friend Marcie discovered, education offers a clear and well-trod pathway for ambitious individuals to give back to the broader community. That impulse to give back, to become involved in creating something of real, lasting value—it is as natural and as human as any of our lesser, more reptilian impulses. It just needs to be given time and space and encouragement—and for us to insist on that time and space and encouragement. And that insistence must come from inside. When my friend Marcie talks about her decision to become a teacher, she describes a tipping point—a moment when she allowed herself to ask a critical question: "Who are we expecting to do these jobs if it's not going to be someone like me?"

This isn't the sort of question we're encouraged to ask in the Impulse Society. Rather, in a society driven by the hunt for yield and the churn of the treadmill and the incessant search for the perfect, personalized satisfactions, we're rarely invited to even consider a reality beyond the short-term and self-regarding. To ask whether we might step beyond that reality—to ask who we are if not for others, and if not now, when?—is to defy the logic of the marketplace and to insist instead on a different, older set of values. It is to recognize that individual freedom and power are only truly realized when they operate in the service of something larger. Most important, to ask that sort of question is to take the first step beyond the Impulse Society by rejecting the idea that sustains it—the idea that a myopic, self-absorbed, destructive status quo is the best that society can do. It only takes one question, and the courage to answer it, to realize that this central "truth" of the Impulse Society is a lie.

Acknowledgments

All books are collaborations, but this one was more than most. The many subjects covered here were complicated and often controversial, and I benefited enormously from long conversations with dozens of experts who were willing not only to share their knowledge, but to consider how it might fit into the big picture I wanted to describe. Special thanks goes to Dean Baker, Bill Bishop, Robert Bixby, Robert Boyd, Ralph Brown, Keith Campbell, Daniel Callahan, Hilarie Cash, Amitabh Chandra, Jonathan Cohen, Tyler Cowen, Richard Curtain, Richard Davies, Michael X. Delli Carpini, Jake Dunagan, Judith Feder, Andrew Haldane, Dacher Keltner, Bill Lazonick, George Loewenstein, Michael Mandel, Sam McClure, Todd Miller, Manoj Narang, Paul Piff, Clyde Prestowitz, Peter Richerson, Judy Samuelson, Walker Smith, Evan Soltas, Dilip Soman, Kenneth Stone, Richard Thaler, and Eric Tymoigne. Thanks as well to those hardy souls who read and commented on early drafts—including Matt Roberts, Molly Roberts, Karen Dickinson, Nina Miller, Claire Dederer, Fred Moody, Paul Bravmann, Susan Kucera, Ralph Brown, Bill Lazonick, and Johann Hari—as well as to those who shared their personal stories from the front lines of the Impulse Society, notably, Brett Walker and Marcie.

Above all, thanks to the crew at Bloomsbury Publishing: George Gibson, Laura Keefe, Nikki Baldauf, Rachel Mannheimer, Summer Smith—and, especially, my editor, Anton Mueller, without whose ideas, curiosity, and (mainly) cheerful willingness to work late and on weekends this book wouldn't have been possible.

Finally, I want to acknowledge those who provided encouragement, support, and/or meals and drinks while the book was being written (and rewritten), among them: the entire Dickinson tribe; Chris and Andrea Brixey; Eric and Ben at Eurosports; Luke, Colin, and Luis; Stephen Sharpe and A Book For All Seasons; Linda and Jake at Homefires, Damian and Susie at Schocolat; Susan at Sage Mountain; Kurt and Nadine at Good Mood Food; Roy Gumpel; Susan Garner; the tandem cyclist; and, last and certainly best, Hannah and Isaac, the two points of my heart's compass.

Bibliography

Alder, Nathan. *New Lifestyles and the Antinomian Personality*. New York: Harper & Row, 1972.

Alexander, Jennifer Karns. *The Mantra of Efficiency: From Water Wheel to Social Control*. Baltimore: Johns Hopkins Press, 2008.

Baker, Dean. *The End of Loser Liberalism: Making Markets Progressive*. Washington, DC: Center for Economic and Policy Research, 2011.

Baker, Dean, and Thomas Frank. *Plunder and Blunder: The Rise and Fall of the Bubble Economy*. San Francisco: PoliPoint Press, 2009.

Bell, Daniel. *The Cultural Contradictions of Capitalism*. New York: Basic Books, 1996.

Bellah, Roberts et al. *Habits of the Heart: Individualism and Commitment in American Life*. Berkeley: University of California Press, 1985.

Bevan, Tom, and Carl Cannon. *Election 2012: The Battle Begins*. The RealClearPolitics Political Download. 2011.

Bishop, Bill. *The Big Sort: Why the Clustering of Like-Minded America Is Tearing Us Apart*. Boston: Houghton Mifflin, 2008.

Bloom, Allan. *The Closing of the American Mind*. New York: Simon & Schuster, 1988.

Bowles, Samuel, and Herbert Gintis. *A Cooperative Species: Human Reciprocity and Its Evolution*. Princeton, NJ: Princeton University Press, 2011.

Bradsher, Keith. *High and Mighty: SUVs—the World's Most Dangerous Vehicles and How They Got That Way*. New York: Public Affairs, 2003.

Braudel, Fernand. *The Structure of Everyday Life: The Limits of the Possible. Civilization and Capitalism, 15th–18th Century*. Vol. I. Translated from the French by Sian Reynolds. Berkeley: University of California Press, 1992.

Brown, Clair, and Greg Linden. *Chips and Change: How Crisis Reshapes the Semiconductor Industry*. Cambridge, MA: MIT Press, 2009.

Brynjolfsson, Erik, and Andrew McAfee. *Race against The Machine: How the Digital Revolution Is Accelerating Innovation, Driving Productivity, and Irreversibly Transforming Employment and the Economy*. Boston: Digital Frontier Press, 2012.

Burnham, Terry, and Jay Phelan. *Mean Genes: From Sex to Money to Food Taming Our Primal Instincts*. New York: Penguin, 2000.

Calder, Lendol. *Financing the American Dream: A Cultural History of Consumer Credit*. Princeton, NJ: Princeton University Press, 1999.

Carr, Nicholas. *The Shallows: What the Internet Is Doing to Our Brains*. New York: W. W. Norton, 2011.

Chandler, Alfred. *Scale and Scope: The Dynamics of Industrial Capitalism*. Cambridge, MA: Harvard University Press, 1994.

———. *The Visible Hand: The Managerial Revolution in American Business*. Cambridge, MA: Harvard University Press, 1977.

Coates, John. *The Hour between Dog and Wolf: Risk Taking, Gut Feelings and the Biology of Boom and Bust*. New York: Penguin Press, 2012.

Cowen, Tyler. *Average Is Over: Powering America beyond the Age of the Great Stagnation*. New York: Dutton, 2013.

———. *The Great Stagnation: How America Ate All the Low-Hanging Fruit of Modern History, Got Sick, and Will (Eventually) Feel Better*. New York: Dutton, 2011.

Davis, Gerald. *Managed by the Markets: How Finance Re-Shaped America*. New York: Oxford University Press, 2009.

Dionne, E. J. *Our Divided Political Heart: The Battle for the American Idea in an Age of Discontent*. New York: Bloomsbury, 2012.

Donaldson-Pressman, Stephanie, and Robert M. Pressman. *The Narcissistic Family: Diagnosis and Treatment*. New York: Macmillan, 1994.

Fishman, Charles. *The Wal-Mart Effect: How the World's Most Powerful Company Really Works—and How It's Transforming the American Economy*. New York: Penguin Press, 2006.

Frank, Robert. *The Darwin Economy: Liberty, Competition, and the Common Good*. Princeton, NJ: Princeton University Press, 2011.

Frank, Robert, and Philip J. Cook. *The Winner-Take-All Society: Why the Few at the Top Get So Much More Than the Rest of Us*. New York: Penguin Books, 1995.

Frank, Thomas, and Matt Weiland, eds. *Commodify Your Dissent: The Business of Culture in the New Gilded Age*. New York: W. W. Norton, 1997.

Friedman, Milton. *Capitalism and Freedom*. Fortieth Anniversary Edition. Chicago: University of Chicago Press, 2002.

Hacker, Jacob S., and Paul Pierson. *Winner-Take-All Politics: How Washington Made the Rich Richer—and Turned Its Back on the Middle Class*. New York: Simon & Schuster, 2011.

Hammond, Phillip E. *Religion and Personal Autonomy: The Third Disestablishment in America*. Columbia: University of South Carolina Press, 1992.

Hirschman, Albert. *The Passions and the Interests: Political Arguments for Capitalism before Its Triumph*. Twentieth Anniversary Edition. Princeton, NJ: Princeton University Press, 1997.

Horowitz, Daniel. *Anxieties of Affluence: Critiques of American Consumer Culture, 1939–1979*. Amherst: University of Massachusetts Press, 2004.

Inglehart, Ronald. *Culture Shift in Advanced Industrial Society*. Princeton, NJ: Princeton University Press, 1990.

Inglehart, Ronald, and Christian Welzel. *Modernization, Cultural Change, and Democracy: The Human Development Sequence*. Cambridge: Cambridge University Press, 2005.

Jackson, Tim. *Inside Intel: Andy Grove and the Rise of the World's Most Powerful Chip Company*. New York: Penguin, 1997.

Kanigel, Robert. *The One Best Way: Frederick Taylor and the Enigma of Efficiency*. New York: Viking, 1997.

Katona, George et al. *Aspirations and Affluence: Comparative Studies in the United States and Western Europe*. New York: McGraw-Hill, 1971.

Kling, Arnold. *Crisis of Abundance: Rethinking How We Pay for Health Care*. Washington, DC: Cato Institute, 2006

Krippner, Greta. *Capitalizing on Crisis: The Political Origins of the Rise of Finance*. Cambridge, MA: Harvard University Press, 2011.

Landes, David. *The Wealth and Poverty of Nations: Why Some Are So Rich and Some So Poor*. New York: W. W. Norton, 1999.

Lasch, Christopher. *The Culture of Narcissism: American Life in an Age of Diminishing Expectations*. New York: W. W. Norton, 1991.

Levins, Richard. *Willard Cochrane and the American Family Farm*. Lincoln: University of Nebraska, 2000.

Lichtenstein, Nelson. *The Retail Revolution: How Wal-Mart Created a Brave New World of Business*. New York: Picador, 2009.

Lichtenstein, Nelson, ed. *Wal-Mart: The Face of Twenty-First-Century Capitalism*. New York: The New Press, 2006.

Lindsey, Brink. *The Age of Abundance: How Prosperity Transformed America's Politics and Culture*. New York: HarperCollins, 2009.

Lowenstein, Roger. *When Genius Failed: The Rise and Fall of Long-Term Capital Management*. New York: Random House, 2000.

Lynch, Michael. *True to Life: Why Truth Matters*. Cambridge, MA: Bradford Books, 2004.

Marin, Peter. *Freedom and Its Discontents: Reflections on Four Decades of American Moral Experience*. South Royalton, VT: Steerforth, 1995.

Marsh, Peter, and Peter Collett. *Driving Passion: The Psychology of the Car*. Boston: Faber & Faber, 1986.

Messick, David M., and Roger M. Kramer, eds. *The Psychology of Leadership: New Perspectives and Research*. Mahwah, NJ: Lawrence Erlbaum Associates, 2005.

McCloskey, Deirdre. *The Bourgeois Virtues: Ethics for an Age of Commerce*. Chicago: University of Chicago Press, 2006.

Mokyr, Joel. *The Lever of Riches: Technological Creativity and Economic Progress*. New York: Oxford University Press, 1992.

Morozov, Evgeny. *To Save Everything, Click Here: The Folly of Technological Solutionism*. New York: Public Affairs, 2013.

Noah, Timothy. *The Great Divergence: America's Growing Inequality Crisis and What We Can Do about It*. New York: Bloomsbury, 2012.

Nordhaus, Ted, and Michael Shellenberger, *Break Through: From the Death of Environmentalism to the Politics of Possibility*. Boston: Houghton Mifflin, 2007.

Packard, Vance. *The Hidden Persuaders*. New York: Pocket Books, 1958.

———. *The Waste Makers*. New York: Pocket Books, 1964.

Pelfrey, William. *Billy, Alfred, and General Motors: The Story of Two Unique Men, a Legendary Company, and a Remarkable Time in American History*.

Phillips, Kevin. *American Theocracy: The Peril and Politics of Radical Religion, Oil, and Borrowed Money in the 21st Century*. New York: Penguin, 2006.

Putnam, Robert. *Bowling Alone: The Collapse and Revival of American Community*. New York: Simon & Schuster, 2000.

Rappaport, Alfred. *Saving Capitalism from Short-Termism: How to Build Long-Term Value and Take Back Our Financial Future*. New York: McGraw-Hill, 2011.

Sennett, Richard. *The Culture of the New Capitalism*. New Haven, CT: Yale University Press, 2006.

Shiller, Robert. *Irrational Exuberance*. Second Edition. Princeton, NJ: Princeton University Press, 2005.

Slade, Giles. *Made to Break: Technology and Obsolescence in America*. Cambridge, MA: Harvard University Press, 2009.

Smith, Adam. *The Wealth of Nations*. New York: Penguin Classics, 1982.

Smith, Merrit Roe, and Leo Marx, eds. *Does Technology Drive History? The Dilemma of Technological Determinism*. Cambridge, MA: MIT Press, 1994.

Sunstein, Cass R. *Republic.com 2.0: Revenge of the Blogs*. Princeton, NJ: Princeton University Press, 2007.

———. *Why Societies Need Dissent (Oliver Wendell Holmes Lectures)*. Cambridge, MA: Harvard University Press, 2003.

Thaler, Richard H. *Quasi Rational Economics*. New York: Russell Sage Foundation, 1991.

Thaler, Richard, and Cass Sunstein. *Nudge: Improving Decisions about Health, Wealth, and Happiness*. New Haven, CT: Yale University Press, 2008.

Turkle, Sherry. *Alone Together: Why We Expect More from Technology and Less from Each Other*. New York: Basic Books, 2011.

Twenge, Jean, and W. Keith Campbell. *The Narcissism Epidemic: Living in the Age of Entitlement*. New York: Free Press, 2009.

Tymoigne, Eric., and L. Randall Wray. *The Rise and Fall of Money Manager Capitalism: Minsky's Half Century from World War Two to the Great Recession*. Routledge Critical Studies in Finance and Stability. Oxford: Routledge, 2013.

Weiss, Eugene H. *Chrysler, Ford, Durant and Sloan: Founding Giants of the American Automotive Industry*. Jefferson, NC: McFarland, 2003.

Wood, Michael, and Louis Zurcher Jr. *The Development of a Postmodern Self: A Computer-Assisted Comparative Analysis of Personal Documents*. New York: Greenwood Press, 1988.

Selected Articles:

Abramowitz, Alan. "Don't Blame Primary Voters for Polarization." *The Forum: Politics of Presidential Selection* 5, no. 4 (2008).

Abramowitz, Alan, Brad Alexander, and Matthew Gunning. "Incumbency, Redistricting, and the Decline of Competition in U.S. House Elections." *Journal of Politics* 68, no. 1 (Feb. 2006): 75–88.

Abramowitz, Alan, and Morris P. Fiorina. "Polarized or Sorted? Just What's Wrong with Our Politics, Anyway?" *American Interest*, March 11, 2013. Accessed November 18, 2013. Doi: http://www.the-american-interest.com/article.cfm?piece=1393.

Auletta, Ken. "Outside the Box." *New Yorker*, Feb. 3, 2014.

Baker, Dean. "The Productivity to Paycheck Gap: What the Data Show," briefing paper, Center for Economic and Policy Research, April 2007. http://www.cepr.net/documents/publications/growth_failure_2007_04.pdf

———. "The Run-Up in Home Prices: Is It Real or Is It Another Bubble?" briefing paper, Center for Economic and Policy Research, August 2002, http://www.cepr.net/documents/publications/housing_2002_08.pdf.

Beinart, Peter. "The Rise of the New New Left." *Daily Beast*, Sept. 12, 2013. Doi: http://www.thedailybeast.com/articles/2013/09/12/the-rise-of-the-new-new-left.html.

Brooks, David. "The Opportunity Coalition." *New York Times*, Jan. 30, 2014, A27.

Cecchetti, Stephen G., and Enisse Kharroubi. "Reassessing the Impact of Finance on Growth." Band for International Settlements Working Paper No. 381, July 2012. Accessed August 4, 2013. Doi: http://www.bis.org/publ/work381.pdf.

Cobb, Clifford, Ted Halstead, and Jonathan Rowe. "If the GDP Is Up, Why Is America Down?" *Atlantic*, Oct. 1995. Accessed November 7, 2012. Doi: http://www.theatlantic.com/past/politics/ecbig/gdp.htm.

Cutler, David, and Mark McClellan. "Is Technological Change in Medicine Worth It?" *Health Affairs* 20, no. 5 (September/October 2001): 11–29.

Daly, Herman E. "A Steady-State Economy." Text delivered to UK Sustainable Development Commission, April 24, 2008.

Davidson, Adam. "Making It in America." *Atlantic*, Dec. 20, 2011.

Duhigg, C. "How Companies Learn Your Secrets." *New York Times Magazine*, Feb. 16, 2012, MM30.

Drum, Kevin. "You Hate Me, Now with a Colorful Chart!" *Mother Jones*, Sept. 26, 2012. Accessed March 14, 2013. Doi: http://www.motherjones.com/kevin-drum/2012/09/you-hate-me-now-colorful-chart.

Easterbrook, Gregg, "Voting for Unemployment: Why Union Workers Sometimes Choose to Lose Their Jobs Rather Than Accept Cuts in Wages." *Atlantic*, May 1983. Accessed September 12, 2013. Doi: http://www.theatlantic.com/past/docs/issues/83may/eastrbrk.htm.

Edsall, Thomas B. "The Obamacare Crisis." *New York Times*, Nov. 19, 2013. Doi: http://www.nytimes.com/2013/11/20/opinion/edsall-the-obamacare-crisis.html?pagewanted=1&_r=2&smid=tw-share&&pagewanted=all.

Field, Alexander J. "The Impact of the Second World War on U.S. Productivity Growth." *Economic History Review* 61, no. 3 (2008): 677.

———. "The Origins of U.S. Total Factor Productivity Growth in the Golden Age." *Cleometrica* 1, no. 1 (April 2007): 19, 20.

Fisher, Richard. "Ending 'Too Big to Fail': A Proposal for Reform before It's Too Late (with Reference to Patrick Henry, Complexity and Reality)." Remarks by the president of the Federal Reserve Bank of Dallas to the Committee for the Republic. Washington, DC, January 16, 2013. Accessed December 1, 2013, Doi: http://www.dallasfed.org/news/speeches/fisher/2013/fs130116.cfm.

Fleck, Susan et al. "The Compensation-Productivity Gap: A Visual Essay." *Monthly Labor Review*, January 2011. Accessed October 13, 2012. Doi: http://www.bls.gov/opub/mlr/2011/01/art3full.pdf.

FRED Economic Data. Federal Reserve Bank of St. Louis. "Graph: Corporate Profits after Tax (without IVA and CCAdj) (CP)/Gross Domestic Product (GDP)." March 13, 2014. Doi: http://research.stlouisfed.org/fred2/graph/?g=cSh.

Fullerton, Robert. "The Birth of Consumer Behavior: Motivation Research in the 1950s." Paper presented at the 2011 Biennial Conference on Historical Analysis and Research in Marketing, May 19–22, 2011.

Good, James A., and Jim Garrison. "Traces of Hegelian *Bildung* in Dewey's Philosophy." In *John Dewey and Continental Philosophy*, edited by Paul Fairfield. Carbondale: Southern Illinois University, 2010. Available at Google Books.

Hagel, John et al. "The 2011 Shift Index: Measuring the Forces of Long-Term Change." Deloitte Center for the Edge, 2011.

Haldane, Andrew. "Financial Arms Races." Essay based on a speech given at the Institute for New Economic Thinking, Berlin, April 14, 2012.

———. "The Race to Zero." Speech given at International Economic Association Sixteenth World Congress, Beijing, China, July 8, 2011.

Haldane, Andrew G., and Richard Davies. "The Short Long." A speech delivered at Twenty-Ninth Société Universitaire Européene de Recherches Financières Colloquium: New Paradigms in Money Finance, Brussels, May 2011. http://www.bankofengland.co.uk/publications/Documents/speeches/2011/speech495.pdf.

Haveman, Ernest, "The Task Ahead: How to Take Life Easy." *Life*, Feb. 21, 1964. Available at Google Docs.

Heller, Nathan. "Laptop U: Has the Future of College Moved Online?" *New Yorker*, May 20, 2013. http://www.newyorker.com/reporting/2013/05/20/130520fa_fact_heller?currentPage=all

Jensen, Michael C., and William H. Meckling, "Theory of the Firm: Managerial Behavior, Agency Costs and Ownership Structure," *Journal of Financial Economics* 3, no. 4 (October 1976): 305–60.

Karabarbounis, Loukas, and Brent Neiman. "Declining Labor Shares and the Global Rise of Corporate Savings." National Bureau of Economic Research Working Paper No. 18154, June 2012. Accessed October 4, 2013. Doi: http://www.nber.org/papers/w18154.

Katz, Daniel. "Quantitative Legal Prediction—Or—How I Learned to Stop Worrying and Start Preparing for the Data-Driven Future of the Legal Services Industry." *Emory Law Journal* 62, no. 909 (2013): 965.

Knowles, John. "The Responsibility of the Individual." *Daedalus* 106, no. 1 (Winter 1977).

Krueger, Alan B. "Fairness as an Economic Force." Lecture delivered at "Learning and Labor Economics" Conference at Oberlin College, April 26, 2013. Accessed August 14, 2013. Doi: http://www.whitehouse.gov/sites/default/files/docs/oberlin_final_revised.pdf.

Krugman, Paul. "Defining Prosperity Down." *New York Times*, July 7, 2013. http://www.nytimes.com/2013/07/08/opinion/krugman-defining-prosperity-down.html?src=recg.

Kuchler, Hannah. "Data Pioneers Watching Us Work." *Financial Times*, February 17, 2014.

Lazonick, William. "The Innovative Enterprise and the Developmental State: Toward an Economics of 'Organizational Success.'" Discussion paper presented at Finance, Innovation & Growth 2011.

Lazonick, William, and Mary O'Sullivan. "Maximizing Shareholder Value: A New Ideology for Corporate Governance," *Economy and Society* 29, no. 1 (Feb. 2000): 19.

Loewenstein, George, "Insufficient Emotion: Soul-Searching by a Former Indicter of Strong Emotions." *Emotion Review* 2, no. 3 (July 2010): 234–39. http://www.cmu.edu/dietrich/sds/docs/loewenstein/InsufficientEmotion.pdf.

Lynd, Robert S. "The People as Consumers." In *Recent Social Trends in the*

United States: Report on the President's Research Committee on Social Trends,
with a Foreword by Herbert Hoover, 857–911. New York: McGraw-Hill, 1933.
Accessed May 11, 2013. Doi: http://archive.org/stream/recentsocialtren02pres
rich#page/867/mode/1up.

Madrigal, Alexis C. "When the Nerds Go Marching In." *Atlantic*, Nov. 16, 2012.
Accessed Sept. 27, 2013. Doi: http://www.theatlantic.com/technology/
archive/2012/11/when-the-nerds-go-marching-in/265325/?single_page=true.

Mankiw, Gregory N. "Defending the One Percent," *Journal of Economic
Perspectives* 27, no. 3 (Summer 2013). http://scholar.harvard.edu/files/ mankiw/
files/defending_the_one_percent_0.pdf.

Maslow, A. H., "A Theory of Human Motivation," originally published in
Psychological Review 50 (1943): 370–96.

McGaughey, William Jr. "Henry Ford's Productivity Lesson." *Christian Science
Monitor*, Dec. 22, 1982. Accessed March 11, 2012. Doi: http://www.csmonitor.
com/1982/1222/122232.html.

McKibben, Bill. "Breaking the Growth Habit." *Scientific American*, April 2010.
Accessed May 8, 2012. Doi: http://www.scientificamerican.com/article.
cfm?id=breaking-the-growth-habit&print=true.

———. "Money ≠ Happiness. QED," *Mother Jones*, March/April 2007.

McLean Bethany, and Joe Nocera. "The Blundering Herd." *Vanity Fair*,
Nov.2010.http://www.vanityfair.com/business/features/2010/11/financial-crisis-
excerpt–201011.

Murphy, Kevin J. "Pay, Politics, and the Financial Crisis." In *Rethinking the
Financial Crisis*, edited by Alan S. Blinder, Andrew W. Lo, and Robert M.
Solow. New York: Russell Sage Foundation, 2012.

Murphy, Tom. "An Angel and a Brute: Self-Interest and Individualism in
Tocqueville's America." Essay for preceptorial on *Democracy in America*. St.
John's College, Santa Fe, NM, Summer 1985. Accessed June 8, 2013. Doi:
http://www.brtom.org/sjc/sjc4.html.

Noah, Timothy, "The United States of Inequality," *Salon*, Sept. 12, 2010. Accessed
September 12, 2013. Doi: http://www.slate.com/articles/news_and_politics/
the_great_divergence/features/2010/the_united_states_of_inequality/the_
great_divergence_and_the_death_of_organized_labor.html.

Parker, Kathleen. "A Brave New Centrist World." *Washington Post*, Oct. 15,
2013. Accessed November 1, 2013. Doi: http://www.washingtonpost.com/opin-
ions/kathleen-parker-a-brave-new-centrist-world/2013/10/15/ea5f5bc6–35c9–
11e3-be86–6aeaa439845b_story.html.

Polsky, G., and Lund, A. "Can Executive Compensation Reform Cure Short-
Termism?" *Issues in Governance Studies* 58 (March 2013). Washington, DC:
Brookings Institute.

Purinton, Edward. "The Efficient Home." *Independent* 86–87 (May 15, 1916):
246–48. Available in Google Docs.

Rappaport, A. et al. "Stock or Cash: The Trade-Offs for Buyers and Sellers in Mergers and Acquisitions." *Harvard Business Review*, Nov.–Dec. 1999, p.147. Accessed July 13, 2013. Doi: http://www2.warwick.ac.uk/fac/soc/law/pg/offer/llm/iel/mas_sample__lecture.pdf

Reguly, Eric. "Buyback Boondoggle: Are Share Buybacks Killing Companies?" *Globe and Mail*, Oct. 24, 2013. Accessed November 4, 2013. Doi: http://www.theglobeandmail.com/report-on-business/rob-magazine/the-buyback-boondoggle/article15004212/.

Rowe, Jonathan. "Our Phony Economy." *Harper's*, June 2008. Accessed November 8, 2012. Doi: http://harpers.org/print/?pid=85583.

Schoetz, David. "David Frum on GOP: Now We Work for Fox." ABCNews, March 23, 2010. Accessed November 18, 2013. Doi: http://abcnews.go.com/blogs/headlines/2010/03/david-frum-on-gop-now-we-work-for-fox/.

Senft, Dexter. "Impact of Technology of the Investment Process." Conference Proceedings of the CFA Institute Seminar "Fixed-Income Management 2004." CFA Institute, 85–90.

Smaghi, Lorenzo Bini (member of the Executive Board of the European Central Bank). "The Paradigm Shift after the Financial Crisis." Speech at the Nomura Seminar.Kyoto, April 15, 2010. http://www.ecb.europa.eu/press/key /date/2010/html/sp100415.en.html.

Smith, Hedrick. "When Capitalists Cared." *New York Times*, Sept. 2, 2012, A19.

Stokes, Bruce. "Europe Faces Globalization—Part II: Denmark Invests in an Adaptable Workforce, Thus Reducing Fear of Change." *YaleGlobal*, May 18, 2006.

The Economist. "Coming Home: Reshoring Manufacturing." Jan. 19, 2013. Accessed January 23, 2913. Doi: http://www.economist.com/news/special-report/21569570-growing-number-american-companies-are-moving-their-manufacturing-back-united.

White, Michelle J., "Bankruptcy Reform and Credit Cards," *Journal of Economic Perspectives* 21, no. 4 (Fall 2007): 175–99.

Will, George F. "Time to Break Up the Big Banks." *Washington Post*, Feb. 9, 2013. Accessed September 2, 2103. Doi: http://www.washingtonpost.com/opinions/george-will-break-up-the-big-banks/2013/02/08/2379498a-714e-11e2-8b8d-e0b59a1b8e2a_story.html.

Wohlfert, Lee. "Dr. John Knowles Diagnoses U.S. Medicine." *People*, May 6, 1974. Accessed April 11, 2013. Doi: http://www.people.com/people/archive/article/0,,20064026,00.html.

Wolfe, Thomas. "The 'Me' Decade and the Third Great Awakening." *New York Magazine*, August 23, 1976.

Wood, Allen W. "Hegel on Education." In *Philosophy as Education*, edited by Amélie O. Rorty. London: Routledge, 1998.

Notes

CHAPTER 1: MORE BETTER

1. Andrew Nusca, "Say Command: How Speech Recognition Will Change the World," *SmartPlanet*, Issue 7, at http://www.smartplanet.com/blog /smart-takes/say-command-how-speech-recognition-will-change-the-world /19895?tag=content;siu-container.
2. Apple video introducing Siri, at http://www.youtube.com/watch?v=8ciagGASro0.
3. *The Independent*, 86–87 (1916), at http://books.google.com/books?id= IZAeAQAAMAAJ&lpg=PA108&ots=L5W1-w9EDW&dq=Edward%20 Earle%20Purinton&pg=PA246#v=onepage&q=Edward%20Earle%20 Purinton&f=false.
4. Daniel Bell, *The Cultural Contradictions of Capitalism* (New York: HarperCollins, 1976), p. 66.
5. James H. Wolter, "Lessons from Automotive History," research paper, presented at the Conference on Historical Analysis and Research in Marketing, Quinnipiac University, New York, 1983, p. 82.
6. Quoted in David Gartman, "Tough Guys and Pretty Boys: The Cultural Antagonisms of Engineering and Aesthetics in Automotive History," Automobile in American Life and Society, at http://www.autolife.umd.umich .edu/Design/Gartman/D_Casestudy/D_Casestudy5.htm.
7. V. G. Vartan, "'Trust Busters' Aim Legal Cannon at GM," *Christian Science Monitor*, Feb. 10, 1959, p. 12.
8. G. H. Smith, 1954, in Ronald A. Fullerton, "The Birth of Consumer Behavior: Motivation Research in the 1950s," paper presented at the 2011 Biennial Conference on Historical Analysis and Research in Marketing, May 19–22, 2011.

9. *Recent Social Trends in the United States: Report on the President's Research Committee on Social Trends, with a Foreword by Herbert Hoover* (New York: McGraw-Hill, 1933), pp. 866–67, at http://archive.org/stream /recentsocialtren02presrich#page/867/mode/1up.

10. Franklin D. Roosevelt Inaugural Address, March 4, 1933, available at History Matters: The U.S. Survey Course on the Web, http://historymatters.gmu.edu /d/5057/.

11. Alexander J. Field, "The Origins of U.S. Total Factor Productivity Growth in the Golden Age," *Cleometrica* 1, no. 1 (April 2007): 19, 20.

12. Alexander J. Field, "The Impact of the Second World War on U.S. Productivity Growth," *Economic History Review* 61, no. 3 (2008): 677.

13. Gary Nash, "A Resilient People, 1945–2005," in *Voices of the American People, Volume 1* (New York: Pearson, 2005), p. 865.

14. "US Real GDP by Year," http://www.multpl.com/us-gdp-inflation-adjusted /table.

15. "US Real GDP per Capita," http://www.multpl.com/us-real-gdp-per-capita.

16. G. Katona et al., *Aspirations and Affluence* (New York: McGraw-Hill, 1971), p. 18.

17. For 1945 median income, see "Current Population Reports: Consumer Income," Series P-60, No. 2, Washington, DC, March 2, 1948, http://www2 .census.gov/prod2/popscan/p60-002.pdf; for 1962 median income, see "Current Population Reports: Consumer Income," Series P-60, No. 49, Washington, DC, Aug. 10, 1966, http://www2.census.gov/prod2/popscan/p60 -049.pdf.

18. Nash, "A Resilient People, 1945–2005," p. 864.

19. Gregg Easterbrook, "Voting for Unemployment: Why Union Workers Sometimes Choose to Lose Their Jobs Rather Than Accept Cuts in Wages," *The Atlantic*, May 1983, http://www.theatlantic.com/past/docs/issues /83may/eastrbrk.htm; and Timothy Noah, "The United States of Inequality," *Salon*, Sept. 12, 2010, http://www.slate.com/articles/news_and_politic s/the_great_divergence/features/2010/the_united_states_of_inequality /the_great_divergence_and_the_death_of_organized_labor.html.

20. Standard Schaefer, "Who Benefited from the Tech Bubble: An Interview with Michael Hudson," *CounterPunch*, Aug. 29–31, 2003, http://www.counter punch.org/2003/08/29/who-benefited-from-the-tech-bubble-an-interview with-michael-hudson/; "Kaysen Sees Corporation Stress on Responsibilities to Society," *The Harvard Crimson*, March 29, 1957, http://www.thecrimson.com /article/1957/3/29/kaysen-sees-corporation-stress-on-responsibilities/; and Gerald Davis, "Managed by the Markets" (New York: Oxford University Press, 2009), p. 11.

21. "Life Expectancy by Age," Information Please, Pearson Education, 2007 http://www.infoplease.com/ipa/A0005140.html.

22. Ernest Haveman, "The Task Ahead: How to Take Life Easy," *Life*, Feb. 21, 1964.

23. Pierre Martineau, "Motivation in Advertising: A Summary," in *The Role of Advertising* (New York: McGraw-Hill, 1957), cited in Fullerton.

24. Bellah et al., *Habits of the Heart: Individualism and Commitment in American Life* (Berkeley: University of California Press, 1985), p. 108.

25. William Shannon, quoted by Richard Rovere in *The American Scholar* (Spring 1962).

26. "U.S. Federal Spending," graph, in U.S. Government Spending, http://www.usgovernmentspending.com/spending_chart_1900_2018USp_XXs1li111mcn_F0f_US_Federal_Spending.

27. Cited in Mary Ann Glendon, "Lost in the Fifties," *First Things* 57 (Nov. 1995): 46–49, http://www.leaderu.com/ftissues/ft9511/articles/glendon.html.

28. A. H. Maslow, "A Theory of Human Motivation," Classics in the History of Psychology: An Internet Resource, http://psychclassics.yorku.ca/Maslow/motivation.htm.

29. Cited in Ellen Herman, "The Humanistic Tide," in *The Romance of American Psychology: Political Culture in the Age of Experts* (Berkeley: University of California Press, 1995), http://publishing.cdlib.org/ucpressebooks/view?docId=ft696nb3n8&chunk.id=d0e5683&toc.depth=1&toc.id=d0e5683&brand=ucpress.

30. Ronald Inglehart and Christian Welzel, *Modernization, Cultural Change, and Democracy: The Human Development Sequence* (Cambridge, UK: Cambridge University Press, 2005), p. 149.

31. Ibid., p. 144.

CHAPTER 2: NO CONFIDENCE

1. "Survey of Consumers," University of Michigan, Survey Research Center, http://www.sca.isr.umich.edu/fetchdoc.php?docid=24776.

2. Michael C. Jensen and William H. Meckling, "Theory of the Firm: Managerial Behavior, Agency Costs and Ownership Structure," research paper, http://www.sfu.ca/~wainwrig/Econ400/jensen-meckling.pdf.

3. Interview with author.

4. Gary Hector and Carrie Gottlieb, "The U.S. Chipmakers' Shaky Comeback," CNNMoney, http://money.cnn.com/magazines/fortune/fortune_archive/1988/06/20/70690/index.htm.

5. "GM Speeds Time to Market through Blistering Fast Processors," FreeLibrary, http://www.thefreelibrary.com/GM+speeds+time+to+market+through+blistering+fast+processors%3a+General..-a0122319616.

6. "S&P 500: Total and Inflation-Adjusted Historical Returns," Simple Stock

Investing, http://www.simplestockinvesting.com/SP500-historical-real-total-returns.htm.

7. William Lazonick and Mary O'Sullivan, "Maximizing Shareholder Value: A New Ideology for Corporate Governance," *Economy and Society* 29, no. 1 (Feb. 2000): 19.

8. Ibid.

9. Ted Nordhaus and Michael Shellenberger, *Break Through: From the Death of Environmentalism to the Politics of Possibility*, p. 156.

10. "Work Stoppages Falling," graph, U.S. Bureau of Labor Statistics, http://old.post-gazette.com/pg/images/201302/20130212work_stoppage600.png.

11. Loukas Karabarbounis and Brent Neiman, "Declining Labor Shares and the Global Rise of Corporate Savings," research paper, October 2012, http://econ.sciences-po.fr/sites/default/files/file/cbenard/brent_neiman_LabShare.pdf.

12. William Lazonick, "Reforming the Financialized Corporation," http://www.employmentpolicy.org/sites/www.employmentpolicy.org/files/Lazonick%20Reforming%20the%20Financialized%20Corporation%2020110130%20(2).pdf.

13. Author interview with William Lazonick, April 15, 2013.

14. Gerald Davis, *Managed by the Markets: How Finance Re-Shaped America* (New York: Oxford University Press, 2009), p. 90–91.

15. Interview with author.

16. "The Rise of Freakonomics," *Wired*, Nov. 26, 2006, http://www.longtail.com/the_long_tail/2006/11/the_rise_of_fre.html.

17. *The Oxford Companion to American Food and Drink*, edited by Andrew F. Smith (New York: Oxford University Press, 2006), p. 266.

18. "Supply Chain News: Will Large Retailers Help Manufacturers Drive Out Supply Chain Complexity?" *Supply Chain Digest*, June 30, 2009, http://www.scdigest.com/assets/On_Target/09-06-30-2.php

19. Robert Peters, "Chronology of Video Pornography: Near Demise and Subsequent Growth," Morality in Media, http://66.210.33.157/mim/full_article.php?article_no=175; and Tony Schwartz, "The TV Pornography Boom," Sept. 13, 1981, http://www.nytimes.com/1981/09/13/magazine/the-tv-pornography-boom.html?pagewanted=all.

20. Press release, "Industry History: A History of Home Video and Video Game Retailing," Entertainment Merchants Association 2013, http://www.entmerch.org/press-room/industry-history.html. Accessed February 3, 2014.

21. "'Father of Aerobics,' Kenneth Cooper, MD, MPH to Receive Healthy Cup Award from Harvard School of Public Health," press release, April 16, 2008, http://www.hsph.harvard.edu/news/press-releases/2008-releases/aerobics-kenneth-cooper-to-receive-harvard-healthy-cup-award.html.

22. J. D. Reed, "America Wakes Up," *Time*, Nov. 16, 1981, http://www.time.com /time/subscriber/printout/0,8816,950613,00.html.

23. Personal communication, October 5, 2012.

24. Kurt Eichenwald with John Markoff, "Wall Street's Souped-up Computers," *New York Times*, Oct. 16, 1988, http://www.nytimes.com/1988/10/16 /business/wall-street-s-souped-up-computers.html.

25. Dean Baker, "The Run-up in Home Prices: Is It Real or Is It Another Bubble?" briefing paper, Center for Economic and Policy Research, August 2002, http://www.cepr.net/documents/publications/housing_2002_08.pdf; and Dean Baker, "The Productivity to Paycheck Gap: What the Data Show," briefing paper, April 2007, http://www.cepr.net/documents/publications /growth_failure_2007_04.pdf.

26. Peter Marin, "The New Narcissism," Harper's, October 1975.

27. Quoted in book review by Scott London, http://www.scottlondon.com /reviews/lasch.html.

28. Glendon, "Lost in the Fifties."

29. All in Putnam, R. *Bowling Alone: The Collapse and Revival of American Community* (New York: Simon & Schuster, 2000), except visiting and close confidants, which is from McKibben, Bill. "Money ≠ Happiness. QED." *Mother Jones*, March/April 2007, http://www.motherjones.com/politics/2007 /03/reversal-fortune?page=3Issue.

30. Ibid.

31. Charles Fishman, "The Revolution Will Be Televised (on CNBC)," FastCompany, http://www.fastcompany.com/39859/revolution-will-be-tele-vised-cnbc.

CHAPTER 3: POWER CORRUPTS

1. Interview with author.

2. Michelle J. White, "Bankruptcy Reform and Credit Cards," *Journal of Economic Perspectives* 21, no. 4 (Fall 2007): 175–99, http://www.econ.ucsd .edu/~miwhite/JEPIII.pdf.

3. Reuven Glick and Kevin J. Lansing, U.S. Household Deleveraging and Future Consumption Growth, Federal Reserve Bank of San Francisco Economic Letter, May 15, 2009, http://www.frbsf.org/publications/economics /letter/2009/el2009-16.html; and "U.S., World's Growing Household Debt," research paper, June/July 2004, http://www.marubeni.com/dbps_data /_material_/maruco_en/data/research/pdf/0407.pdf.

4. White, "Bankruptcy Reform and Credit Cards."

5. Richard H. Thaler, *Quasi Rational Economics*, p. 78.

6. Smith, "The Theory of Moral Sentiments." In "Adam Smith, Behavioral

Economist", Carnegie Mellon University, www.cmu.edu/dietrich/sds/docs
/loewenstein/AdamSmith.pdf.

7. Personal communication.

8. Ibid.

9. Michael E. Lara, "The New Science of Emotion: From Neurotransmitters
to Neural Networks," SlideShare, http://www.slideshare.net/mlaramd
/science-of-emotion-from-neurotransmitters-to-social-networks.

10. George Loewenstein, "Insufficient Emotion: Soul-Searching by a Former
Indicter of Strong Emotions," *Emotion Review* 2, no. 3 (July 2010):
234–39.

11. Richard Sennett, *The Culture of the New Capitalism* (New Haven, CT: Yale
University Press, 2006), p. 23.

12. Vivian Yee, "In Age of Anywhere Delivery, the Food Meets You for
Lunch," *New York Times*, Oct. 5, 2013, http://www.nytimes.com/2013/10
/06/nyregion/in-age-of-anywhere-delivery-the-food-meets-you-for-lunch
.html?hp.

13. Hilary Stout, "For Shoppers, Next Level of Instant Gratification," *New York
Times*, Oct. 8, 2013, http://www.nytimes.com/2013/10/08/technology/for
-shoppers-next-level-of-instant-gratification.html?hpw.

14. Jonah Lehrer, "DON'T! The Secret of Self-Control," *The New Yorker*, May
18, 2009, http://www.newyorker.com/reporting/2009/05/18/090518fa_fact
_lehrer?currentPage=all.

15. Cited in Thomas Frank, *Commodify Your Dissent*, p.32.

16. Leonard N. Fleming, "David Kipnis, 74, Psychology Professor," obituary,
Philly.com, http://articles.philly.com/1999-08-29/news/25482558_1_psychology
-professor-social-psychology-absolute-power; Kipnis quoted in David M. Messick
and Roger M. Kramer, eds., *The Psychology of Leadership: New Perspectives and
Research* (Mahwah, NJ: Lawrence Erlbaum Associates, 2005).

17. Fleming, "David Kipnis, 74."

18. Interview with author.

19. Interview with author.

20. Jeremy Laurance, "4x4 Debate: Enemy of the People," *The Independent*,
June 23, 2006, http://www.independent.co.uk/life-style/health-and-families
/health-news/4x4-debate-enemy-of-the-people-405113.html.

21. Jon Bowermaster, "When Wal-Mart Comes to Town," April 2, 1989, http://
www.nytimes.com/1989/04/02/magazine/when-wal-mart-comes-to-town
.html?pagewanted=all&src=pm.

22. "The Sovereignty of the Consumers," Ludwig von Mises Institute, http://
mises.org/humanaction/chap15sec4.asp.

23. "Robert Nisbet and the Conservative Intellectual Tradition," Ludwig von
Mises Institute, http://mises.org/media/4211.

24. Bell, *The Cultural Contradictions of Capitalism*, pp. xxiv.

25. R. Putnam, *Bowling Alone: The Collapse and Revival of American Community* (New York: J. Simon & Schuster, 2000) p. 335.

CHAPTER 4: SOMETHING FOR NOTHING

1. Interview with author.
2. Interview with author.
3. Interview with author.
4. Leith van Onselen, "Ireland, the Greatest Property Bust of All," *Macro Business*, April 8, 2013, http://www.macrobusiness.com.au/2013/04/ireland-the-greatest-property-bust-of-all/.
5. Matthew Benjamin, "Bond Traders Who Gave Bush a Pass May Ambush Obama or McCain," Bloomberg, Aug. 10, 2008, http://www.bloomberg.com/apps/news?pid=newsarchive&sid=ayrMJ4R.bmLY&refer=home.
6. Bob Woodward, *The Agenda: Inside the Clinton White House* (New York: Simon & Schuster), 1994.
7. Brian J. Hall, "Six Challenges in Designing Equity-Based Pay," NBER Working Paper 9887, July 2003, http://www.nber.org/papers/w9887.pdf?new_window=1.
8. Ben Heineman, Jr. and Stephan Davis. "Are Institutional Investors Part of the Problem or Part of the Solution?" Yale School of Management, 2011. http://www.ced.org/pdf/Are-Institutional-Investors-Part-of-the-Problem-or-Part-of-the-Solution.pdf.
9. Ibid., but see also Sennett, *The Culture of the New Capitalism*, p. 40, who argues that it is from four years in 1960s to four months today.
10. "The Short Long," speech delivered by Andrew G. Haldane and Richard Davies.
11. "Shooting the Messenger: Quarterly Earnings and Short-Term Pressure to Perform," Wharton–University of Pennsylvania, July 21, 2010, http://knowledge.wharton.upenn.edu/article.cfm?articleid=2550.
12. G. Polsky and A. Lund, "Can Executive Compensation Reform Cure Short-Termism?" *Issues in Governance Studies* 58, Brookings, March 2013.
13. "Shooting the Messenger."
14. Google Inc. (Nasdaq-Goog), graph, Google Finance, https://www.google.com/finance?cid=694653.
15. Interview with author.
16. "A National Conversation on American Competitiveness," panel discussion, Wilson Center, March 28, 2012, http://www.wilsoncenter.org/event/regaining-americas-competitive-edge.
17. Gustavo Grullon and David Eikenberry, "What Do We Know about Stock Repurchases?" Bank of America and *Journal of Applied Corporate Finance*

15, no. 1 (Spring 2000), http://www.uic.edu/classes/idsc/ids472/research /PORTFOLI/JACFSU~1.PDF.

18. Patrick Bolton, Wei Xiong, and Jose A. Schienkman, "Pay for Short-Term Performance: Executive Compensation in Speculative Markets," ECGI Finance Working Paper No. 79/2005, April 2005, http://papers.ssrn.com/sol3 /papers.cfm?abstract_id=691142.

19. Al Lewis, "Record Number of Companies Restate Earnings in 2005," *Denver Post*, Jan. 2, 2006, http://blogs.denverpost.com/lewis/2006/01/02/record -number-of-companies-restate-earnings-in-2005/75/.

20. Interview with author.

21. Bethany McLean and Andrew Serwer, "Goldman Sachs: After the Fall," *Fortune* Nov. 9, 1998, http://features.blogs.fortune.cnn.com/2011/10/23 /goldman-sachs-after-the-fall-fortune-1998/.

22. Bethany McLean and Joe Nocera, "The Blundering Herd," *Vanity Fair*, Nov. 2010.

23. "Home Equity Extraction: The Real Cost of 'Free Cash,'" Seeking Alpha, April 25, 2007, http://seekingalpha.com/article/33336-home-equity-extraction-the -real-cost-of-free-cash.

24. Interview with author.

25. Sameer Khatiwada, "Did the Financial Sector Profit at the Expense of the Rest of the Economy? Evidence from the United States," discussion paper, Digital Commons@ILR, Jan. 1, 2010, http://digitalcommons.ilr.cornell.edu /cgi/viewcontent.cgi?article=1101&context=intl; "Wages and Human Capital in the U.S. Finance Industry: 1909–2006," *Quarterly Journal of Economics* (Oct. 9, 2012), http://qje.oxfordjournals.org/content/early/2012/11/22/qje .qjs030.full; and Thomas Philippon, "Are Bankers Over-Paid?" EconoMonitor, Jan. 21, 2009, http://www.economonitor.com/blog/2009/01/are-bankers-over -paid/.

26. "A Paradigm Shift after the Financial Crisis." Speech by Lorenzo Bini Smaghi.

27. Stephen G. Cecchetti and Enisse Kharroubi, "Reassessing the Impact of Finance on Growth."

28. Gregory N. Mankiw, "Defending the One Percent," *Journal of Economic Perspectives* 27, no. 3 (Summer 2013).

29. Kevin J. Murphy, "Pay, Politics, and the Financial Crisis," in *Rethinking the Financial Crisis*, edited by Alan S. Blinder, Andrew W. Lo, and Robert M. Solow. (New York: Russell Sage Foundation, 2012).

30. U.S. Chamber of Commerce Foundation, "Manufacturing's Declining Share of GDP Is a Global Phenomenon, and It's Something to Celebrate" March 22, 2012, http://emerging.uschamber.com/blog/2012/03/manufacturing%E2%80%99s -declining-share-gdp; "U.S Manufacturing In Context" Advanced Manufacturing Portal, U.S. government website, http://manufacturing.gov/mfg_in_context.html.

31. Justin Latiart, "Number of the Week," *The Wall Street Journal*, Dec. 10, 2011.

32. Adam Mellows-Facer, "Manufacturing a Recovery," Publications and Records, Parliament.uk, http://www.parliament.uk/business/publications /research/key-issues-for-the-new-parliament/economic-recovery/modern -manufacturing-and-an-export-led-recovery/.

33. Stephen Burgess, "Measuring Financial Sector Output and Its Contribution to UK GDP," *Bank of England Quarterly Bulletin 2011* (Sept. 19, 2011), http://www.bankofengland.co.uk/publications/Documents/quarterlybulletin /qb110304.pdf.

34. Cecchetti et al.

35. All finance shares at L. Maer, et al., "Financial Services: Contribution to the UK Economy," House of Commons, England, August 2012, p4 http://www .parliament.uk/briefing-papers/sn06193.pdf; all manufacturing shares at "Manufacturing, value added (% of GDP)," The World Bank at data.world bank.org/indicator/NV.IND.MANF.ZS.

36. Lydia Depillis, "Congrats, CEOs! You're Making 273 Times the Pay of the Average Worker," *Wonkblog, Washington Post*, June 26, 2013, http://www .washingtonpost.com/blogs/wonkblog/wp/2013/06/26/congrats-ceos-youre -making-273-times-the-pay-of-the-average-worker/.

37. Ahmed Abuiliazeed and Al-Motaz Bellah Al-Agamawi, "AOL Time Warner Merger: Case Analysis, Strategic Management of Technology," SlideShare, http://www.slideshare.net/magamawi/aol-time-warnercase-analysis.

38. A. Rappaport, et al., "Stock or Cash: The Trade-offs for Buyers and Sellers in Mergers and Acquisitions," *Harvard Business Review*, Nov.-Dec. 1999, p. 147. http://www2.warwick.ac.uk/fac/soc/law/pg/offer/llm/iel/mas_sample _lecture.pdf

39. According to research by Dean Baker at Center for Economic and Policy Research.

40. William Lazonick, "The Innovative Enterprise and the Developmental State: Toward an Economics of 'Organizational Success.'" Discussion paper presented at Finance, Innovation & Growth 2011.

41. H. Minsky, in E. Tymoigne and R. Wray, *The Rise and Fall of Money Manager Capitalism* (Oxford: Routledge, 2013).

42. "IBG YBG," review of Jonathan Knee, *The Accidental Investment Banker* (Oxford University Press, 2006), in *Words, Words, Words*, http://wordsthrice .blogspot.com/2006/12/ibg-ybg.html.

43. Yexin Jessica Li, Douglas Kenrick, Vladas Griskevicius, and Stephen L. Neuberg, "Economic Decision Biases in Evolutionary Perspectives: How Mating and Self-Protection Motives Alter Loss Aversion," *Journal of Personality and Social Psychology* 102, no. 3 (2012), http://www.csom.umn .edu/marketinginstitute/research/documents/HowMatingandSelf -ProtectionMotivesAlterLossAversion.pdf.

44. Interview with author.

45. William Lazonick, "The Innovative Enterprise and the Developmental State: Toward an Economics of 'Organizational Success.'" Discussion paper presented at Finance, Innovation & Growth 2011.

46. William Lazonick, "Everyone Is Paying Price for Share Buybacks," FT.com, Sept. 25, 2008, http://www.ft.com/intl/cms/s/0/e75440f6-8b0e-11dd-b634 -0000779fd18c.html#axzz2r21JdHWo.

47. In Kevin Phillips, *American Theocracy: The Peril and Politics of Radical Religion, Oil, and Borrowed Money in the 21st Century* (New York: Penguin, 2006), p. 312.

48. Richard Fisher, "Ending 'Too Big to Fail': A Proposal for Reform Before It's Too Late (With Reference to Patrick Henry, Complexity and Reality)

49. "Get Shorty," lecture given by Andrew Haldane for the Sir John Gresham annual lecture, 2011. Cited at Financial Services Club Blog http:// thefinanser.co.uk/fsclub/2011/11/get-shorty-andrew-haldane-speech.html.

50. Eric Reguly, "Buyback Boondoggle: Are Share Buybacks Killing Companies?" *The Globe and Mail*, Oct. 24, 2013, http://www.theglobeandmail.com/report -on-business/rob-magazine/the-buyback-boondoggle/article15004212/.

CHAPTER 5: HOME ALONE

1. "Bike + Walk Maps," Portland Bureau of Transportation, City of Portland, OR, http://www.portlandoregon.gov/transportation/39402.

2. Interview with author.

3. Bill Bishop, *The Big Sort: Why the Clustering of Like-Minded America Is Tearing Us Apart*. (Boston: Houghton Mifflin, 2008), p. 5–6; and personal communication with the author.

4. "2012 General Presidential Election Results," table, Dave Leip's Atlas of U.S. Presidential Elections, http://uselectionatlas.org/RESULTS/.

5. Cited in Tom Murphy, "An Angel and a Brute: Self-Interest and Individualism in Tocqueville's America," essay for preceptorial on *Democracy in America*, St. John's College, Santa Fe, NM, http://www.brtom.org/sjc/sjc4.html.

6. Michio Kaku, "The Next 20 Years: Interacting with Computers, Telecom, and AI in the Future," keynote address, RSA Conference 2011, https://www .youtube.com/watch?v=Y6kmb16zSOY.

7. Nicholas Carr, *The Shallows: What the Internet Is Doing to Our Brains* (New York: W. W. Norton, 2011), p. 117.

8. Kent Gibbons, "Advanced Advertising: Obama Campaign Showed Value of Targeting Viewers," MultichannelNews, Nov. 13, 2012, http://www .multichannel.com/mcnbc-events/advanced-advertising-obama-campaign -showed-value-targeting-viewers/140262.

9. C. Duhigg, "How Companies Learn Your Secrets," *New York Times Magazine*, Feb. 16, 2012.

10. Cass R. Sunstein, *Republic.com 2.0: Revenge of the Blogs* (Princeton, NJ: Princeton University Press, 2007), p. 5.

11. Cass R. Sunstein, *Infotopia: How Many Minds Produce Knowledge* (New York: Oxford University Press, 2006), p. 95.

12. Cass R. Sunstein, *Why Societies Need Dissent (Oliver Wendell Holmes Lectures)* (Cambridge, MA: Harvard University Press, 2003), cited in Bishop p. 67.

13. Interview with author.

14. Putnam, *Bowling Alone*, p. 332.

15. "Community connectedness linked to happiness and vibrant communities" Social Capital Community Benchmark Survey John F. Kennedy School of Government of Harvard University. http://www.hks.harvard.edu/saguaro /communitysurvey/results4.html; This Emotional Life, Public Broadcasting System, January 2010. http://www.pbs.org/thisemotionallife/topic/connecting /connection-happiness.

16. In Putnam, *Bowling Alone,* p. 333.

17. Ibid.

18. Belinda Goldsmith, "Friendships Cut Short on Social Media as People Get Ruder," Reuters, Apr 10, 2013, http://www.reuters.com/article/2013 /04/10/us-socialmedia-behaviour-survey-idUSBRE9390TO20130410.

19. Christopher Lasch, *The Culture of Narcissism: American Life in an Age of Diminishing Expectations* (New York: W. W. Norton, 1979), p. 47.

20. Personal communication.

21. James A. Good and Jim Garrison, "Traces of Hegelian *Bildung* in Dewey's Philosophy," in Paul Fairfield, ed., *John Dewey and Continental Philosophy* (Carbondale, IL: Board of Trustees, Southern Illinois University, 2010).

22. Allen W. Wood, "Hegel on Education," in Amélie O. Rorty, ed., *Philosophy as Education* (London: Routledge, 1998), www.stanford.edu/~allenw/webpapers /HegelEd.doc.

23. Quoted by Ken Auletta in "Outside the Box," *The New Yorker*, Feb. 3, 2014.

CHAPTER 6: HARD LABOR

1. Alex Aldridge, "Law Graduates Face a Bleak Future at the Bar," *The Guardian*, Nov. 25, 2011, http://www.guardian.co.uk/law/2011/nov/25 /law-graduates-bleak-future-bar.

2. Daniel Katz, "Quantitative Legal Prediction—Or—How I Learned to Stop Worrying and Start Preparing for the Data-Driven Future of the Legal Services Industry," *Emory Law Journal*, 62, no. 909 (2013): 965.

3. Laura Manning, "65 Students Chasing Each Training Contract Vacancy," Lawyer 2B, June 28, 2011, http://l2b.thelawyer.com/65-students-chasing-each-training-contract-vacancy/1008370.article.

4. John Markoff, "Armies of Expensive Lawyers, Replaced by Cheaper Software," The New York Times, March 4, 2011, http://www.nytimes.com/2011/03/05/science/05legal.html?pagewanted=1&_r=1&hp.

5. Thor Olavsrud, "Big Data Analytics Lets Businesses Play Moneyball," ComputerworldUK, Aug. 24, 2012, http://www.computerworlduk.com/in-depth/it-business/3377796/big-data-analytics-lets-businesses-play-moneyball/.

6. Daniel Martin, Katz "Quantitative Legal Prediction—Or—How I Learned to Stop Worrying and Start Preparing for the Data-Driven Future of the Legal Services Industry," Emory Law Journal, 62, no. 909 (2013): 938.

7. Gary Burtless, "How Far Are We From Full Employment?" Brookings, Aug. 27, 2013.

8. Paul Krugman, "Defining Prosperity Down," The New York Times, July 7, 2013, http://www.nytimes.com/2013/07/08/opinion/krugman-defining-prosperity-down.html?src=recg; "Median Household Income, by Year," table, DaveManuel.com, http://www.davemanuel.com/median-household-income.php; Robert Pear, "Median Income Rises, but Is Still 6% below Level at Start of Recession in '07," The New York Times, Aug. 21, 2013, http://www.nytimes.com/2013/08/22/us/politics/us-median-income-rises-but-is-still-6-below-its-2007-peak.html; past years' data was adjusted using the CPI Inflation Calculator at the U.S. Bureau of Labor Statistics—http://www.bls.gov/data/inflation_calculator.htm.

9. John Kenneth Galbraith, "The Winner Takes All . . . Sometimes," review of Robert H. Frank and Philip J. Cook, The Winner-Take-All Society (Free Press, 1995), Harvard Business Review (Nov. 1995), http://hbr.org/1995/11/the-winner-takes-allsometimes/ar/1.

10. "The New Normal? Slower R&D Spending," Federal Reserve Bank of Atlanta Macroblog, Sept. 26, 2013, http://macroblog.typepad.com/macroblog/2013/09/the-new-normal-slower-r-and-d-spending.html.

11. Adam Davidson, "Making It in America," The Atlantic, Dec. 20, 2011, http://www.theatlantic.com/magazine/archive/2012/01/making-it-in-america/308844/.

12. Patrice Hill, "The Mean Economy: IBM workers suffer culture change as jobs go global Technological advances demand new skill sets, lower labor costs," The Washington Times, August 26, 2012, http://www.washingtontimes.com/news/2012/aug/26/innovators-working-their-way-out-of-a-job/?page=all.

13. Vinay Couto, Mahadeva Mani, Arie Y. Lewin, and Dr. Carine Peeters, "The Globalization of White-Collar Work: The Facts and Fallout of

Next-Generation Offshoring," Booz Allen Hamilton, https://offshoring .fuqua.duke.edu/pdfs/gowc_v4.pdf.

14. Fareed Zakaria, "How Long Will America Lead the World?" *Newsweek*, June 11, 2006, http://www.thedailybeast.com/newsweek/2006/06/11/how-long-will -america-lead-the-world.html; and "Graphic: Going Abroad," *BloombergBusinessWeek*, Feb. 2, 2003, http://www.businessweek.com /stories/2003-02-02/graphic-going-abroad.

15. Sam Ro, "The Case for the Robot Workforce," *Business Insider*, December 4, 2012, http://www.businessinsider.com/robot-density-for-select-countries -2012-11. Accessed February 1, 2014.

16. Interview with author.

17. Bruce Stokes, "Europe Faces Globalization – Part II: Denmark Invests in an Adaptable Workforce, Thus Reducing Fear of Change." YaleGlobal, May 18, 2006, http://yaleglobal.yale.edu/content/europe-faces-globalization-%E2% 80%93-part-ii.

18. Personal communication.

19. John Hagel et al., "The 2011 Shift Index: Measuring the Forces of Long-Term Change," Deloitte Center for the Edge, pp. 10-11.

20. Diana Farrell et al., "Offshoring: Is It a Win-Win Game?" McKinsey and Company: Insights and Publications, Aug. 2003, http://www.mckinsey.com /insights/employment_and_growth/offshoring_is_it_a_win-win_game.

21. Hedrick Smith, "When Capitalists Cared," *The New York Times*, Sept. 2, 2012, http://www.nytimes.com/2012/09/03/opinion/henry-ford-when-capitalists -cared.html?_r=0.

22. William McGaughey Jr., "Henry Ford's Productivity Lesson," *Christian Science Monitor*, Dec. 22, 1982, http://www.csmonitor.com/1982/1222 /122232.html.

23. Nathan Heller, "Laptop U," May 20, 2013

24. Interview with author.

25. Interview with author.

26. Lazonick and O'Sullivan, "Maximizing Shareholder Value," p. 31.

27. Personal communication, January 10, 2014.

28. "Coming Home: Reshoring Manufacturing," *The Economist*, Jan. 19, 2013, http://www.economist.com/news/special-report/21569570-growing -number-american-companies-are-moving-their-manufacturing-back -united.

29. Alan B. Krueger, "Fairness as an Economic Force," lecture delivered at "Learning and Labor Economics" Conference at Oberlin College, April 26, 2013, http://www.whitehouse.gov/sites/default/files/docs/oberlin_final revised.pdf.

30. Richard Sennett, *The Culture of the New Capitalism*, pp. 4–5.

31. Christopher Null and Brian Caulfield, "Fade to Black: The 1980s Vision of

'Lights-Out' Manufacturing, Where Robots Do All the Work, Is a Dream No More," CNNMoney, http://money.cnn.com/magazines/business2/business2 _archive/2003/06/01/343371/index.htm.

32. "Coming Home: Reshoring Manufacturing."

33. "Robots Are Coming, Part 2," SoundCloud discussion on InnovationHub, https://soundcloud.com/innovationhub/robots-are-coming-part-2.

34. Interview with author.

35. NPR Staff, "Tired of Inequality? One Economist Said It'll Only Get Worse," NPR.org, Sept. 12, 2013, http://www.npr.org/2013/09/12/221425582/tired-of -inequality-one-economist-says-itll-only-get-worse.

36. Ibid.

37. Hannah Kuchler, "Data Pioneers Watching Us Work," *Financial Times*, February 17, 2014.

38. NPR, "Tired of Inequality."

39. Paul Sullivan, "Twitter Tantalizes, but Beware the I.P.O." *The New York Times*, Oct. 25, 2013, http://www.nytimes.com/2013/10/26/your-money/asset -allocation/twitter-tantalizes-but-beware-the-ipo.html?hpw.

40. "IPO Performance," graph, Renaissance Capital IPO Center, http://www .renaissancecapital.com/ipohome/press/mediaroom.aspx?market=us.

41. Susan Fleck, John Glasser, and Shawn Sprague, "The Compensation-Productivity Gap: A Visual Essay," *Monthly Labor Review* (Jan. 2011).

42. Jacob S. Hacker and Paul Pierson, *Winner-Take-All Politics: How Washington Made the Rich Richer—and Turned Its Back on the Middle Class* (New York: Simon & Schuster, 2011), pp. 3-4.

43. "Graph: Corporate Profits after Tax (without IVA and CCAdj) (CP)/Gross Domestic Product (GDP)," Federal Reserve Bank of St. Louis: Economic Research, http://research.stlouisfed.org/fred2/graph/?g=cSh.

44. Krueger, "Fairness as an Economic Force."

45. Mina Kimes, "Caterpillar's Doug Oberhelman: Manufacturing's Mouthpiece," BloombergBusinessWeek, May 16, 2013, http://www.businessweek.com/articles /2013-05-16/caterpillars-doug-oberhelman-manufacturings-mouthpiece#p4.

46. Lydia Depillis, "Britain's Chamber of Commerce Says Corporations Should Share Their New Prosperity with Line Workers. Wait, What?" *Washington Post*, Dec. 30, 2013, http://www.washingtonpost.com/blogs/wonkblog/wp /2013/12/30/britains-chamber-of-commerce-says-corporations-should-share -their-new-prosperity-with-line-workers-wait-what/.

47. Eliezer Yudkowsky, "The Robots, AI, Unemployment Anti-FAQ," *LessWrong* (blog), July 25, 2013, http://lesswrong.com/lw/hh4/the_robots_ai_and _unemployment_antifaq/.

48. King, Ian and Beth Jinks, "Icahn seeks $150 million Apple stock buyback," *San Francisco Chronicle*, October 1, 2013. http://www.sfgate.com/business /article/Icahn-seeks-150-million-Apple-stock-buyback-4860812.php.

CHAPTER 7: IN SICKNESS AND IN WEALTH

1. "Benefits, Costs, and Policy Considerations of Proton Therapy," *Asco Daily News*, June 1, 2013, http://am.asco.org/benefits-cost-and-policy-considerations-proton-therapy.

2. Dani Fankhauser, "Google Wants You to Live 170 Years," Oct. 24, 2013, Mashable.com, http://mashable.com/2013/10/24/google-calico/; and Harry McCracken and Lev Grossman, "Google vs. Death," *Time*, Sept. 30, 2013, http://content.time.com/time/subscriber/printout/0,8816,2152422,00.html.

3. Amy Goldstein and Juliet Eilperin, "Healthcare.gov: How Political Fear Was Pitted against Technical Needs," *Washington Post*, Nov. 3, 2013, http://www.washingtonpost.com/politics/challenges-have-dogged-obamas-health-plan-since-2010/2013/11/02/453fba42-426b-11e3-a624-41d661b0bb78_print.html.

4. Lee Wohlfert, "Dr. John Knowles Diagnoses U.S. Medicine," *People*, May 6, 1974, http://www.people.com/people/archive/article/0,,20064026,00.html.

5. John Knowles, "The Responsibility of the Individual," *Daedalus* 106, No. 1, The MIT Press (Winter 1977): p. 59.

6. Ibid., p. 75.

7. Ibid., p. 59.

8. David Brown, "A Case of Getting What You Pay For: With Heart Attack Treatments, as Quality Rises, So Does Cost," *The Washington Post*, July 26, 2009, http://www.washingtonpost.com/wp-dyn/content/article/2009/07/25/AR2009072502381_pf.html.

9. David M. Cutler and Mark McClellan, "Is Technological Change in Medicine Worth It?" *Health Affairs* 20, no. 5 (September/October 2001): 11–29.

10. Interview with author.

11. Fareed Zakaria, "Health Insurance Is for Everyone," *Fareed Zakaria* (blog), March 19, 2012, http://fareedzakaria.com/2012/03/19/health-insurance-is-for-everyone/.

12. Interview with author.

13. Courtney Hutchison, "Provenge Cancer Vaccine: Can You Put a Price on Delaying Death?" ABCNews, July 29, 2010, http://abcnews.go.com/Health/ProstateCancerNews/provenge-cancer-vaccine-months-life-worth-100k/story?id=11269159.

14. Zakaria, "Health Insurance Is for Everyone."

15. Jonathan Rowe, "Our Phony Economy," *Harper's*, June 2008, http://harpers.org/print/?pid=85583.

16. Interview with author.

17. Jeffrey M. Jones, "Majority in U.S. Favors Healthcare Reform This Year," Gallup, July 14, 2009, http://www.gallup.com/poll/121664/majority-favors-healthcare-reform-this-year.aspx.

18. Benjamin Zycher, "Obamacare Inhibits Medical Technology," *Washington Times*, Jan. 9, 2012, http://www.washingtontimes.com/news/2012/jan/9 /obamacare-inhibits-medical-technology/.

19. Thomas B. Edsall, "The Obamacare Crisis," *New York Times*, Nov. 19, 2013, http://www.nytimes.com/2013/11/20/opinion/edsall-the-obamacare-crisis .html?pagewanted=1&_r=2&smid=tw-share&&pagewanted=all.

20. Interview with author.

21. Interview with author.

CHAPTER 8: FOREVER WAR

1. Sam Stein, "Robert Draper Book: GOP Anti-Obama Campaign Started Night of Inauguration," *Huffington Post*, April 25, 2012, http://www.huffingtonpost .com/2012/04/25/robert-draper-anti-obama-campaign_n_1452899.html.

2. Ibid.

3. Ibid.

4. "Vote Tallies for Passage of Medicare in 1965," Official Social Security Website, http://www.ssa.gov/history/tally65.html.

5. Alan Abramowitz, "Don't Blame Primary Voters for Polarization," *The Forum: Politics of Presidential Selection* 5, no. 4 (2008), http://www.themonkeycage .org/wp-content/uploads/2008/01/Abramowitz.Primary.Voters.pdf.

6. David Schoetz, "David Frum on GOP: Now We Work for Fox," ABCNews, March 23, 2010, http://abcnews.go.com/blogs/headlines/2010/03/david-frum -on-gop-now-we-work-for-fox/.

7. "Q3 2013 Cable News Ratings: Fox #1 Overall, MSNBC #2 in Primetime, CNN #2 in Total Day," *Mediate*, Oct. 2, 2013, http://www.mediaite.com/tv/q3 -2013-cable-news-ratings-fox-1-overall-msnbc-2-in-primetime-cnn-2-in -total-day/.

8. Abramowitz, "Don't Blame Primary Voters for Polarization."

9. "Polarized or Sorted? Just What's Wrong with Our Politics, Anyway?" *American Interest*, March 11, 2013, http://www.the-american-interest.com /article.cfm?piece=1393.

10. Interview with the author.

11. Kevin Drum, "You Hate Me, Now with a Colorful Chart!" *Mother Jones*, Sept 26, 2012, http://www.motherjones.com/kevin-drum/2012/09/you-hate -me-now-colorful-chart.

12. Steven Pearlstein, "Turned off from Politics? That's Exactly What the Politicians Want," *The Washington Post*, April 20, 2012, http://www.washing tonpost.com/opinions/turned-off-from-politics-thats-exactly-what-the -politicians-want/2012/04/20/gIQAffxKWT_story.html.

13. Alex C. Madrigal, "When the Nerds Go Marching In," *The Atlantic*, Nov. 16,

2012. http://www.theatlantic.com/technology/archive/2012/11/when-the-nerds-go-marching-in/265325/?single_page=true.

14. Michael Scherer, "How Obama's Data Crunchers Helped Him Win," *Time*, Nov. 8, 2012, http://www.cnn.com/2012/11/07/tech/web/obama-campaign-tech-team/index.html.

15. Madrigal, "When Nerds Go Marching In."

16. Tom Agan, "Silent Marketing: Micro-Targeting," a Penn, Schoen, and Berland Associates White Paper, http://www.wpp.com/wpp/marketing/reportsstudies/silentmarketing/.

17. Interview with author.

18. Schoetz, "David Frum on GOP."

19. Nicholas Confessore, "Groups Mobilize to Aid Democrats in '14 Data Arms Race," *New York Times*, http://www.nytimes.com/2013/11/15/us/politics/groups-mobilize-to-aid-democrats.html?hp=&adxnnl=1&adxnnlx=1384974279-yMZXrvK1b5WLU7mXxrJ6yg.

20. "Data Points: Presidential Campaign Spending," *U.S. News & World Report*, http://www.usnews.com/opinion/articles/2008/10/21/data-points-presidential-campaign-spending.

21. David Knowles, "U.S. Senate Seat Now Costs $10.5 Million to Win, on Average, while U.S. House Seat Costs $1.7 Million New Analysis of FEC Data Shows," (New York) *Daily News*, http://www.nydailynews.com/news/politics/cost-u-s-senate-seat-10-5-million-article-1.1285491.

22. "The Cost of Winning an Election, 1986–2012," table, http://www.cfinst.org/pdf/vital/VitalStats_t1.pdf.

23. "The Money behind the Elections," OpenSecrets, http://www.opensecrets.org/bigpicture/.

24. Alan Abramowitz, Brad Alexander, and Matthew Gunning, "Incumbency, Redistricting, and the Decline of Competition in U.S. House Elections," *Journal of Politics* 68, no. 1 (Feb. 2006): 75–88, http://www.stat.columbia.edu/~gelman/stuff_for_blog/JOParticle.pdf.

25. Cited in A. Lioz, "Breaking the Vicious Cycle: How the Supreme Court Helped Create the Inequality Era and Why a New Jurisprudence Must Lead Us Out," *Seton Hall Law Review* 43, no. 4, Symposium: The Changing Landscape of Election Law, Nov 1, 2013.

26. Sabrina Siddiqui, "Call Time for Congress Shows How Fundraising Dominates Bleak Work Life," *Huffington Post*, Jan. 8, 2013, http://www.huffingtonpost.com/2013/01/08/call-time-congressional-fundraising_n_2427291.html.

27. "Tom Perriello: President & CEO of the Center for American Progress Action Fund, Counselor to the Center for American Progress," staff bio, http://www.americanprogress.org/about/staff/perriello-tom/bio/.

28. Interview with author.

29. "Finance/Insurance/Real Estate Long-Term Contribution Funds," graph, http://www.opensecrets.org/industries/totals.php?cycle=2014&ind=F.

30. "Ideology/Single-Issue: Long-Term Contribution Trends," graph, OpenSecrets, http://www.opensecrets.org/industries/totals.php?cycle=2014&ind=Q.

31. Patrick Basham, "It's the Spending, Stupid! Understanding Campaign Finance in the Big-Government Era," Cato Institute Briefing Paper No. 64, July 18, 2001, http://www.cato.org/sites/cato.org/files/pubs/pdf/bp64.pdf.

32. "Ranked Sectors," table, OpenSecrets, http://www.opensecrets.org/lobby/top.php?showYear=2012&indexType=c.

33. Eric Lipton, "For Freshman in the House, Seats of Plenty," New York Times, Aug. 10, 2013, http://www.nytimes.com/2013/08/11/us/politics/for-freshmen-in-the-house-seats-of-plenty.html.

34. Ibid.

35. Jeffrey Rosen, "Citizens United v. FEC Decision Proves Justice Is Blind—Politically," The New York Times, Jan. 25, 2012, http://www.politico.com/news/stories/0112/71961.html.

36. Ibid.

37. Peter Beinart, "The Rise of the New New Left," The Daily Beast, Sept. 12, 2013, http://www.thedailybeast.com/articles/2013/09/12/the-rise-of-the-new-new-left.html.

38. "Man and Woman of the Year: The Middle Americans," Time, Jan. 5, 1970, http://www.time.com/time/subscriber/printout/0,8816,943113,00.html.

39. Clifford Cobb, Ted Halstead, and Jonathan Rowe, "If the GDP Is Up, Why Is America Down?" The Atlantic, Oct. 1995, http://www.theatlantic.com/past/politics/ecbig/gdp.htm.

40. Beinart, "The Rise of the New Left."

41. Kathleen Parker, "A Brave New Centrist World," The Washington Post, Oct 15, 2103, http://www.washingtonpost.com/opinions/kathleen-parker-a-brave-new-centrist-world/2013/10/15/ea5f5bc6-35c9-11e3-be86-6aeaa439845b_story.html.

42. E. J. Dionne, Our Divided Political Heart: The Battle for the American Idea in an Age of Discontent: (New York: Bloomsbury, 2012), p. 270.

CHAPTER 9: MAKING SPACE

1. Book 1, chapter 8, http://econlib.org/library/Smith/smWN3.html#I.8.35.

2. Book 2, chapter 2, http://econlib.org/library/Smith/smWN7.html#II.2.94.

3. "The Real Adam Smith Problem: How to Live Well in Commercial Society," The Philosopher's Beard (blog), Sept. 12, 2013, http://www

.philosophersbeard.org/2013/09/the-real-adam-smith-problem-how-to
-live.html.

4. Peter S. Goodman, "Emphasis on Growth Is Called Misguided," *New York Times*, Sept. 22, 2009, http://www.nytimes.com/2009/09/23/business /economy/23gdp.html?ref=business&_r=0.

5. Herman E. Daly, "A Steady-State Economy," text delivered to UK Sustainable Development Commission, April 24, 2008.

6. Bill McKibben, "Breaking the Growth Habit," *Scientific American*, April 2010, http://www.scientificamerican.com/article.cfm?id=breaking-the-growth -habit&print=true.

7. Coral Davenport, "Industry Awakens to Threat of Climate Change," *New York Times*, Jan. 23, 2014, http://www.nytimes.com/2014/01/24/science/earth /threat-to-bottom-line-spurs-action-on-climate.html?hp.

8. Goodman, "Emphasis on Growth Is Called Misguided."

9. Gregg D. Polsky and Andrew C. W. Lund, "Can Executive Compensation Reform Cure Short-Termism."

10. Susanne Craig, "Cuomo, Frank Seek to Link Executive Pay, Performance," *Wall Street Journal*, March 13, 2009, http://online.wsj.com/news/articles /SB123690181841413405?mg=reno64-wsj&url=http%3A%2F%2Fonline .wsj.com%2Farticle%2FSB123690181841413405.html#mod=testMod.

11. Gretchen Morgenson, "An Unstoppable Climb in C.E.O. Pay," *New York Times*, June 29, 2013, http://www.nytimes.com/2013/06/30/business /an-unstoppable-climb-in-ceo-pay.html?pagewanted=all.

12. Diane Stafford, "High CEO Pay Doesn't Mean High Performance, Report Says," *Kansas City Star*, Aug. 28, 2013, http://www.kansascity.com/2013/08 /28/4440246/high-ceo-pay-doesnt-mean-high.html.

13. Brian Montopoli, "Ronald Reagan Myth Doesn't Square with Reality," CBSNews, Feb. 4, 2011, http://www.cbsnews.com/news/ronald-reagan-myth -doesnt-square-with-reality/.

14. Peter Beinart, "The Republicans' Reagan Amnesia," *The Daily Beast*, Feb. 1, 2010, http://www.thedailybeast.com/articles/2010/02/01/the-republicans -reagan-amnesia.html.

15. Richard W. Fisher, "Ending 'Too Big to Fail.'"

16. Evan Pérez, "First on CNN: Regulator Warned against JPMorgan Charges," CNN, Jan. 9, 2014, http://www.cnn.com/2014/01/07/politics/jpmorgan-chase -regulators-prosecutors/.

17. Fisher, "Ending 'Too Big to Fail.'"

18. George F. Will, "Time to Break Up the Big Banks," *Washington Post*, Feb. 9, 2013, http://www.washingtonpost.com/opinions/george-will-break-up-the -big-banks/2013/02/08/2379498a-714e-11e2-8b8d-e0b59a1b8e2a_story .html.

19. Fisher, "Ending 'Too Big to Fail.'"

20. Communication with author.

21. Liz Benjamin, "What Would Cuomo Do to Get Public Financing?" *Capital New York*, Jan. 20, 2014, http://www.capitalnewyork.com/article/albany/2014/01/8539039/what-would-cuomo-do-get-public-financing.

22. Liz Kennedy, "Citizens Actually United: The Bi-Partisan Opposition to Corporate Political Spending and Support for Common Sense Reform," Demos, Oct. 25, 2012, http://www.demos.org/publication/citizens-actually-united-bi-partisan-opposition-corporate-political-spending-and-support.

23. Chris Myers, "Conservatism and Campaign Finance Reform: The Two Aren't Mutually Exclusive," *RedState*, April 24, 2012, http://www.redstate.com/clmyers/2013/04/24/conservatism-and-campaign-finance-reform/.

24. David Brooks, "The Opportunity Coalition," *The New York Times*, Jan 30, 2014.

25. "2013 Report Card for America's Infrastructure," American Society of Civil Engineers, http://www.infrastructurereportcard.org/.

26. In Robert Frank, *The Darmn Economy: Liberty, Competition, and Common Good*.

27. Brooks, "The Opportunity Coalition."

Index

A NOTE ON THE TYPE

Caledonia (the Latin name for Scotland) is a transitional serif typeface designed by William A. Dwiggins for Linotype in 1939, based on elements of the Scotch Roman and Bulmer typefaces. It is one of the most widely used book types of all time.

ALSO AVAILABLE BY PAUL ROBERTS

THE END OF OIL

'*The End of Oil* does what it says. It looks at an energy economy that is "falling apart" because global oil demand will soon begin to outstrip supply . . . It looks, in short, at a world beyond oil'
SUNDAY TIMES

Billions of people around the world enjoy an unprecedented standard of living based on one thing: oil. And each year we demand more. Everything we buy, from a McDonald's hamburger to cancer drugs, represents a measure of energy produced and consumed. But how can this sustain itself, when already we have burned our way through half the easily available oil? Yet the pursuit of fuel is relentless. In this devastating piece of reportage, Paul Roberts shows what is likely to happen, why the transition from oil will be complicated, traumatic and possibly dangerous, and what it will mean for our daily lives.

'This book may very well become for fossil fuels what *Fast Food Nation* was to food'
PUBLISHERS WEEKLY

BLOOMSBURY

ALSO AVAILABLE BY PAUL ROBERTS

THE END OF FOOD

'Indispensable . . . The best analysis of the global food economy you
are likely to find'
MICHAEL POLLAN, AUTHOR OF IN DEFENCE OF FOOD

The emergence of large-scale food production gave us unprecedented abundance
– but at a steep and ultimately unsustainable price. Relentless cost-cutting has
made our food systems vulnerable to contamination and disease. More than a
billion people are overweight or obese, yet roughly the same number are still
malnourished. Over-crowded countries like China are already planning for
tightened global food supplies. As the world veers back to a time of hunger
and uncertainty, Paul Roberts explores the vulnerable miracle of our modern
food economy and pinpoints the decisions we must make to avoid the coming
meltdown.

'The coming food crisis . . . is as intractable as global warming, and no less urgent'
THE ECONOMIST

ORDER YOUR COPY:

By phone: +44 (0)1256 302 699; BY EMAIL: DIRECT@MACMILLAN.CO.UK

DELIVERY IS USUALLY 3–5 WORKING DAYS. FREE POSTAGE AND PACKAGING FOR ORDERS OVER £20.

ONLINE: WWW.BLOOMSBURY.COM/BOOKSHOP

PRICES AND AVAILABILITY SUBJECT TO CHANGE WITHOUT NOTICE.

WWW.BLOOMSBURY.COM

B L O O M S B U R Y